# BORDER WALLS
# GONE GREEN

# BORDER WALLS GONE GREEN

## NATURE AND ANTI-IMMIGRANT POLITICS IN AMERICA

## JOHN HULTGREN

UNIVERSITY OF MINNESOTA PRESS
Minneapolis · London

Elements of the introduction appeared in "Natural Exceptions to Green Sovereignty: American Environmentalism and the 'Immigration Problem,'" *Alternatives: Global, Local, Political* 37, no. 4 (2012): 300–316. Elements of chapters 2 and 3 appeared in "The 'Nature' of American Immigration Restrictionism," *New Political Science* 36, no. 1 (2014): 52–75.

Published by the University of Minnesota Press
111 Third Avenue South, Suite 290
Minneapolis, MN 55401-2520
http://www.upress.umn.edu

Library of Congress Cataloging-in-Publication Data

Hultgren, John.
  Border walls gone green : nature and anti-immigrant
  politics in America / John Hultgren.
  Includes bibliographical references and index.
  ISBN 978-0-8166-9497-6 (hc)—ISBN 978-0-8166-9498-3 (pb)
  1. United States—Emigration and immigration—Public opinion.
  2. Immigrants—United States—Public opinion. 3. Emigration
  and immigration—Environmental aspects. 4. United States—
  Emigration and immigration—Government policy. 5. Emigration and
  immigration—Political aspects—United States. 6. Environmentalism—
  Political aspects—United States. 7. Nature—Effect of human beings
  on—United States. 8. United States—Environmental conditions. I. Title.
JV6456.H85    2015
325.73—dc23          2014049430

Printed in the United States of America on acid-free paper

The University of Minnesota is an equal-opportunity educator and employer.

21 20 19 18 17 16 15    10 9 8 7 6 5 4 3 2 1

To those migrants who continue to struggle for the right "to live, love, and work where they please."

The first frontier was the water's edge, and there was a first moment, because how could there not have been such a moment, when a living thing came up from the ocean, crossed that boundary and found that it could breathe.

**SALMAN RUSHDIE,** "Step across This Line"

# CONTENTS

# ABBREVIATIONS

AICF     American Immigration Control Foundation
ALT      America's Leadership Team Coalition
AMREN    American Renaissance
AP3      American Third Position
ASUSA    Alliance for a Sustainable USA (formerly Diversity Alliance for a Sustainable USA)
CAPS     Californians for Population Stabilization
CCC      Council of Conservative Citizens
CCN      Carrying Capacity Network
CIS      Center for Immigration Studies
CJPE     Center for Justice, Peace, and Environment (has been renamed FCCAN)
CNC      Center for New Community
CWPE     Committee on Women, Population, and Environment
EHC      Environmental Health Coalition
FAIR     Federation for American Immigration Reform
FCCAN    Fort Collins Community Action Network (formerly CJPE)
NCIR     Northern Coloradoans for Immigration Reduction
NPG      Negative Population Growth
PEG      Political Ecology Group
PFIR     Progressives for Immigration Reform
SCBC     Sierra Club Borderlands Campaign
SUSPS    Support U.S. Population Stabilization or Sierrans for Population Stabilization
ZPG      Zero Population Growth (renamed Population-Connection)

# EARTH DAY EXCLUSIONS

In April 2012, viewers tuning into "progressive" American television news station MSNBC were faced with a surprise. In celebration of Earth Day, the immigration-reduction organization Californians for Population Stabilization (CAPS) had launched a national advertising campaign aimed at persuading the American left that immigration is a driving force behind the contemporary global ecological crisis:

> Concerned about America's ecological footprint? Then you should be concerned about immigration. Sound crazy? Immigrants produce four times more carbon emissions in the U.S. than in their home countries. Left alone, immigration will drive a population increase equal to the entire American West in just thirty years. Reducing immigration won't solve global warming, but it is part of the solution.

The ad provoked considerable controversy, even catching the attention of faux-conservative political satirist Stephen Colbert, who skewered the message on his nightly Comedy Central program *The Colbert Report*. Colbert began the segment, titled "United We Can't Stand Them," by reflecting on the immigration–environment connection and its potential for bridging the American political divide:

> I don't believe global warming exists, and even if it does, you could never convince me it's man-made. But now I know it's caused by immigrants. Saving the planet by demonizing immigrants gives liberals and conservatives something they can do together. Now, when a liberal yammers on about the record heat we had this winter, a conservative can say, "Let's save the environment by building an electrified border fence that runs on alternative energy."[1]

Colbert clearly intended this facetiously, but he inadvertently stumbled onto something very real: *border walls are going green*.

The central thesis of this book is that nature is increasingly being deployed as a form of *walling*—providing a subtle means of reinforcing "traditional" territorial borders and national identities without having to revert to racial and cultural logics that are no longer socially acceptable within mainstream political discourse. Nature, in this sense, provides a way for immigration restrictionists to expand their alliances beyond the far right while still maintaining the support of nativists. The implications of this are far-reaching. I contend that in the American context, in particular, progressive, leftist, and even radical ecological efforts to "green" sovereignty—to render the nation-state more sustainable—are, in many cases, actually serving to shore up exclusionary forms of political community.

The difficulties that American greens have faced in grappling with the issue of immigration are not new. Environmental activists are well aware of hotly contested Sierra Club and Earth First! debates that have waxed and waned from the mid 1970s until today; many of the so-called fathers of the modern American environmental movement—including Edward Abbey, Garrett Hardin, David Brower, Gaylord Nelson, Paul Ehrlich, "Captain" Paul Watson, and Dave Foreman—were or are themselves restrictionists; and the logic has even attracted the attention of several Democratic members of Congress who have echoed environmental restrictionist talking points in legislative debates.[2]

What is new, however, is the institutional setting within which these debates are occurring. In 2008, a coalition calling itself "America's Leadership Team for Long-Range Population-Immigration-Resource Planning" (ALT) placed a series of advertisements in left-leaning news sources (including *Mother Jones, The Nation,* and the *New York Times*) proclaiming that immigration poses a grave threat to the natural environment of the United States. In 2009, Roy Beck of immigration-reduction organization NumbersUSA appeared before the U.S. Senate Judiciary Committee testifying against a bill that would have provided green cards to same-sex partners of U.S. citizens on the grounds that "every new immigrant increases the total U.S. carbon footprint and ecological footprint." And in 2012, an organization calling itself Progressives for Immigration Reform launched the Immigration Environmental Impact Statement Project, seeking justification for immigration restrictions under the U.S. National Environmental Policy Act. Add to this the recent CAPS advertisement, and a clear trend emerges: the environmental restrictionist logic is now being forcefully advanced by traditional immigration-reduction organizations and newly emerging alliances between greens and immigration-reduction organizations formed for the specific purpose of promoting restrictionist policies. "Nature," it seems, occupies an increasingly prominent position in the American immigration-restriction movement—particularly in materials geared toward public consumption.

But what, exactly, is "nature" for restrictionists? How does it intersect with narratives of political community, political economy, race, class, and gender? How is it strategically deployed to broaden and/or deepen restrictionist alliances? And, conversely, how might opponents of restrictionism articulate alternative conceptions of nature and embed them in counternarratives in ways that lead toward social and ecological justice? Although American debates over the environmental impacts of immigration have received attention elsewhere (Reimers 1998; Hartmann 2004; Muradian 2006; King 2008; Urban 2008; Pearce 2010; Angus and Butler 2011; Park and Pellow 2011), commentators have yet to systematically analyze the variety of ways that commitments to nature are woven into restrictionist thought.

This shortcoming is reflective of a broader theoretical lacuna in environmental thought: greens lack an adequate understanding of the political terrain on which struggles over nature intersect with the norms, practices, and institutions of sovereignty. As nature is increasingly being deployed in projects of boundary drawing—working in the service of exclusion, coercion, and dispossession—a failure to grapple with this emerging form of territorialization disables effective responses to "environmental restrictionism"[3] and opens up space for anti-immigrant logics to subtly influence well-intentioned greens. This book seeks to provide environmental scholars and activists a better understanding of this phenomenon, shedding light on the discursive and institutional pathways through which nature is subtly woven into exclusionary political projects.

## MAKING SENSE OF ENVIRONMENTAL RESTRICTIONISM

American debates over the environmental impacts of immigration raise important questions about the relationship between nature—almost universally assumed to be a commitment of "liberals,"[4] progressives, or radicals—and the politics of social exclusion. In addition to the American right's disavowal of all things environmental (Dunlap, Xiao, and McCright 2001; Bryner 2008; Anderson 2011),[5] nature's location on the left of the political spectrum is reinforced by its perceived function as a counterscreen to neoliberalism. Nature provides a feeling of place amid the dislocations of capital, a space of leisure as demands of work increase, a sense of tradition as many yearn for simpler times, and a symbol of purity in a period in which seemingly little is sacred and all is commodified. Nature is widely seen to exist outside of, or even in contrast to, neoliberal political economy; it represents both an escape from late capitalism and a progressive bulwark against its advance.

That nature now occupies a space on the left of American political imaginaries has left many observers baffled and struggling to make sense of how environmentalists could possibly support anti-immigrant politics.[6] Not surprisingly, the solution to this apparent puzzle has been to assert that those advancing this logic *could not possibly be actual environmentalists*. Antiracist organizations, such as the Southern Poverty Law Center and Center for New Community, have aggressively publicized the "John Tanton Network," revealing the connections between one of the architects of the American restrictionist movement, immigration-reduction logics, and overt racism (Southern Poverty Law Center 2002b; Center for New Community 2009). The argument here is that environmental restrictionists are not "real environmentalists" but "wolves in sheep's clothing" (Beirich 2010).

Such a response is not unfounded; several prominent restrictionist organizations, such as the American Immigration Control Foundation, use environmental rhetoric for the sole purpose of advancing their xenophobic ideologies, and other organizations, such as Californians for Population Stabilization, have been quick to strategically latch on to anti-immigrant allies and agendas. However, this response is incomplete and continues to portray the relationship between nature and social exclusion in dichotomous terms: either you are committed to nature, or you are committed to anti-immigrant politics. You cannot be both. And if you are one of the few activists—like Edward Abbey or Garrett Hardin—who are undoubtedly both, it is a mere coincidence.

Although I sympathize with this narrative, it rests on a flawed vision of nature and culture as separate ontological spheres, neglecting to consider how conceptions of nature are imbued with cultural assumptions, and vice versa. It posits, on one side, Nature, that emancipatory field made intelligible through ecological sciences, romantic aesthetics, and eastern philosophy, and, on the other side, Culture, wherein lurk the exclusionary institutions and norms of sovereignty, nationalism, racism, militarism, neoliberalism, and so on. Such a narrative, however, doesn't mesh with the complexities of natural–cultural interconnection. As opponents of restrictionism point out, nature's perceived location within progressive politics enables it to be used for exclusionary purposes by a variety of actors who seek to naturalize their (usually privileged) location within the political community while marginalizing others. Nature, in this sense, functions as a progressive signifier deployed by individuals and groups for whom a sense of place underscores the connections between blood and soil; "simpler times" is a thinly veiled code for "whiter times," and purity refers to the national culture as much as the natural environment. My argument, however, is that there is also something *internal to environmental thought* that renders nature so easily appropriable by anti-immigrant advocates and that renders restrictionism so attractive to many greens. Nature is not merely *captured* to advance exclusionary social agendas; it is commitments to certain conceptions of nature that *give rise* to such agendas.

Examples of commitments to nature intersecting with socially exclusionary politics abound in the United States and abroad: from American greens employing tactics of NIMBYism that protect the nature in their local communities while leaving poor, minority, and immigrant populations disproportionately exposed to pollutants and pesticides (Bullard 2000; Pulido 2000; Park and Pellow 2004), to northern environmentalists seeking to prevent indigenous peoples from accessing land and resources in efforts to save "Third World" wildernesses (Neumann 1998; Peluso and Watts 2001; Hartmann 2004), to neo-Malthusians placing the blame for climate change squarely on population growth from the developing world (Hartmann 2004). Drawing on the same logics, environmental restrictionism has been advanced by individuals, organizations, and political parties in many countries of the world, including Australia (Sustainable Population Party), Belgium (Vlams Blok), Canada (Canadian Centre for Immigration Policy Reform), England (Optimum Population Trust), France (alliances between local-level greens and le Front Nationale), Germany (Christian Social Union, Christian Democratic Union), Italy (Northern League), the Netherlands (Center Democrats), Russia (Rasputin), Switzerland (Social Democrats), and Mongolia (Olsen 1999, 135–40; Angus and Butler 2011, 28–35, 118–19; Barria 2013).

To better understand—and ultimately resist—these political realities, this book uses American debates over the environmental impacts of immigration as a lens into the complex ways that nature cuts across a diverse array of social registers, intersecting with ideals of political community, political economy, race, class, and gender. My contention is that only by recognizing the role that nature—specifically "ecocentric" conceptions of nature[7]—plays in restrictionist thought, and reflexively grappling with it, can environmentalists who seek socioecological justice resist the incursions of border walls gone green.

## "Natural" Borders in Crisis

American environmental restrictionism is best understood by considering its location at the intersection of two borders that cut to the core of contemporary political struggles: the ontological borders that separate "Nature" from "Culture" and the geopolitical borders that separate one "Sovereign Nation-State" from another. Both of these borders are in crisis. How the crises of nature and sovereignty are resolved will play a major role in determining the trajectory of twenty-first-century politics.

That nature is in crisis might initially appear obvious: climate change, resource shortages, extreme weather patterns, species extinctions, and environmental pollution of all types abound. Indeed, it has become customary for any book on environmental politics to begin with a list of these crises. What I mean here is slightly different: the nature–culture dualism is in crisis. Over the past twenty years, scholars have sought to politicize this binary, asserting that rather than providing any stable ontological footing from which to base political claims, nature is irrevocably bound up in cultural norms, practices, and institutions, and vice versa (Bennett and Chaloupka 1993; Castree and Braun 2001; Braun 2002). The assumption that nature and culture are discrete spheres of life has only emerged through epistemological practices that purify one from the other (Latour 1993). Nature, in this respect, is a signifier that is conventionally understood to represent the vast multiplicity of the nonhuman realm; it is not a timeless representation of a material reality but a contingent effect of power.

The social construction of nature is reflected in the widely varying conceptions that prevail at different times and places: nature is romanticized and aestheticized or villainized and deemed threatening; it is rationalized and instrumentalized or sacralized and worshiped; it is an enclosed space of equilibrium or a wild space of untamed and overlapping flows. Nature is also raced, classed, gendered, and sexualized. It is often *raced* by linking a specific population (for instance, indigenous peoples) with "nature" and another (generally white Europeans) with "culture" or civilization (Braun 2002; Moore, Kosek, and Pandian 2003; Kosek 2006); it is *classed* by transforming "wilderness" into a space of leisure or recreation over one of labor (White 1995; Williams [1972] 2005); it is *gendered* in constant appeals to a Mother Nature (who is variously nurturing, vindictive, irrational, etc.) who can be tamed or controlled by a masculinized scientific regime (Sandilands 1999); and it is often *sexualized* ("barren wasteland," "fertile wilderness," "impenetrable forest") and linked with these racial, gendered, or class-based anxieties (McClintock 1995; Braun 2002) in ways that shore up some vision of how power relations (naturally) ought to be.

At the same time as the idea that *nature is a social construction* has become increasingly accepted among academics, *actually existing environmental crises*—that is, existential threats to forests, rivers, lakes, plants, and animals—have themselves increased. Driven by these crises, environmental politics is coming to occupy an increasingly prominent, if still marginalized, position on political agendas. This conjuncture has opened the door for debates over nature to influence issue areas—like security, development, and immigration—that have traditionally been governed by anthropocentric logics. The discursive terrain of nature is growing more and more complex. As such, attention to how nature is produced, and to the power relations that accompany various constructions of nature, becomes a central task of environmental political analysis. Throughout the book, I demonstrate how restrictionists and their opponents both concur that our current reality is unsustainable, yet I show that there is little agreement on what sustainability truly entails, and for whom. This disconnect emerges from divergent ways of conceptualizing nature and relating it to the foundational political concept of sovereignty.

## Natural Sovereigns, Political Interventions

At first glance, it may seem unorthodox to study ostensibly societal organizations—like the anti-immigrant groups, environmentalists, and immigrants' rights advocates involved in this debate—through the lens of sovereignty. Sovereignty is conventionally understood to refer to the supreme power of the nation-state—a possession that reflects the state's monopoly on the use of coercive force, authority to control borders, recognition by other states, and overall supremacy on matters related to the domestic territory and the populations that reside within. In such an account, the "sovereign nation-state" is defined by its separation from society; it is a relatively autonomous entity that captures authority and rules according to its own methods, logics, and sense of self-interest.

The problem is that this dominant account erases the mutually constitutive relationship between "the nation-state" and "society" that exists in democratic states, in particular. Political struggles dispersed throughout society (forms of knowledge, cultural norms, and political rationales) not only seep into the actions and logics of the nation-state; they produce a vision of what the nation-state is, how it ought to function, and who it should represent—and they produce subjects who demand this vision be enacted. The dominant account of sovereignty (as detached from society) can only explain why the sovereign's vision of nationalism, sense of social purpose, and conception of self-interest all wax and wane through time by appealing to internal shifts in the state itself (e.g., a new president or shifting bureaucratic logics). While these internal variables certainly wield some explanatory weight, they fail to identify the societal shifts that produce changes in executive and bureaucratic logics. As a consequence, this account leaves many questions unanswered. Why has the relationship of certain populations to ideals of nationalism shifted through time? Why does the nation-state exclude certain immigrants while including others? Why have many nation-states gradually incorporated environmental goals into their senses of purpose and identity? To understand these questions, it is necessary to brush aside the dubious analytical separation that equates sovereignty with the nation-state and parcels "it" off from society. It makes more sense to examine how sovereignty emerges as an "effect of power" forged through discourses, institutions, and practices dispersed throughout social life (Mitchell 1991).[8]

Debates over the environmental impacts of immigration are instructive in this regard. The success of the environmental restrictionist argument is dependent on the naturalization of visions of sovereignty that resonate with carefully targeted segments of the American public— visions that rely on particular *articulations* between territorial borders, national and racial identities, political economic ideologies, forms of governance, and claims surrounding ecological integrity.[9] To unpack the assumptions that undergird environmental restrictionism, my analysis of the case engages with recent work that examines the processes through which—amid the myriad flows and ruptures of globalization—certain populations (e.g., immigrants) become perceived as "threats" against which the "sovereign nation-state" comes to understand and reproduce its identity, boundaries, and sense of social and ecological purpose (Weber 1995; Shapiro 2004; Doty 2009; Brown 2010). As R. B. J. Walker (1992) has noted, dominant narratives of sovereignty function through *depoliticization,* transforming historically and culturally specific assumptions about the relationship between political community, space, and time into "natural," "objective," or "universal" givens from which analysis of the world, and action in the world, proceeds. For example, many anti-immigrant movements are founded on the assumption that the self-interested, "sovereign nation-state"—conceived as a clearly demarcated entity with a uniform culture and absolute autonomy and control over territorial borders—is natural (Perea 1997; Doty 2009). A critical reading of sovereignty aims to *repoliticize* such an account by revealing the discursive processes—the struggles over knowledge, social norms, and, ultimately, meaning—through which sovereignty is constantly being (re)produced (Walker 1992; Weber 1995; Doty 1996; Shapiro 2004). Thus, in contrast with works that define sovereignty as a timeless reflection of the nation-state's *natural* supremacy (and its concomitant ability to legitimately deploy violence), I conceive of sovereignty as the process through which authority backed by coercive force is "constituted and legitimated" (Shaw 2008, 1; see also Lindner 2012, 45).[10]

To analyze struggles over how environmental restrictionists and their opponents seek to reconfigure sovereignty—to constitute and legitimate a particular type of authority backed by coercive force—I draw heavily on the work of two political theorists: Michel Foucault and Giorgio Agamben. I turn to these particular thinkers because of the insight they provide into the relationship between sovereignty and, what Foucault famously termed, "biopolitics." Biopolitics refers to Foucault's assertion that whereas earlier forms of sovereign power were content to merely "take life or let live," today's predominant mode of power is defined by an attempt to intervene at the level of the population in pursuit of a whole host of political ends; it seeks to "foster life or disallow it to the point of death" (Foucault [1978] 1990, 138). Theorists emphasizing biopolitics evaluate the ways in which various populations emerge as targets of governmental rationalities that attempt to mold, distribute, and regularize forces of biological life (population movements, literacy rates, fertility rates, levels of production, modes of consumption, etc.) in line with certain political ends. In opposition to, though frequently operating in tandem with, the spectacular, violent manifestations of sovereign power, biopolitics set into motion relations of power that subtly function through the deployment of scientific, "objective" knowledge (demography, political economy, biology, etc.) (142–43).[11] It is here, according to Foucault, where the major political struggles of our time—"the 'right' to life, to one's body, to health, to happiness, to the satisfaction of needs"—will play out (145).

Agamben agrees with Foucault that an attention to biopolitics is necessary to understand modern social life, but he suggests that Foucault's conception fails to capture the actual enigma of contemporary power. Although Foucault repeatedly notes that sovereign power and biopower are related to one another, Agamben contends that he fails to specify "the point at which the voluntary servitude of individuals comes into contact with objective power" (Agamben 1998, 6). In other words, how do the biopolitical practices—*the relations of power*—that Foucault identifies intersect with forms of sovereign power defined by *relations of violence* (Edkins and Pin-Fat 2004, 3–9)? To illuminate this connection, Agamben makes the case that in contrast with Foucault's narrative in which "the biological" becomes a target of state power in the nineteenth century, "the production of the biopolitical body is the originary activity of sovereign power" (Agamben 1998, 5). His argument is that sovereignty and biopolitics are historically wedded to one another through the ability of the sovereign to declare a "state of exception" (or "state of emergency") in which the normal juridical order is suspended in the very name of saving that order. These periods of crisis create the potential for the sovereign to deploy coercive force in ways that would not be permitted under "normal" modes of rule, relegating populations deemed threats to the sovereign's rule to, what Agamben terms, "bare life"—biological life abandoned to the perpetual administration of the sovereign, without any of the protections that have historically characterized politically qualified life.[12]

Whereas the state of exception was once a temporary aberration in political life, Agamben (1998, 9) suggests that we live in a period in which the exception has effectively become the rule, with far-reaching implications:

> The decisive fact is that, together with the process by which the exception everywhere becomes the rule, the realm of bare life—which is originally situated at the margins of the political order, gradually begins to coincide with the political realm, and exclusion and inclusion, outside and inside, *bios* and *zoē*, enter into a zone of irreducible indistinction.

As such, the line between democracy and totalitarianism is fast becoming indistinguishable as power invests the most intimate minutiae of biological life in the very name of saving democracy, without providing recourse to the sorts of political rights that have historically characterized democratic societies. In this period, Agamben asserts that we are all in danger of becoming bare life.

And yet, although bare life may be a universal potentiality, a number of critics have pointed out that it is only actualized through the production of difference—across, often interlocking, lines of race, class, gender, nationality, religion, and sexuality (Pratt 2005; Giroux 2006; Ong 2006; Biswas and Nair 2010). Put differently, sovereignty is biopolitical, as Agamben claims, but the terrain linking biopolitics to sovereignty is more relational and dispersed than he accounts for. The "threats" that create the conditions of existence for any state of exception are not merely conjured out of thin air by a "nation-state" that "decides" the exception; they have historically depended upon claims to objectivity that have naturalized the distinctions separating "the civilized" and/or "the nation" from indigenous populations, racial minorities, women, the "Third World," the poor, and immigrants (Deloria and Lytle 1984; Tully 1995; Soguk and Whitehall 1999; Bruyneel 2007; Mongia 2007).[13] While conventional accounts of sovereignty have worked to reinforce these "threats," a biopolitical reading suggests that sovereignty is produced through discourses that deploy knowledge (e.g., claims to truth emerging from orthodox international relations theory, neoliberal political economy, Darwinian natural science) and social norms (e.g., appeals to national identity, culture, legality) in the strategic ordering, management, and distribution of specific populations—for the supposed good of the body politic (Shapiro 2004; Lindner 2012). Biopolitical struggles are central to the operation of sovereign power. In working to reinforce or reconfigure distinctions between "politically qualified life" and "bare life," sovereignty is always already biopolitical.[14]

## NATURE AND SOVEREIGNTY: FROM SPACES
## OF FLOW TO SPACES OF EXCEPTION

How does this approach to sovereignty shed light on environmental restrictionism? My argument is that struggles over sovereignty are dispersed throughout social life, imbricated in claims to knowledge, scientific methodologies, social norms, and political strategies. As Karena Shaw (2008, 205) observes, "the resolutions and practices of sovereignty are constitutive of conceptual frameworks we use to understand the world." One such concept that has been articulated in a mutually constitutive relationship with sovereignty is nature.[15] Accounts of "nature as sovereign"—that is, of nature cleansed of all political and cultural residues—work to naturalize certain assumptions of political sovereignty. For instance, Hobbes, Locke, and Rousseau famously turned to visions of nature to legitimate their normative ideals of civil society. Conversely, ostensibly "cultural" norms of sovereignty (e.g., territoriality, nation, and race) themselves meld into ideals of nature. Most notoriously, racialized notions of national purity were historically articulated with romantic ideals of natural purity in early-twentieth-century German and American contexts (Bramwell 1989; Biehl 1994; Olsen 1999). This entangled, potentially insidious relationship between sovereignty and nature becomes particularly clear in examining debates over the environmental impacts of immigration. On September 23, 2008, an advertisement from the aforementioned ALT appeared in the *New York Times* (2008):

> As America's population races from the current 300 million to a projected 400 million in the next 30 years, progressive thinkers are confronted with a debate among themselves—and Others—as to our nation's capacity to absorb domestic population growth and growth due almost entirely to immigration. What price will we pay in terms of the environment? What will be the impact on resources from water to energy? What additional challenges will be created by this growth? What is our responsibility to future generations?

Framed against a backdrop of an apparently pristine landscape, the ad portrays a man standing in front of two paths: one presumably leads to a sustainable future, the other to certain ecological destruction (Figure 1). Throughout other publications that composed the umbrella coalition's yearlong ad campaign—six pieces appearing in fifteen news sources (*The American Prospect, The Atlantic, Forbes, Foreign Affairs, Harpers, The Hill,* the *LA Times, Mother Jones, The Nation, Nature, Newsweek, The New Republic,* the *New York Times, Roll Call,* and the *Washington Post*)—a similar narrative emerged: U.S. citizens have taken significant steps toward adopting a progressive environmental culture (having fewer children, recycling, and developing renewable energy sources), however, "we" continue to import population growth. This offsets "our" (allegedly) diminishing consumptive habits and puts serious stress on ecosystems that are already at or above their carrying capacities. Throughout the advertisements, this overarching neo-Malthusian logic is interspersed with forays into postmaterialist values, place-based identities, romantic aesthetics, geopolitics, and cultural consumptive patterns.

The ALT coalition proceeds by strategically directing its arguments at progressive, environmentalist audiences while, at the same time, recognizing that its position is controversial in such circles and attempting to anticipate unease with its exclusionary policy prescriptions:

> We want it all. We want a clean environment, adequate natural re-
> sources, good housing, plenty of food, first rate healthcare, and so
> on. We also feel the need to welcome the world to our front door, or,
> in many cases, our back door. But America is rapidly approaching
> the point of no return. Either we opt for preserving the quality of
> life that has attracted so many millions in the past by limiting some
> in the future. Or we continue to accept millions, knowing that our
> children and grandchildren will continue to pay a huge price. No-
> body wants to close the doors. Nobody wants to totally abandon
> our heritage of immigration and the rich tapestry it has woven. But
> with more sensible numbers we could actually restore it. More and
> more progressive thinkers are saying it's time to connect the dots . . .

While this addendum speaks to progressive concerns over natural
resources, intergenerational justice, and even multiculturalism, the
ease with which the nonhuman realm is rhetorically transformed into
a national possession is telling; the preservation of our shared national heritage is explicitly linked with the fate of our environment.
A commentator in a popular restrictionist journal frames the issue in
even starker terms: "Mexico is sweeping its people and problems into
the United States. . . . If we don't solve these problems ourselves, then
Mother Nature will solve them for us" (Duncan 2007).

Though the coalition is more strategic in its presentation, the narrative that emerges is quite similar: the visual appeal to the "road less
traveled" works to conjure up emotions of radical independence and
populism (ideals that lay at the heart of both American and environmentalist identities), while the text serves to fill the two distinct paths with
metaphoric and symbolic meanings. One road, polluted and crowded
with, presumably Mexican, immigrants, leads from "our back door"
to certain ecological destruction. The other, pristine and inhabited by a
treasured line of "Americans" (past, present, and future), proceeds along
a sacred path to the preservation of our wilderness, natural resources,
and, by extension, "rich" multicultural heritage. Ecological health, in
other words, functions as the foundation on which this national imaginary is sustained; the fate of nature is the fate of the American nation.
As I detail throughout the book, environmental restrictionists claim
that steering the mutually constitutive relationship between nature and
sovereignty in a sustainable direction requires a biopolitical intervention
targeting the movements, reproductive practices, economic activities,

FIGURE 1. Population, immigration, and the "progressive conundrum." Advertisement by America's Leadership Team appearing in the *New York Times*, September 23, 2008.

and environmental cultures of immigrant populations. In forging these linkages, environmental restrictionists foster a sociopolitical environment in which immigrant bodies are increasingly subject to sovereign violence.

## Sovereignty: To Green or Not to Green?

The relationships that environmental restrictionists articulate between nature and sovereignty initially appear odd. After all, environmental flows—rivers, oceans, mountain ranges, forests, species migrations, and pollution—traverse boundaries and often evade sovereign control. It thus seems paradoxical for restrictionists to argue that national sovereignty ought to be reinforced to protect nature. The relationship between nature and sovereignty, however, has been the focus of considerable debate among environmental scholars and practitioners, and many environmentalists view the nation-state's sovereignty, in one form or another, as a necessary requirement for environmental protection. This raises the question, is greening sovereignty a viable path toward socioecological transformation? Or does it inevitably tend toward exclusion, violence, and socioecological injustice?

It should first be noted that many greens do not take an explicit position in these debates, favoring localized practices (e.g., farmers markets, urban gardens, municipal-level lobbying) or normative ideals (e.g., bioregions, appeals to "planetary patriotism," ambiguous "glocalisms") that avoid sovereignty or even implicitly disavow it but suggesting few strategies for moving from *what is* toward *what ought to be*. There is also great variability among those who do engage with sovereignty, ranging from calls for a global green sovereignty guided by scientific expertise (see Ehrlich, Ehrlich, and Holdren 1977; Barbier 2010; for a critique, see Wainwright and Mann 2013), to a confederal system of bioregions or ecovillages (Mische 1989; Deudney 1998), to a variety of subaltern ecosovereignties espoused by indigenous actors and environmental justice activists in the food sovereignty and climate justice movements (see, e.g., Barker 2005; Alkon and Agyeman 2011). However, among those who take a concrete stance on sovereignty, two dominant—and contrasting—positions have emerged.

On one hand are those who argue that the "sovereign nation-state" remains the primary terrain for environmental protection and that strengthening its regulatory capacity will provide a necessary check on the excesses of transnational capital (Eckersley 2004; 2006; 2007a; Barry and Eckersley 2005; Hunold and Dryzek 2005; Meadowcroft 2005). The most prominent of these thinkers is Robyn Eckersley (2004, 5), who contends that because states are "likely to persist as major sites of social and political power for at least the foreseeable future," greens should focus their strategic energies on building a radically different type of ecological state. Her basic premise is that the state is a contingent discursive construction open to contestation (34–35, 62–64). It is therefore possible to reconfigure the contours of public responsibility and obligation to allow the state's regulatory and steering mechanisms to work toward green projects pushed forward by an amended *demos*.

To guide the trajectory of such shifts toward an inclusive sovereignty, Eckersley proposes a political community founded on a blend of communitarian concerns with cultural solidarity and cosmopolitan emphasis on transnational affect. Her "transnational state" would gain legitimacy through its organization around principles of "cosmopolitan nationalism" that strategically reorient the insular ethos of traditional nationalism outward to extend to nonhumans, nonmembers, and future generations (Eckersley 2004, chapter 7; 2007a, 677). In this sense, "the people would remain sovereign, but would be a more variable and fluid community made up of nations and all those who happen to belong, or are likely to belong, to the relevant community at risk" (Eckersley 2004, 197). Eckersley attempts to institutionalize this inclusive form of sovereignty through a mutually reinforcing interaction between a "green constitution" and a "green public sphere." The former would solidify certain social and ecological norms in law (e.g., the precautionary principle, rights to environmental information, public participation) (193), whereas the latter would guarantee that a fluctuating array of actors could voice their social and ecological realities in debates that have direct implications for their lives.

While Eckersley's normative ideal is more nuanced than that echoed by activists, the drive to green sovereignty is reflected in the politics of many environmentalists—from calls for a "Green New Deal" (Jones 2008; Stein 2012), to appeals to national sovereignty by environmentalists contesting the environmentally destructive rulings of the World Trade Organization, to the assertions of steady statists that "we" need to strengthen the nation-state to maintain socioecological equilibrium (Daly 2006). For many contemporary scholars and activists, greening the territorial state—and, for some, the nation[16]—is the chief goal of environmentalism; it is the primary terrain on which environmental struggles should be fought.

On the other hand are those who contend that sovereignty is inherently violent, exclusionary, and anthropocentric (Gould 2006; Smith 2008; 2009; 2011; Wainwright and Mann 2013). For example, philosopher Mick Smith (2011, 200–201) asserts that the green statists have overestimated the malleability of sovereignty. He argues that "while we can recognize historically different discourses surrounding and informing the normal practices of state sovereignty . . . its ordering principle is precisely not one that is protean. . . . In the last instance sovereign power is wielded by a 'body' which 'decides on the exception'" (Smith 2009, 113). This "body" is the nation-state, and "the decision" is—given the track record of the nation-state—likely to invoke ecological emergency as a cover for motives that are definitely anthropocentric (112–14). In this sense, calls to green sovereignty, no matter how well intentioned, are likely to end in exceptional decisions that eschew radical ecological solutions in defense of the stability wrought by a capital-friendly logic of ecological modernization. Indeed, "the possibility of this ultimately arbitrary decisionistic assumption of absolute territorial power underlies all claims to state sovereignty, no matter what kind of political constitutions such states espouse" (113). A complete and total rejection of sovereign power is, for Smith, the only path forward.

This apparently self-evident disconnect between nature and sovereignty is one articulated by a broad array of theorists and practitioners, from orthodox international relations scholars emphasizing the purely instrumental role that natural resources play in the high politics of military affairs (see, e.g., Levy 1995) to deep ecological activists juxtaposing the violent realities of human-created institutions with the liberatory promise of a deterritorialized nature (Earth First! 2011). The latter is also an argument taken up by critics of environmental restrictionism who emphasize that a focus on nature will itself provide pathways to a world without the destructive forces of sovereignty. Following this line of thought, Smith (2008, 9) suggests that the only way out of sovereignty is through the deterritorializing impulses of radical ecology:

> radical ecology tries to save politics and ethics (and not only the natural world), to recognize their "relative autonomy" and their vital importance in constituting a good life for human communities within, and not constitutionally positioned as a sovereign power above, a "more than human" world.

It is through an ethicopolitical commitment to nature that the geopolitical and capitalistic instrumentalities that breed bare life give way to the freedom of a life unmarked by sovereign power: "to save the whales is to free them from all claims of human sovereignty, to release them into the flows of evolutionary time, of natural history" (3). A *real* commitment to nature not only points out cracks and fissures in the machinations of sovereignty; it offers unmediated guidance toward a normatively preferable future.[17]

## The Contingent Contours of Green Sovereignty

The two aforementioned approaches are directly conflicting; the green statists urge us to consider the potentially progressive potentialities that might be latent in current institutional forms, while their critics call attention to the underlying biopolitical structure of sovereignty, which is said to negate any potentially radical shifts in environmental governance (turning instead to the emancipatory power of nature itself). The latter contention suggests that whereas green statists seek a mode of sovereignty that is more socially inclusive and ecologically sustainable, their approach leaves undertheorized the interstices in which environmental politics, subtle biopolitical practices, and the often violent spectacles of sovereign power meet. "Progressive" environmental projects routinely rely on managing the biological lives of various populations; concerns over population reduction, for instance, seek to channel fertility rates, distribute movement, and control the productive and consumptive capacities of select populations in efforts to construct a particular type of environmental society. Such projects are often bound up in exclusionary politics of race, class, and gender and, in periods of "crisis," are likely to be imposed rather than subject to democratic debate.

These exclusionary residues persist even within the most radical calls for greening sovereignty. Eckersley (2007a, 685), for instance, insists on the necessity of national solidarity as a precondition for ecological democracy—a strategy that ignores the real risk that nature may be woven into insidious schemes to reconsolidate imagined communities through the exclusion of Others. Historically, certain constitutive elements of nature have materialized within narratives of exception: discourses of Linnaean classification, romantic wilderness, Malthusian political economy, and Darwinian natural science have all served as markers of difference enabling the erasure of indigenous and marginalized inhabitants from the national landscape or constructing them as biopolitical threats to the vitality of the nation (Braun 2000; 2002, Tsing 2005; Kosek 2006). These "natural" concepts, which have worked to efface the violence through which hegemonic national forms have proceeded, are more likely to reemerge today under a commitment to "progressive" environmental politics rather than an overt commitment to nationalism.

And while the green statists tend to overlook the way that nature is bound up in biopolitical struggles, those explicitly rejecting sovereignty too often "cut the head off the king"[18] only to fashion his ghost into a biopolitical God whose exceptional decisions are a fait accompli. Both the declaration of the state of exception and the trajectory through which it emerges appear inevitable. In his universal rejection of sovereignty, for example, Smith does not unpack the contingent conjunctures that suture "the nation" to "the state" at a particular point in time. This leaves him open to the same critique that political theorist William Connolly (2004, 29) levels against Agamben:

> He does not ask whether disturbing developments in the logic of sovereignty are bound not merely to a conjunction between biopolitics and sovereignty, *but to a conjunction between them and renewed attempts to consolidate the spirituality of the nation during a time when it is even more difficult to do so.* If and as the reactive drive to restore the fictive unity of the nation is relaxed, it becomes more possible to negotiate a generous ethos of pluralism that copes in more inclusive ways with the nexus between biology, politics, and sovereignty. . . . The shape of the ethos infusing the practice of sovereignty is therefore critical, and not a mere conjugation of sovereignty and biopolitics.

Connolly's emphasis on the *ethos of sovereignty* is significant, because it suggests that sovereignty—particularly in governmental arrangements that are influenced, to some degree, by democratic processes—is, far from being reducible to a single static logic, subject to contingent struggles between shifting ideals of the sacred that emanate throughout society. Two prominent secular manifestations of the sacred have been found in nationalism (epitomized by godlike depictions of "Founding Fathers" and the veneration of national anthems and flags) and nature (epitomized by romantic depictions of Wilderness as "sublime"). While those holding the formal levers of power might "declare" a state of exception when these sacred ideals are perceived as threatened, they are reliant on the presence of preexisting discourses that will legitimate their actions and allow them to retain the degree of popularity necessary to prolong or extend their authority. This is not to advance a naive pluralism—historical path dependencies, institutional sedimentations, and material asymmetries of power matter—but to recognize the existence of complex, mutually constitutive interrelations between state, economy, and society that must be empirically fleshed out.

In this light, Connolly (2004, 30) notes that "within the idea of the exception 'decided' by sovereignty, an oscillation flows between a juridically established authority that authoritatively decides the exception and social powers that insert themselves irresistibly in and around the decision." The logics pushing forth these sovereign projects do not emerge within an autonomous site irrevocably wedded to predetermined interests but through forms of "statecraft from below" that struggle among themselves for institutionalization in diverse macropolitical realms (Doty 2001). For instance, in her analysis of American vigilante justice groups, Roxanne Doty (2007, 130) argues that "the decision that ushers in both the enemy and 'we,' 'the people,' 'the nation,' 'the society,' is in fact a plurality of decisions made from diverse locales." Discursive struggles over the scope of political community, and over the scale and social purpose of governance (as well as over the racial, gendered, class-based, and sexualized norms that are embedded within these discussions), create the conditions of existence for any formal declaration of exception. Nature plays an increasingly vital role within this process.

My argument is that those who are quick to embrace the greening of sovereignty frequently neglect to consider how the territorialized assumptions hedged within specific constructions of nature might be translated into violent exclusions during periods of crisis. At the same time, however, those who reject sovereignty altogether too often harken back to an image of a singular sovereign body—the nation-state—declaring a state of exception, when such a declaration emerges from a multiplicity of enunciative sites dispersed throughout society. As a consequence, the anti-statists often fail to identify and resist the broader biopolitical terrain (i.e., the norms, forms of knowledge, and cultural identities that are galvanized in efforts to construct sustainable societies) that continues to give rise to violence, exclusion, and inequality. The alternative ideals that they strive for (e.g., anarchoprimitivism, bioregionalism) thus stand in danger of subtly reproducing the very biopolitical agendas they aim to resist—a danger borne out by the surprisingly large number of primitivists and bioregionalists advocating restrictionist positions.[19]

Both approaches frame their projects in opposition to neoliberal globalization; both work from the radical (or critical) ecological tradition; and both seek an inclusive, equitable, and just future. However, both approaches also pay insufficient attention to how nature is contingently produced and woven into the norms, practices, and institutions of sovereignty at particular political conjunctures. This is problematic because environmental politics is an issue area in which there exists no definitive voice that renders nature intelligible for all. And as environmental advocates strategically latch on to traditionally anthropocentric discourses of security, jobs, development, and migration, the ethos that green sovereignty might take on depends on hotly contested struggles—between the scientist, capitalist, deep ecologist, bureaucrat, economist, social justice advocate, and, at times, xenophobe—to articulate a particular conception of nature and its relation to ideals of political community, political economy, governmental institutions, race, class, and gender. The outcomes of these struggles are not predetermined.

Analyzing how these forms of *statecraft from below* work to reconfigure the *ethos of sovereignty* provides insight into how power relations are produced in ways that enable and disable specific types of interactions with a host of differentially positioned Others (human and more-than-human). Within American debates over the environmental impacts of immigration, there exists significant variability—both *within* restrictionist alliances and *between* restrictions and opponents—in the ethos of sovereignty that social actors are attempting to sculpt. As such, conceptualizing environmental restrictionism as a form of statecraft from below can offer a more holistic understanding of the discursive pathways through which the nature–sovereignty nexus is being reproduced and resisted. In contrast with universalizing accounts that reject or embrace green sovereignty, examining the discourses embedded in these forms of statecraft from below can provide strategic direction to environmental and social activists working on the ground at specific locales and conjunctures to ameliorate the violent, exclusionary, or environmentally destructive manifestations of sovereign power.

## LOOKING FORWARD

As nature is valued and deployed in ways that have vastly differing social and environmental consequences—many of which are antithetical to inclusion and justice—it is crucial to better grasp how varied conceptions of nature intersect with the foundational political construct of sovereignty. Rather than engaging in this debate through an abstract theoretical analysis (as much of the existing literature has done), I employ a case study of how this relationship is produced in a heated environmental struggle, asking, how do social actors conceptualize and work to reconfigure the relationship between nature and sovereignty?

To explore this question, I examine the various discourses through which efforts to green sovereignty proceed among environmental restrictionists and their opponents. Following Maarten Hajer (1995, 44), I define discourse as the "ensemble of ideas, concepts and categories through which meaning is given to social and physical phenomena and which is produced and reproduced through an identifiable set of practices." What I seek to understand in this analysis is not the simple "empirical" relationship between immigration and environmental degradation in the United States—which has been studied elsewhere (Squalli 2009; 2010; Price and Feldmeyer 2012)—but how the concept of sovereignty and its constituent parts (e.g., "the nation," "the state," "the border," "culture") influence the ways in which American environmental and social actors conceptualize nature, and, conversely, how particular constructions of nature (e.g., Malthusian, romantic,

Darwinian) influence the ways in which American environmental and social actors conceptualize sovereignty.

My contention is that positivist analyses, centered on the question of the impact of immigration on the natural environment of the United States, are shot through with normative assumptions that remain unquestioned. For example, the positivist discourse insists that the health of nature can be measured through national-level proxies (e.g., American carbon dioxide emissions). This effectively transforms socially constructed borders into natural facts while a priori purging any ecosystemic or transnational forms of analysis from discussion. Implicit here is a claim that the nation-state is the appropriate lens through which environmental impacts can be examined and understood. And while those employing this form of analysis highlight the impact the transnational movement of bodies has on environmental health, the transnational political economic logics, processes, and institutions that push forward migration and, in many cases, environmental degradation are cleansed from the analytical terrain. Those who are concerned about the exclusionary social implications of environmental restrictionism, but continue to employ positivist analyses, effectively allow their opponents to set the terms of the debate.

By contrast, a discursive approach to the nature–sovereignty relationship enables insight into the ontological and epistemological assumptions that are embedded in the efforts of both environmental restrictionists and their opponents to grapple with the so-called immigration problem. Drawing on textual analysis of websites, publications, and advertisements of organizations supporting and opposing environmental restrictionism, as well as thirteen semistructured interviews with activists who have publicly taken positions within this debate, I sketch the contours of the discursive terrain on which individuals and organizations are currently seeking to reconfigure American sovereignty by appealing to nature.

It is important to note that, like all methods, discourse analysis has its limitations. My discourse analysis alone cannot explain the coercive force that the U.S. Border Patrol wields against migrant bodies or the chains of production that drive migrant workers from Sonora to Arizona. My analysis of American debates over the environmental impacts of immigration does, however, reveal the multiple channels through which nature and sovereignty come to intersect. Although other scholars and activists have critiqued environmental restrictionists, they have often portrayed them as a homogeneous grouping of irrational, anthropocentric nativists appropriating environmental discourses to advance their xenophobic ends (a notable exception is Angus and Butler 2011). My discursive account, though highly critical of environmental restrictionism, recognizes that there exists significant variability within environment restrictionism and clarifies the internal logics of three restrictionist discourses. This approach enables me to identify the subtle pathways through which environmental restrictionism advances; not only among overt nativists and racists but among well-intentioned greens. I thus make the case that challenging discourses of environmental restrictionism is a necessary (although insufficient) step toward destabilizing and resisting the structural realities that produce sovereign violence and exclusion. Discourse functions as a key material foundation through which biopolitics and sovereignty are contingently related to one another; discourses imbued with biopolitical assumptions become sedimented within institutions that possess the capacity to visit coercive force on supposedly deviant, dangerous, or resistant bodies. In this case, the apparently progressive discourse of green sovereignty advances a biopolitical project that legitimates attempts to reduce immigrant populations to bare life.

My analysis proceeds as follows. Chapter 1 traces the historical trajectory of the relationship between nature and immigration restrictionism, asserting that commitments to nature and restrictionist politics are not *mutually exclusive* but *mutually constitutive*. To show this, I detail how three ways of knowing nature—Malthusianism, romanticism, and Darwinism—have historically intersected with American restrictionism. I find that from the late 1800s to the late 1930s, an articulation between romantic and Darwinian natures intersected with a hegemonic, racial nationalism through a shared commitment to natural and national purity. By contrast, from the early 1940s to the early 2000s, the overt racial essentializations present in the earlier wave of restrictionism were subsumed by a dominant neo-Malthusian nature that cut across an increasingly complex social terrain, enabling restrictionists to reinforce American sovereignty through the exclusion of immigrants, but provoking strong opposition in the process.

This historical overview begins to highlight how the nature–sovereignty relationship is mediated by a variety of sociopolitical struggles over race, gender, nationalism, and capitalism. My analysis pays particular attention to how changing notions of race have enabled and disabled particular forms of environmental restrictionism.[20] Dominant conceptions of both nature and sovereignty have historically been racialized. With regard to sovereignty, American political supremacy and white supremacy have been intimately entwined in ways that have limited political participation and economic opportunities for populations deemed nonwhite, while disproportionately exposing them to state and societal violence (Olson 2004).[21] In recent years, however, the overt forms of white supremacy that once undergirded American sovereignty have given way to "neoracism"—racial discrimination premised not on assertions of biological inferiority but on appeals to cultural signifiers that have been historically imbued with racial assumptions (Balibar [1991] 2005; Doty 1999).[22]

As neoracism comes to dominate anti-immigrant discourse, explicit concerns over racial inferiority are displaced into ostensibly nonracial categories, and racial anxieties over increased immigration are recast in terms of cultural values, economic costs, security threats, and—in this case—environmental degradation. In her analysis of "new nativism," Robin Jacobson (2008, 3) points out that race is "no longer a central platform on which immigration restrictionists stand publicly." Immigration scholar Kevin Johnson (1997, 175) concurs, remarking that "race normally is submerged in public discourse about immigration." In such a conjuncture, the natures that worked to legitimate the *biological* racism of eugenics have morphed into natures that justify racialized *cultural* essentializations on the basis of "objective" and "ecocentric" concerns over population growth.

The difficulty in grappling with neoracism is that, in addition to a strategy, the displacement of immigration debates onto (what appear to be) nonracial terrains also attracts adherents who are not driven by overtly racist agendas. The environment, because of its perceived location on the left of the political spectrum, thus provides a unique strategy for restrictionists and a unique challenge for opponents of restrictionism. The nature that emerges from environmental restrictionism reflects both an instrumental strategy to depoliticize controversial questions (overpopulation, identity, borders, inclusion, etc.) and a genuine onto-logical and epistemological commitment of many greens. The key point is that racial formations do not rely on ecocentric ideals of nature to merely cover up their real (i.e., cultural) ideological goals. Rather, certain ideals of nature themselves give rise to racialized iterations of sover-eignty. In this sense, dominant racial formations have rested on visions of nature that were articulated, in part, *from within environmentalism*.

The argument that I begin to flesh out here is that the articulations between nature and sovereignty create space for political maneuver, playing the ostensibly "cultural" politics of sovereignty off against the "natural" politics of the environment in ways that justify social hierar-chies while speaking in languages that seem color-blind. In this sense, the history of racism, coupled with the continually shifting terrain of race, has ensured that racial hierarchies are at times reflected in both "natural" (e.g., carrying capacity, wilderness, purity and pollution) and "cultural" (e.g., nationalism, citizenship, legality) concepts. Out of this history, we (greens) have inherited a seemingly contradictory conjunc-ture: on one hand, most American environmentalists have adopted core cultural commitments—to liberal equality, multiculturalism, and, in many cases, social justice—that place them on the left of the American political spectrum and lead them to extend some form of ethical and political recognition to immigrants; but on the other hand, contempo-rary commitments to nature remain bound up in epistemologies that have close historical linkages with conservative, restrictionist politics. Contemporary political debates continue to be filtered through the dichotomous nature–culture ontology, and the social and ecological commitments that flow from this ontology are often at odds. This cre-ates an ambivalence that cuts to the core of American political debates and renders nature a pivotal site of discursive struggle.

Chapter 2 begins to shed light on this struggle by analyzing two dis-courses of contemporary environmental restrictionism: *social nativism* and *ecological nativism*. Social nativism refers to traditional nativist and white nationalist ideologies that seek to secure American sovereignty against the "nonwhite invasion." While social nativists routinely draw on nature as a symbol of disorder, they periodically (and instrumentally) deploy ecocentric concerns in attempts to appeal to those beyond the far right. By contrast, econativism refers to individuals and organizations for whom ecocentric commitments to nature have come to intersect with commitments to sovereignty driven by racial and cultural essentializations. The logic of econativism is grounded in neo-Malthusian, Darwinian, and romantic traditions through which nature is intricately woven into a celebration of Anglo-European culture. I argue that econativism represents a form of neoracism through which "natural" visions of sovereignty serve to shore up visions of natural purity, and vice versa. I conclude by arguing that because the cultural essentializations prevalent in the discourse are so clearly racialized, it is unlikely that either of these discourses could work to broaden the support for environmental restrictionism, though they may deepen anti-immigrant sentiment within the far right. For this reason, a new discourse is emerging in an attempt to appeal to "progressive environmentalists."

Chapter 3 introduces a discourse of environmental restrictionism that is typically, and problematically, ignored by opponents: *ecocommunitarianism*. Although there is a long tradition of communitarianism in environmental thought and practice (e.g., social ecology, bioregionalism, indigenous ecologies), ecocommunitarian restrictionism is the logic being articulated in restrictionist material geared toward public consumption. These restrictionists move away from the cultural essentializations of econativism, embedding their commitments to nature in a discourse of communitarianism that emphasizes multiculturalism, democratic processes, and shared national sacrifices. Ecocommunitarianism provides a forceful critique of neoliberalism, brings nonhumans and future generations into its discussion of political community, and makes repeated reference to saving "wild places."

Ecocommunitarians also move beyond the neoracism of nativist forms of restrictionism in embedding their commitments to a national nature within a discourse of "postracism" (or "color-blind racism") (Bonilla-Silva 2006). In articulating their own internal logic, racial anxieties and cultural essentializations are avoided at all cost; however, race is continually emphasized as a preemptive response to critics. Their argument—one that appears time and again in journal articles, on websites, and in interviews—is that anyone bringing race into discussions of population is seeking to close off debate. The ecocommunitarian restrictionists thus discuss race constantly, but in a way that is rhetorically distanced from the logic of ecocommunitarianism itself. I observe that, for environmental restrictionists, ecocommunitarianism represents the next logical strategic step beyond econativism, but also signifies an ideological breaking point. Race is displaced to such an extent that it becomes illegitimate to talk about, yet the policies supported by eco-communitarians further entrench the racialized structures producing environmental injustice—thus threatening to shatter the very postracial narrative that ecocommunitarians rely upon. The shattering of this narrative is not preordained, however; it requires opponents who can articulate an alternative vision of the relationships between nature, sovereignty, and race. The problem is that the ecocommunitarian logic has received little attention from opponents of restrictionism despite the fact that it is the discourse of environmental restrictionism that is most likely to persuade social progressives and mainstream environmentalists. How should opponents respond to the relative nuances of ecocommunitarian restrictionism?

Chapter 4 reviews responses to environmental restrictionism, identifying the main discourse on which opponents have relied. I find that while opposition to restrictionism is varied, critics—mainly environmental justice and immigrants' rights advocates—have generally adopted a discourse of *global environmental justice* founded on an opposition between the deterritorialized realities of nature and the territorialized realities of sovereignty. Their arguments vary, but the overall thrust is that sovereignty is inherently anthropocentric and exclusionary, whereas nature is an inherently borderless, emancipatory force. By truly listening to and knowing nature, "we" (humanity and nature writ large) will be guided toward inclusive, sustainable modes of governance.

Though I am sympathetic to the global environmental justice discourse, I argue that it is politically disabling on three interrelated grounds: (1) it pays insufficient attention to the discursive production of nature; (2) it levels a critique of environmental restrictionism that is excessively reliant on a portrayal of individual restrictionists as racist and, in doing so, actually disables broader considerations of structural racism; and (3) it introduces a counterdiscourse that rests on an ahistorical and oversimplified vision of immigrants as "noble savages," which prevents immigrants from full inclusion and participation in environmental politics. I conclude by suggesting that though the activists who oppose restrictionism effectively respond to its nativist iterations, their current efforts have proven incapable of combating the more politically savvy discourse of ecocommunitarianism.

As a consequence, an alternative discursive intervention is needed to destabilize the seemingly beneficent articulations between nature and sovereignty on which ecocommunitarian restrictionists rely.

Chapter 5 attempts to develop an alternative approach to the nature–sovereignty relationship. I begin from the observation that whereas environmental theorists have focused tremendous attention of late on greening traditionally territorialized, anthropocentric institutions (e.g., the nation, the state, citizenship), social theorists have turned to migration to critically reconsider sovereignty. Migration, in these accounts, functions as a lens into (1) the political economic contours of sovereignty during a period of neoliberal globalization, (2) the securitization of sovereignty amid the threats produced by neoliberal globalization, and (3) the modes of resistance that are emerging in relation to these dominant forms of sovereignty. Drawing these insights into environmental political struggles, I sketch the contours of, what I term, an environmental political theory of migration. I make the case that by placing migration at the center of their ontologies, epistemologies, strategies, and ethics, socioecological activists could imbue their practice with a critical cosmopolitan ethos that severs nature from its nationalistic foundations, working to construct a global movement that is better equipped to identify the structural sources of socioecological degradation, more ethical in its inclusion of human and nonhuman others, and more effective in its alliance building.

As environmental crisis worsens and migration intensifies, the way that we react to these borders-in-crisis will shape efforts to construct alternative forms of socioecological communities, economies, and institutions. Will we wall off nation-states through the deployment of nature? Or will we use socioecological interconnectedness to forge transnational modes of obligation and communal identity? Will we scapegoat migrants as ecological savages who pose a threat to national natures? Or will we turn to migrants as those whose experiences might provide insight into diverse iterations of sovereign power and how they might be resisted and reconfigured?

The goal of this book is threefold. First, I attempt to render environmental restrictionism transparent—to invert the gaze away from migrants and toward the networks, logics, and strategies of their restrictionist opponents. My contention is that an in-depth analysis of American debates over the environmental impacts of immigration tells us more about the "nature" of American environmental politics—that is, how greens and their interlocutors conceptualize nature, relate it to foundational political ideals, and internalize it as part of their identities—than it does about the impacts of immigrants on "America's environment."

Second, I attempt to provide a deep description of the discourses through which struggles over greening sovereignty are likely to play out in the coming years. For activists working on the ground against social injustice and ecological degradation, understanding the linkages between nature and social exclusion ought to provide both a reflexive self-awareness and a broader array of strategies in negotiating more just, inclusive futures. My study is anchored in American debates, but the approach that I employ to analyze the relationship between nature and sovereignty could be extended beyond this particular context: shedding light on the promises and perils of environmental nationalism; delineating the contexts within which the securitization of nature might lead to a militarized state of exception; and mapping out the discourses within which debates over ethical obligations to a variety of human and nonhuman Others (e.g., climate refugees and environmental migrants) are likely to take place.

Finally, I attempt to push back against the way that the "immigration problem" has been framed within environmentalist debates. Instead of asking, "What is the impact of immigrants on the national environment?" I shift the discussion to, "What would an activist movement founded on the socionatural realities of migration enable?" In this sense, the idea is to invite environmentalists to step across the lines—geographically, conceptually, strategically—that have artificially constrained their practice, so that "we" might move toward an environmentalism that is both more ethical and effective.

The hope in developing such an alternative would be to convince those well-intentioned environmentalists, currently so captivated by the nature put forth by the restrictionists, not to insulate their nationalized landscapes through the exclusion of the already marginalized so that nature doesn't continue to function as another wedge issue dividing the left on immigration. And so that commitments to nature work to break down walls rather than building them up.

# 1

# WE HAVE ALWAYS BEEN RESTRICTIONISTS

Never, since the Greeks' earliest discussions on the
excellence of public life, have people spoken about politics
without speaking of nature; or rather, never has anyone
appealed to nature except to teach a political lesson.

**BRUNO LATOUR,** *The Politics of Nature*

In a 1751 essay that would influence English political economist Thomas Malthus,[1] Ben Franklin wrote the following:

The Number of purely white People in the World is proportionately very small. All *Africa* is black or tawny. *Asia* chiefly tawny. America (exclusive of the new Comers) wholly so. And in *Europe,* the *Spaniards, Italians, French, Russians* and *Swedes,* are generally of what we call a swarthy Complexion; as are the *Germans* also, and *Saxons* only excepted, who with the *English,* make the principal Body of White People on the face of the Earth. I could wish their Numbers were increased. And while we are, as I may call it, *Scouring* our Planet, by clearing *America* of Woods, and so making this Side of our Globe reflect a brighter Light to the Eyes of Inhabitants in *Mars* or *Venus,* why should we in the Sight of Superior Beings, darken its People? Why increase the Sons of *Africa,* by *Planting* them in America, where we have so fair an Opportunity, by excluding all Blacks and Tawneys, of increasing the lovely White and Red? But perhaps I am partial to the Complexion of my Country, for such Kind of Partiality is natural to Mankind. (10)

Employing the familiar trope of "mankind" taming a dark and dangerous wilderness, the metaphor of light functions to draw a parallel between the civilization of nature and the civilization of the nation—both of which are rhetorically transformed into white spaces. Franklin, thus, links an attempt to secure a racialized nation with his discontent over the impacts of a growing population. While, at this time, this may well have been a "progressive" argument against the importation of slaves, "Civilized" whites have the agency—they can "Plant" Africans here—and nonwhite migrants are passive threats to the nation, its nature, and culture. In Franklin's vision, American popular sovereignty could only be secured through a concomitant process of whitening. What's more, preference for a racialized nation was deemed natural.

Writing on the precipice of modernity, Franklin's writings deploy Nature and Culture as foundational ontological assumptions that work to legitimate specific normative desires. This binary mode of thinking, Bruno Latour has argued, constitutes a hallmark of modern political thought. At the same time, however, Latour insists that these apparently autonomous spheres of life are an illusion—albeit one on which our "modern" realities have been constructed. Nature and Culture only emerge as separate spheres of life through practices of purification that erase the natural–cultural interconnection inherent in the world as it actually exists. Latour (1993, 11) writes,

> The word modern designates two sets of entirely different practices which must remain distinct if they are to remain effective, but have recently begun to be confused. The first set of practices, by "transla-tion," creates mixtures between entirely new types of beings, hybrids of nature and culture. The second, by "purification," creates two en-tirely distinct ontological zones: that of human beings on one hand; that of nonhumans on the other.

Latour thus makes the case that if modern thought, institutions, and actions flow from the binaries between nature and culture, human and nonhuman, then, in all reality, "we have never been modern."

In this chapter, I suggest that this modern nature–culture dualism has been forcefully deployed to advance restrictionist politics: commitments to sovereign natures have served to legitimate cultural ideologies and institutions at the same time as commitments to the cultural politics of sovereignty (nationalism, state self-interest, racism, etc.) have seeped into efforts to know nature in ways that exclude migrants. By decon-structing these logics and revealing the ontological interconnection inherent in ostensibly "natural" projects, I aim to show that modern environmental thought has long been bound up in restrictionist politics.

As I detailed in the introduction, dominant political perceptions suggest that commitments to nature and immigration restriction are fundamentally opposing: commitments to nature emanate from the "progressive" or even "radical" left, whereas commitments to the ideals of sovereignty that lead to immigration restriction are necessarily products of the "conservative" right. This chapter begins to push back against this now-engrained logic, asserting that commitments to nature and restrictionist politics are *not mutually exclusive but mutually constitutive*. Despite the popular tendency to treat ecocentric ideals of nature as inherently progressive, the historical intersections between nature and restrictionism are intense, and the contemporary remnants of these intersections are readily apparent. To play on Latour's famous phrase, "we" greens may never have been modern, but we have always been restrictionists.[2]

The analysis that follows attempts to trace the historical trajectory of this relationship between nature and restrictionism, engaging in what Park and Pellow (2004, 407) term the "environmentalization of racial history" and the "racialization of environmental history." The purpose of my analysis, it should be noted, is not to give a holistic account of the ways in which nature has intersected with exclusionary social projects (an effort that exceeds the scope of this project) but to (1) demonstrate how "nature" is filtered through a variety of epistemological frames that emanate, respectively, from the natural sciences, political economy, social movements, and orthodox international relations and, by doing so, to (2) provide background on several claims to "knowing nature" (specifically Malthusian, romantic, and Darwinian) that are explicitly deployed in contemporary environmental restrictionist projects. The natures articulated by environmentalists over the course of the twentieth century have linked up with visions of nationalism, race, class, and gender in attempts to reconfigure American sovereignty toward an ethos that, in the environmental restrictionist case, is explicitly exclusionary.

## THE HISTORICAL TRAJECTORY OF NATURE AND IMMIGRATION RESTRICTIONISM

The historical intersections between nature and social exclusion have been widely detailed: early naturalists—like Linnaeus and Buffon—employed emerging concepts of biology to build systems of racial classification that they deemed objective and natural (Grove 1996, 163; Koerner 1999); Malthusian political economy constructed a nature of scarcity and competition that enabled England to portray poverty in Ireland, India, and elsewhere as a product of overpopulation (a tendency of "uncivilized" populations) rather than colonial coercion (Ross 1998, 31–32; Pearce 2010, 58); from this Malthusian nature, Darwin derived his theories of natural selection and survival of the fittest—concepts that were soon employed to explain away inequalities of race and class (Bramwell 1989; Worster 1994); and, in the United States, the romantic ideal of experiencing "empty wilderness" to cultivate national subjectivity formed a vital cog in a racialized "frontier mentality" that legitimated the erasure of claims to nature made by Native Americans, Hispanos, African Americans, and eastern European immigrants (Cronon 1996, 27–28; Spence 1999; Jacoby 2001; Kosek 2006).

Less understood, however, are the connections between commitments to nature and commitments to movements for immigration restriction. Interestingly enough, the immigration restriction movement and the environmental movement both took off in the late nineteenth century, and they've been entwined ever since. My analysis begins here—with what I term *first wave environmental restrictionism*—where efforts to protect nature first explicitly converged with efforts to restrict immigration, largely through the intermediary of eugenics. I then observe that the 1940s marked a shift to *second wave environmental restrictionism*, where the relationship between nature and restrictionism took on new discursive forms that were not as overtly connected to racist and nativist logics. I conclude by suggesting that we are on the precipice of a *third wave* of environmental restrictionism that relies on new articulations between nature and sovereignty that resonate with contemporary "progressive" environmentalists.

### First Wave Environmental Restrictionism: Natural–National Purity

The demographic flux of the late nineteenth and early twentieth centuries changed the racial composition of the United States,[3] provoking an anti-immigrant backlash that both seeped into and was reinforced by popular environmental thinking. In the early decades of the twentieth century, romantics expressed fear that immigrants were unable to appreciate wilderness as well as a revulsion against the closeness to nature exhibited by southern, central, and eastern European immigrants (Rome 2008, 433–35; see also Taylor 2002). Specifically, immigrant populations were labeled "pot hunters"—a term referring to those who practiced subsistence hunting—and deemed threats to bird and animal populations (Rome 2008, 434–36). References to *savage* Italian pot hunters abound in the journal *Forest and Stream* and were echoed by early greens like William Hornaday[4] and Madison Grant.[5] These concerns spurred some states to define hunting as a privilege of citizenship and others to institute a tiered system of hunting fees designed to make the practice unaffordable for "foreigners" (Higham 1983, 162; Rome 2008, 435–36).

Romantic efforts to protect a wilderness tinged with race and class were buttressed by the widespread popularity of the social Darwinian "science" of eugenics.[6] Interestingly, proponents of eugenics[7] were not always far right conservatives; many were opposed to traditionalism and militarism and aligned with ecological science and the "Progressive" political ideology (Bramwell 1989, 49–53). For example, eugenics occupied a prominent place in the Progressive[8] agenda of Teddy Roosevelt. Roosevelt's "New Nationalism" speech, written by Gifford Pinchot, the first chief of the Forest Service, articulated the interconnections between nature, race, and nationalism in stark terms:

> Of all the questions which can come before this nation, of the actual preservation of its existence in a great war, there is none which compares in importance with the great central task of leaving this land even a better land for our descendants than it is for us, and training them into a better race to inhabit the land and pass it on. (Roosevelt and Abbott 1910, 21–22, cited by Wohlforth 2010, 28)

Pinchot, along with a prestigious group of scientists and social activists, also submitted a three-volume National Conservation Commission report to Roosevelt titled *National Vitality, Its Wastes and Conservation*:

> The problem of the conservation of our natural resources is therefore not a series of independent problems, but a coherent, all-embracing whole. . . . If our nation cares to make any provision for its grandchildren and its grandchildren's grand-children, this provision must include conservation in all its branches—but above all, the conservation of the racial stock itself. (Fischer 1909, 126, as quoted by Wohlforth 2010, 24–25)

The report included a chapter titled "Conservation through Heredity" that detailed and voiced support for the "science of eugenics." According to journalist Charles Wohlforth, "Roosevelt transmitted the report to Congress with the statement that it was 'one of the most fundamentally important documents ever laid before the American people'" (24).

Pinchot was far from the only environmentally active proponent of eugenics in the United States. The nation's earliest environmental organization, the Boone and Crockett Club (1887), included eugenicists Henry Fairfield Osborn, Hornaday, Grant, and Roosevelt himself. Political geographer Gray Brechin (1996, 233) observes that "members of the Club became key players in the American Museum of Natural History, New York Zoological Park (Bronx Zoo) and San Francisco's Save-the-Redwoods League, as well as eugenics and immigration restriction movements." Examining the political commitments of members of these organizations, it becomes clear that the pull of eugenics was not limited to conservationists espousing progressive ideals of efficiency, scientific rationalism, and economic development; it extended into preservationism as well.[9] In her analysis of the relationship between eugenics and early environmental efforts in California, historian Alexandra Minna Stern (2005, 119–20) finds that eugenic anxieties of racial pollution and "species endangerment" were highly influential in the early years of the Sierra Club, Sempervirens Club, and Save the Redwoods League (see also Allen 2013). Prominent members of these organizations, including Grant, Charles Goethe, John C. Merriam, and David Starr Jordan, viewed the preservation of nature as intimately bound up in the preservation of the national race. Reflecting on the relationship between race and the redwood, Stern writes,

> The redwood—its stateliness, grandeur, and perseverance—represented the "great race." Like Anglo-Saxon America, which was being engulfed by hordes of defectives and mongrels and menaced by the excessive breeding of undesirables, the redwood was imperiled by "race suicide" from rampant logging, urban encroachment, and human ignorance. (124)

Underscoring this commitment to natural and national purity, Goethe, an avid member of virtually every environmental and eugenics organization in existence in the early 1920s, created the Immigration Study Committee to lobby for immigration restrictions from Mexico (home to a "degenerate race" of "peons" and "savages" that would only "mongrelize" its Nordic superiors) (Platt 2005, 17–33; Allen 2013, 53–56).

Even more notoriously, a cofounder of the Save the Redwoods League, Madison Grant (a preservationist who also founded the New York Zoological Park), wrote *The Passing of the Great Race,* in which he cautioned that white Americans "lack the instinct of self-preservation in a racial sense" and argued that "unless such an instinct develops their race will perish, as do all organisms which disregard this primary law of nature" (Grant 1921, 90). Hitler referred to this work as his bible (Spiro 2009, 1), and in his seminal work on American nativism, John Higham (1983, 155) called Grant "intellectually the most important nativist in recent American history."

While I do not wish to draw too close an equivalence between environmentalism, eugenicism, and nativism—each of which has a distinct and heterogeneous history—the three converged in this period in ways that had profound policy implications. Harry Laughlin, president of the Eugenics Record Office, was made the "expert eugenics agent" of the House Committee on Immigration and Naturalization, while Representative Albert Johnson, a close confidant of Grant, deployed eugenic arguments in advocating for the inclusion of racial quotas in the immigration overhaul that he sponsored (Higham 1983, 313–14; Reimers 1998, 21). In addition, Charles Davenport, the founder of the Eugenics Records Office and member of several early environmental organizations, aggressively lobbied Congress to pass eugenics-inspired immigration restrictions (Kosek 2006, 153–54).[10] Ultimately, this thinking was reflected in Calvin Coolidge's oft-quoted statement from immigration debates of the early 1920s:

> There are racial considerations too grave to be brushed aside for sentimental reasons. Biological laws tell us that certain divergent people will not mix or blend. The Nordics propagate themselves successfully. With other races, the outcome shows deterioration. . . . Quality of mind and body suggests that observance of ethnic law is as great a necessity to a nation as immigration law. (1921, 14, quoted by Reimers 1998, 22)

Though the Immigration Act of 1924 strictly curtailed immigration from southern and eastern Europe, the ethnic quota system that it put into place—despite the best efforts of Laughlin and his fellow eugenicists—was not applied to countries in the western hemisphere (Stern 2005, 69–70). However, the eugenic logic institutionalized in the law and embedded in popular imaginaries had impacts that would be felt along the United States–Mexico border (which, up to this point, had been relatively loosely regulated). Stern writes that, in the 1920s, constructions of Mexican migrants as carriers of disease—which had resulted in a "quarantine" in border towns[11]—came to intersect with eugenic concerns over their supposedly inferior racial biology: "reflecting the conflation of germs and genes, the image and description of Mexicans as filthy, lousy carriers that had been spawned by the border quarantine merged with eugenic arguments about the bad hereditary 'stock' of immigrants" (Stern 2005, 68). And although the quarantine was originally put in place to combat a specific public health crisis, Stern suggests that the popular resonance of the eugenics logic enabled this exceptional measure to become the norm. The quarantine lasted until World War II and had impacts that reverberated far and wide:

> The border quarantine helped to solidify the boundary line that had previously been much more nebulous and, in doing so, helped to racialize Mexicans as outsiders and demarcate Mexico as a distinct geographical entity despite topographic and climatic similarity. It not only intensified racial tensions in the borderlands, it also catalyzed anti-Mexican sentiment on a national level and fueled nativist efforts to ban all immigration from the Southern Hemisphere. (Stern 2005, 67)

Of particular importance is the 1921 establishment of a Mounted Quarantine Guard, which came about out of the recognition that many migrants were seeking to avoid the intrusive quarantines by entering into the United States at other points along the border.[12] After the Border Patrol was created as part of the Immigration Act of 1924—a compromise between eugenicists and nativists who wanted strict restrictions on Mexican migration (on the grounds of its impact on public health and national "stock") and southwestern agricultural interests who wanted unfettered access to labor—the relatively limited powers of the Mounted Quarantine Guard were transferred to a Border Patrol emboldened by its authority to "arrest, without warrant, any 'alien' suspected of entering the country illegally or violating federal law" (Stern 2005, 74; see also Ngai 2004, 56–57; Hernandez 2010, 32–36).

Although a detailed engagement with the history, logics, and practices of the Border Patrol is outside the scope of my analysis, Stern contends that "from multiple angles, the Border Patrol can be understood as a facet of a larger eugenic movement rooted in anxieties about biological purity and attendant to contracting and shifting categories of race" (81). In detailing the dramatic increase in the deportation of Mexican immigrants that occurred throughout the 1920s, Mae Ngai (1999, 91) concurs:

> "Illegal" became constitutive of "Mexican," referring, not to citizens of Mexico, but to a wholly negative racial category, which comprised both Mexican immigrants and Mexican Americans in the United States.

As the Great Depression hit, economic hardship, combined with racial animus toward Mexicans, provoked an upsurge in nativism. The Border Patrol's efforts to secure American sovereignty from these racialized "threats" expanded, and American industries turned toward a new pool of surplus labor (the Okies and other out-of-work Americans) (Massey, Durand, and Malone 2003, 34). As a consequence, more than four hundred thousand Mexicans (citizen and noncitizen alike) were "repatriated" during the Depression (Ngai 2004, 72–74; see also Massey, Durand, and Malone 2003, 34–35; Nevins [2002] 2010, 38). Soon enough, however, World War II created a new, dire need for workers, and the United States again turned to Mexican labor via the Bracero program: a temporary, seasonal labor regime that provided Mexican peasants an opportunity to earn the money they needed to return home and farm (Massey, Durand, and Malone 2003, 36).[13] This new wave of migration would face a new wave of restrictionist attacks, anchored in an emergent conception of nature.

## Second Wave Environmental Restrictionism:
## Neo-Malthusianism and Neoracism

Wohlforth (2010, 26) asserts that "World War II's horrors saved our country from going farther down the eugenic path." Eric Ross (1998, 73) amends this observation, arguing that the war did not put an end to eugenics but forced such concerns to be packaged in more subtle, nuanced ways: "As eugenic concerns were muted in the shadow of the Third Reich, environmental catastrophism became the principle vehicle for Malthusian fears." The influence of eugenics, in fact, extends well beyond this restrictionist era to debates over the environmental impacts of population that would, to use Paul Ehrlich's phrase, "explode" in the 1960s. On one hand, eugenics gave rise to the institutional structures—for example, the Population Reference Bureau, Population Council, Office of Population Research, and Pioneer Fund—through which Darwinian and Malthusian logics would be advanced, and the eugenics-inspired Immigration Act of 1924 solidified numerical restriction as the norm in immigration policy (Ngai 2004, 227–28). On the other hand, collective memory of the atrocities of eugenicism, coupled with growing movements for liberal equality, guaranteed that romantic constructions of environmental primitivism and overt social Darwinism would have to be expressed in terms that were less explicitly racist and nativist.

It was in this context that "new Malthusian" thinking emerged, propelled by the works of two American scholars: Fairfield Osborne, director of the Bronx Zoo and New York Zoological Society, and William Vogt, an ornithologist. Both thinkers embraced the central thesis of Malthus: population grows exponentially in a manner that outstrips food production and puts stress on social and ecological resources alike. Both, however, couched this Malthusian political economic logic within a natural scientific narrative derived from the burgeoning science of ecology. Vogt and Osborne drew on new ideas of "carrying capacity," a concept that had first been developed in the shipping industry but had since been adapted and deployed by population biologists and wildlife ecologists such as Aldo Leopold (Sayre 2008, 122–23; Robertson 2012, 38–43). The application of carrying capacity to human population dynamics (i.e., the number of lives that a particular spatial area can sustainably support) was integral to neo-Malthusianism, providing natural scientific legitimation for ecological concerns over overpopulation (Angus and Butler 2011, 86–87; Robertson 2012, 15–19).

Though ecology played a major role in shaping the views of the neo-Malthusians, they were also heavily influenced by recent social upheavals—the Great Depression, World War II, and the impending Cold War. Both Osborne's *Our Plundered Planet* (1948) and Vogt's *Road to Survival* (1948) used the prism of (over)population to explain the outbreak of World War II and to express anxieties over looming conflicts in the post–World War II era. Osborne, for instance, introduced *Our Plundered Planet* by comparing World War II with "the other war, the silent war" that is "man's conflict with nature" (vii). The two wars, he argued, were not unrelated; the "spawn" of the "silent world-wide war" (on nature) "are armed conflicts such as World Wars I and II" (ix).

Given the explicit linkages Osborne and Vogt made between population growth, resource shortages, and national security, it is no surprise that neo-Malthusian concerns over environmental conservation soon dovetailed with Cold War geopolitics. The neo-Malthusian nature intersected with a shifting social agenda in a variety of ways, resulting in varieties of populationism, some hedged firmly within environmental politics and others adopting decidedly anthropocentric worldviews informed by realist international relations theory and orthodox geopolitics. Despite their differences, among both environmental and non-environmental neo-Malthusians, overpopulation was related to a whole host of social ills, including rural poverty, urban riots, and "ideological extremism" (i.e., communism, postcolonial nationalisms)—all of which were assumed to threaten geopolitical stability and, by extension, American sovereignty.

The notion that overpopulation led to violent conflict was reinforced by the frequent tendency of neo-Malthusians to explain the non-Western world in ethnocentric terms (Barker 2011). Vogt, for one, claimed that Asia was populated with "ignorant, backward peoples" (Robertson 2012, 53, citing Vogt 1948), viewed a high death rate as "one of the greatest natural assets of poor countries," and argued that programs to feed the Third World were counterproductive to natural evolutionary laws (Vogt 1948, 186, cited by Desrochers and Hoffbauer 2009, 83). This ethnocentric—and, in some cases, overtly racist—attitude at times extended into environmentalism as well. At the Sierra Club's 1959 Wilderness Conference, ecologist Raymond Cowles warned that if immediate action wasn't taken, America's wilderness would end up like South Africa's:

> I am convinced that preservation of South Africa's wildlife and wilderness areas, any time beyond the next generation, can continue only so long as there is White Domination. (as quoted in Robertson 2012, 120–21)

Cowles's overt racism was outside of the norm, but his presentation, "The Meaning of Wilderness to Science," demonstrated the close connection between neo-Malthusian population anxieties and romantic commitments to untouched national wilderness that were absolutely central to mid-twentieth-century environmentalism. In a foreword to Ehrlich's *Population Bomb* (1968), longtime Sierra Club executive director David Brower wrote, "It was Professor Raymond Cowles who shook us loose with a provocative address before a Sierra Club conference" (xiv). At that very conference, the club first "adopted a resolution warning of over-population and urging the government to give it 'urgent attention'" (Robertson 2012, 122).

The use of Third World countries as foils against which "we" needed to protect "our" wilderness continued over the course of the 1960s and 1970s in a variety of environmentalist forums. Robertson details how the Sierra Club's 1960 campaign for wilderness protection included a photo book, *This Is the American Earth,* that featured several images of crowded slums and warned of the "Chinification" of the United States (Robertson 2012, 122–23). In a 1966 article in *National Parks Magazine,* General William Draper connected overpopulation to both poverty abroad and the crowding of American National Parks (10–13, as cited by Robertson 2012, 85). And Stanford biologist Paul Ehrlich famously began *The Population Bomb* by describing the otherworldly misery he observed on a trip with his family to Delhi, India:

> As we crawled through the city, we entered a crowded slum area. The temperature was well over 100, and the air was a haze of dust and smoke. The streets seemed alive with people. People eating, people washing, people sleeping. People visiting, arguing, and screaming. People thrusting their hands through the taxi window, begging. People defecating and urinating. People clinging to buses. People herding animals. People, people, people, people. (1)

The message being communicated by these constructions of a "savage" Third World was clear: the problems facing "them" would soon spread to "us" if immediate action was not taken. American sovereignty, therefore, needed to be secured against these cultural, environmental, and ideological menaces. Insofar as Erhlich's depiction of India helped to attract American environmental adherents, it was in reference to this uncivilized "outside" that the American environmental subject came to perceive herself. Once these connections had been made, it was only a short logical leap from restricting population growth writ large to restricting immigration.

This new conjuncture—in which nature was constructed not through overtly racist social Darwinian epistemologies but through the ostensibly ecological and geopolitical assumptions of neo-Malthusianism—is reflected in post–World War II immigration policy,[14] where reforms ended racist national origin quotas (which had primarily impacted immigrants from Southern and Eastern Europe) but also institutionalized, for the first time, numerical restrictions in the Western hemisphere. To justify these numerical restrictions, the racial anxieties that eugenics helped to bolster were recast by opponents of immigration in the terms of Cold War geopolitics. Neo-Malthusianism played a central role in these efforts, functioning as an epistemological bridge through which the "teeming" populations "out there" could be connected to the ideological threats of communism. The discursive construction of migrants as potentially impure ideologically served to reinvigorate a racialized nationalism in which "Mexicans"—citizens and immigrants alike—were marked as savage, foreign threats without any overt reference to race or eugenics. In reflecting on the Hart–Cellar Act (the Immigration and Nationality Act of 1965), Mae Ngai (2004, 257) finds that while previous legislative proposals

> had exempted Western immigration from numerical quotas . . . a group of moderates in Congress intervened in the final moments of negotiation over the legislation in 1965 . . . [and] held repeal of the national origins quotas hostage to Western Hemisphere quotas, citing "fairness" and "*worldwide population explosion.*" (emphasis added)[15]

### Environmental Restrictionism amid a Shifting Social Terrain

While those emphasizing the population explosion in Congress during the 1960s were generally Cold War (rather than environmental) neo-Malthusians, the issue of immigration soon burst onto the modern environmentalist agenda after publication of Ehrlich's *The Population Bomb*. Ehrlich did not, at this point, directly address immigration, but his dire warnings over population growth spurred the Sierra Club to establish a Population Committee. As American fertility rates neared replacement levels and immigration to the United States continued increasing,[16] it was not long until these concerns over population were connected to efforts to restrict immigration. The organization Zero Population Growth (ZPG, today renamed Population-Connection), comprising many Sierra Club activists, was founded in 1968. Then, in 1972, Negative Population Growth (NPG) emerged out of a perception that ZPG had failed to effectively advance strict immigration restrictions. Attention to the "population problem" had national repercussions as well, as President Nixon's Commission on Population Growth and the American Future, chaired by John D. Rockefeller, concluded with the measured, yet significant, recommendation that "immigration levels not be increased and that immigration policy be reviewed periodically to reflect demographic conditions and considerations" (1969).

Despite considerable concern among its membership and frequent statements stressing the need for global and national population stabilization, the Sierra Club itself did not directly address the issue of immigration until 1978, when it urged Congress to examine the impacts of immigration on the environment (Bender 2003; Sierrans for U.S. Population Stabilization 2011). In 1980, club members communicated a similar position to the Select Commission on Immigration and Refugee Reform, and in 1989, the Population Committee formally recommended that immigration be limited, stating that "immigration to the U.S. should be no greater than that which will permit achievement of population stabilization in the U.S." (Sierra Club Population Committee 1989).

Yet, since its emergence, the immigration question has been controversial within U.S. environmental organizations, conjuring up the connections between natural and racial purity that have plagued greens since the days of first wave environmental restrictionism. Part of this controversy can be attributed to the fact that, in this period, neo-Malthusianism was under fire from two directions. First, it had become clear that policies aiming to achieve population reduction were often violent and exclusionary in practice. In addition to the American experience with eugenics (which, shockingly, lingered until the 1970s in states like North Carolina) (Schoen 2001), Indira Gandhi received international notoriety when she declared a national state of emergency and used coercive sterilization in an unsuccessful attempt to control the Indian population (Hartmann 1995).

Second, partly because of these atrocities, new social movements expressed skepticism about the underlying ideologies driving neo-Malthusian agendas. For African American activists, for example, the ways in which neo-Malthusians used population to explain the "urban problem" failed to address the real grievances and the root causes of urban poverty (e.g., segregation, workplace and housing discrimination, exclusion from social welfare state protections). As comedian and author Dick Gregory put it,

> first, the white man tells me to sit at the back of the bus. Now it looks like the white man wants me to sleep under the bed. Back in the days of slavery, black folks couldn't grow kids fast enough for white folks to harvest. Now that we've got a little taste of power, white folks want to call a moratorium on having children. (1971, cited by Robertson 2012, 178–79)

It certainly didn't help that a select group of neo-Malthusians, like ecologist Garrett Hardin, continued to support eugenic logics or that ostensibly liberal neo-Malthusians, like Ehrlich (1968, 53–54), blamed urban social unrest on overpopulation.[17]

Civil rights activists were far from the only group critical of neo-Malthusians. For feminists, neo-Malthusianism provided yet another means to control women's bodies and choices. At the very moment when they were finally being liberated from the constraints of patriarchy, populationists were portraying women who chose to have children as socially and ecologically irresponsible (see, e.g., Gordon 1976). For those writing from the so-called Third World, neo-Malthusianism represented an extension of colonialism, explaining away poverty in newly colonized countries without recourse to their violent histories of dispossession (see, e.g., Mamdani 1972). And for Marxists, neo-Malthusianism represented a conservative red herring that steered activists away from the structural, political economic sources of environmental and social ills (see, e.g., Harvey 1974).

The controversies surrounding environmental Malthusianism were reflected in the sheer acrimony of environmentalist debates over immigration in the 1980s and 1990s. Misanthropic tendencies within environmental Malthusian thought can be illustrated most clearly by looking at population-related dialogues within *Earth First!* in the

1980s. Specifically, a member referring to himself as Miss Ann Thropy (1987) wrote an essay celebrating the AIDS virus as a preferable way to decrease human population—a position that found a supporter in deep ecological hero Dave Foreman (1983), who proposed mandatory sterilization for those with "genetic defects" and opposed foreign aid to any countries without a "serious population reduction strategy" (i.e., one child per couple). Foreman (1987) also rehashed deep ecological hero Edward Abbey's argument for immigration restrictions, concluding that continuing to allow sanctuary would "postpone . . . revolutions or effective democratic reform movements" in Latin America and have a variety of negative ecological consequences within the United States. For these environmental Malthusians, wild spaces needed to be preserved through population reduction at all scales and by virtually any means— including the institutionalization of exclusionary modes of sovereignty.

However, these socially exclusionary positions were forcefully rebutted by other environmental activists both within and outside of Earth First! Within the organization, a sizeable social justice faction argued that the logic reflected a failure to address the root causes of both environmental degradation and social injustice. The tensions came to a head at the 1987 Earth First! Round River Rendezvous, an annual gathering for the organization held at the Grand Canyon, where a social justice faction called "Alien Nation" was harassed by a faction faithful to Abbey and Foreman, who disrupted their campsite, cracking a bullwhip and chanting "no more Earth First! wimps . . . down with humans" (Lee 1995, 106; see also Park and Pellow 2011, 158–60). The social justice advocates within Earth First![18] were joined by a number of greens outside the organization. For example, social ecologist Murray Bookchin (1991, 30–31) critiqued the misanthropic and xenophobic bearings of many in the population-control movement:

> The ultimate moral appeal of *Earth First!* is that it urges us to safeguard the natural world from our ecologically destructive societies, that is, in some sense, from ourselves. But, I have to ask, who is this "us" from which the living work has to be protected? Is it "humanity?" . . . Or is it our particular society, our particular civilization, with its hierarchical social relations which pit men against women, privileged whites against people of color . . . and ultimately a cancer-like, "grow or die" industrial capitalist economic system against the

natural world and other life-forms? Is this not the social root of the popular belief that nature is a mere object of social domination, valuable only as a "resource"?

From these responses, it becomes clear that a shifting social–ecological terrain was challenging the ontological, epistemological, strategic, and ethical assumptions undergirding second wave environmental restrictionism: opposition to immigration came to be seen by many greens as a disingenuous means of advancing socially unjust policy goals or as a strategically problematic blow to green alliance building—a mode of thinking that was likely to harm outreach to groups that had historically been undermobilized on environmental issues (King 2008). Strengthening opposition to environmental restrictionism, debates over neo-Malthusian population anxieties reached their pinnacle at the same time as environmental justice was starting to gain ground among mainstream environmental activists. The neo-Malthusian nature, where wilderness is threatened by civilization writ large, came into sharp conflict with the nature of environmental justice—where the environment is extended beyond wilderness to places where people "live, work and play" and universal assertions of a destructive civilization gave way to an emphasis on the particular ways that different populations relate to and encounter nature (Bullard 1994). Environmental justice advocates responded to initial iterations of environmental restrictionism by pointing out that immigrants tended to be disproportionately exposed to environmental hazards, emphasizing the role of consumption in producing environmental degradation and calling attention to the need for structural political economic shifts to truly live sustainably (I detail these responses in chapter 4).

In the Sierra Club, the restrictionist controversy was so great that, in 1996, the club reversed course and formally adopted a position of neutrality on immigration, declaring that "the Sierra Club, its entities, and those speaking in its name will take no position on immigration levels or on policies governing immigration into the United States. . . . The Club remains committed to environmental rights and protections for all within our borders, without discrimination based on immigration status" (Sierra Club 2011). It appears to be this declaration that truly ignited the opposing camps and brought debates over the environmental impacts of immigration to the attention of national media outlets. Out of this impasse, several internal splinter groups emerged: on one side, Sierrans for U.S. Population Stabilization, which was led by former Colorado Democratic governor Dick Lamm, former director of the Congressional Black Caucus Frank Morris, professor of ecology David Pimentel, and activist Alan Kuper, and on the other, Groundswell Sierra, which included thirteen former Sierra Club directors and numerous members worried about the ethical and strategic implications of an anti-immigrant position (Adler 2004; *USA Today* 2005; Dorsey 2011).

As the issue gained greater attention, a variety of outside social interests leapt into this environmental fray. In the restrictionists' corner was former Sierra Club Population Committee and ZPG chair John Tanton, a controversial figure who began his activist career a committed environmentalist but has since founded a whole network of organizations whose fundamental goal is restricting immigration (the Federation for American Immigration Reform, the Center for Immigration Studies, and the Social Contract Press, among others). Additionally, a variety of nativist and white supremacist organizations, such as the Council of Conservative Citizens and *VDARE*,[19] which had previously voiced little concern for the environment, began encouraging their members to join the Sierra Club so that they might use it to advance their xenophobic agendas (see, e.g., Walker 2004). The potential for this was so great that the Southern Poverty Law Center warned, "Without a doubt, the Sierra Club is the subject of a hostile takeover attempt by forces allied with [John] Tanton and a variety of right-wing extremists" (Potok 2003).

In response, opponents of restrictionism were joined by a variety of environmental justice and immigrants' rights organizations, including the Committee on Women, Population, and Environment, the San Francisco–based Political Ecology Group, the Chicago-based Center for New Community, and the Southern Poverty Law Center. Opponents argued that, within these debates, the environment was being appropriated to serve alternative social ends. Their discursive strategy was to challenge the motivations of restrictionists by asserting that they were disingenuously advancing the "greening of hate" (Political Ecology Group 1999). Some in this group rejected neo-Malthusian population concerns out of hand, asserting that environmentalists should focus on decreasing consumption, challenging environmentally destructive modes of production, and redistribution of resources and access to nature. Others agreed with this opposition to restrictionism but also insisted that population growth was a vital environmental issue—just not one that should be dealt with at the national scale (King 2007; 2008). Efforts to reduce population, according to opponents, needed to be unhinged from American sovereignty.

The shouting match between the two alliances was punctuated by a 1998 national referendum where members voted, by a three (60 percent) to two (40 percent) ratio, in favor of keeping in place the club's policy of neutrality (Salazar and Hewitt 2001; Barringer 2004). The winning position statement—while explicitly one of neutrality—contains a strong, if measured, rebuff to restrictionists insofar as it grounds a commitment to nature within a broader politics of social responsibility that is cognizant of structural inequalities:

> The Sierra Club reaffirms its commitment to addressing the root causes of global and United States population problems and offers the following comprehensive approach: The Sierra Club will build upon its effective efforts to champion the right of all families to maternal, infant, and reproductive health care, and the empowerment and equity of women. . . . The Sierra Club will continue to address the root causes of migration by encouraging sustainability, economic security, human rights, viable ecosystems, and environmentally responsible consumption. . . . The Sierra Club supports the decision of the Board of Directors to take no position on U.S. immigration levels and policies.

Despite this convincing defeat, the restrictionist coalition continued to press the issue, and it was revisited in both 2003 and 2005, when restrictionists attempted to stack the Board of Directors of the Sierra Club with sympathizers (Sierrans for U.S. Population Stabilization 2011). Although these efforts did succeed in electing several restrictionist candidates (including Sea Shepherds founder, reality-TV persona, and ardent restrictionist "Captain" Paul Watson) to the board of directors, the restrictionists have ultimately failed to gain a controlling stake.

Since the club's last major public debate in 2005, discussions of immigration within environmental organizations themselves have, to an extent, quieted. Today the vast majority of environmental organizations in the United States have adopted positions of neutrality on immigration.[20]

This does not, however, mean that environmental restrictionism has gone away; in fact, the logic is perhaps now more prominent than ever before. The difference is that environmental restrictionism has been advanced not within environmental organizations but by immigration-reduction organizations and alliances between greens and immigration reductionists formed for the specific purpose of advocating immigration restrictions.

**CONCLUSION: TOWARD A THIRD WAVE?**

In the introductory chapter to *We Have Never Been Modern* (1993), Bruno Latour writes,

> As soon as we direct our attention simultaneously to the work of purification and the work of hybridization, we immediately stop being wholly modern, and our future beings to change. At the same time we stop having been modern, because we become retrospectively aware that the two sets of practices have always already been at work in the historical period that is ending. Our past begins to change. (11)

This chapter was an attempt to recalibrate the future of American commitments to nature by rereading the past, paying particular attention to the close historical intersection between environmental thought and immigration restrictionism. My contention is that, in giving up the idea that commitments to nature are inherently progressive, radical, deterritorializing, or emancipatory, environmentalists are forced to more reflexively consider the contingent production of the nature–culture dualism and to start critically analyzing how this dualism intersects with the norms, institutions, and practices of sovereignty.

The diverse conceptions of nature that I have outlined in this chapter were made legible through prisms founded on natural scientific, political, economic, and geopolitical knowledges. During first wave restrictionism, romanticism worked to construct immigrants as environmentally savage and unable to appreciate wilderness, while social Darwinian eugenics naturalized racial hierarchies that fueled nativism. The message being communicated by eugenic-minded greens was that nonwhite immigrants posed a biopolitical threat to national and natural purity and thus needed to be scrutinized, controlled, and—in some cases—deported through the use of sovereign power.

As second wave restrictionism emerged, neo-Malthusianism provided an objective, ecocentric register through which to filter a wide variety of political projects. The strength of environmental Malthusianism lies in this hypermalleability. For some, like Cowles, neo-Malthusianism was clearly bound up in cultural essentializations and a desire to protect Anglo-European sovereignty from the incursion of nonwhites. For others, like Vogt, neo-Malthusianism was subtly imbued with images of southern savagery that worked to secure American sovereignty from a threatening "outside." For still others, like Osborne and Erhlich in his later work, the social slate was completely cleansed from consideration, and a discourse of scientific universalism was advanced at the same time as national borders were naturalized through methodological choices. In this sense, neo-Malthusianism served as an epistemic bridge connecting a wide variety of projects and attracting a broad array of adherents: from geopolitical cold warriors to ecological scientists to capitalists to immigration restrictionists—with significant overlap between these categories. By 1970, Paul Ehrlich was regularly appearing on *The Tonight Show* with Johnny Carson; population reduction—advocated by prominent politicians such as Morris Udall and Gaylord Nelson—was a central theme of the first Earth Day; and immigration was becoming a common, if contentious, topic in environmental conversations.

But by the 1980s, neo-Malthusianism was losing steam in popular thought, stymied by a changing political economic landscape (e.g., Reagan's neoliberal opposition to environmentalism, global markets and technological shifts ushering in the era of "globalization") and by emerging shifts within environmental organizations themselves that questioned the authenticity and efficacy of populationism (Robertson 2012, 218–20). And yet, despite a dramatic decline in birthrates, the overall population continued to grow—both in the United States and worldwide—and, as such, neo-Malthusianism continued to attract adherents within the environmental movement. From this context, two distinct strands of environmental neo-Malthusianism have emerged. The first is indebted to the works of Garrett Hardin and Edward Abbey; it has unabashedly rejected all opposition to environmental restrictionism as a form of political correctness, has doubled down on a logic of "lifeboat ethics," and—in a manner characteristic of neoracist strategies—has adopted a hypernationalist ethos that portrays immigration as the foremost threat to American national and cultural sustainability. The second is influenced by Paul and Anne Ehrlichs' efforts to couch their concerns over population in a universalist narrative of "spaceship earth" (Robertson 2012, 150–51). The Ehrlichs' internalized some of their opponents' criticisms and began to weave their neo-Malthusian population anxieties into a far more complex, nuanced discourse that combined communitarian visions of political community with a language of scientific rationalism (Robertson 1999; 2012; see also Ehrlich, Bilderback, and Erhlich 1979). As I detail in the following chapters, contemporary environmental restrictionism continues to be animated by these two strands, although the latter has provided the ontological and epistemological foundations for a major discursive shift among environmental restrictionists—the emergence of a third wave of environmental restrictionism.

In the early twenty-first century, growing recognition of nature's intrinsic value has thrust matters of environmental degradation onto political agendas, opening the discursive terrain linking nature and sovereignty to new epistemological practices but remaining in important respects wedded to the historical articulations that I have outlined. While I have focused on the links between nature and restrictionism here, it goes without saying that many conceptions of nature—including Malthusian, romantic, and Darwinian—have been deployed for quite beneficent, even inclusive, purposes. But plenty of scholars and practitioners are singing the praises of these benign articulations. The more insidious iterations, on the other hand, can be witnessed in the contemporary intersection of environmental restrictionism and nativism.

# 2

# NATURALIZING NATIVISM

Even though nature has been a central site of a particularly
potent and exclusionary idea of US nationalism . . . the
connections between nature and nation and the historical
and contemporary material effects of these exclusionary
couplings continue to go largely unexplored.

**JAKE KOSEK,** *Understories: The Political Life of Forests in
Northern New Mexico*

Peter O'Neill drew a deep breath, flustered by the question that had been
posed to him. It was Wednesday, April 29, 2009, and the Fort Collins,
Colorado, resident had just finished a presentation in front of a crowd
of roughly a hundred at a town hall panel titled "Immigration and
Sustainability: How Many People Can the United States Absorb?" The
panel, part of a local celebration of immigration and its rich contribution
to the community, came about after conveners had been pressured by
an organization O'Neill was involved with, Northern Coloradoans for
Immigration Reduction, to include several panels critical of immigration. In the question-and-answer segment following the presentations, a
Latina woman rose and pointed out what seemed to be a contradiction
in O'Neill's logic: "Your talk is called 'Immigration and Sustainability:
How Many People Can the U.S. Absorb?,' but I think a better title would
have been 'How Many Mexicans Can the U.S. Absorb?'" Setting her
sights on one of his comments, she continued, "When I hear about the
dominant culture being wiped out . . . that's confusing to me . . . what
[do] you mean by the dominant culture?"

Despite the audible groans of the three middle-aged Caucasian
males seated behind me, the audience member was on to something.

Throughout his presentation, O'Neill had explicitly disavowed racism, instead emphasizing demographic projections that were purported to result in ecological and social disaster. "It's not immigrants that are the problem, it's the number of immigrants," he repeatedly stated. But late in his presentation, he stopped and, with an air of profundity, made the following remark:

> Then [by 2050] we will become a country that's all minorities. The Europeans will then only be forty-seven percent, so we might not have any dominant culture anymore . . . so you can think about the implications of that. (Immigration and Sustainability 2009)

What *are* the implications of that? To the audience member, there is a tension between O'Neill's assertion that he is concerned with the numbers only and his explicitly stated preference for a dominant Anglo-European culture. To O'Neill, the answer is clear, and there lies no contradiction in his seemingly disparate statements. He forcefully responded to the audience member's observation:

> I meant a *dominant culture,* not a *dominant race.* . . . If you look at why America is so successful, it is ultimately the culture. The culture of free-markets, of democracy, of respect for people, of upward mobility, of valuing education . . . it's that culture that makes us so successful. That culture primarily got its start from people of European descent coming here . . . and I think we can be proud of that. (emphasis added)

O'Neill's talk juxtaposed the "dominant Anglo-European culture" against a sweeping "Third World culture" that, he argued, is democratically deficient, is immature, lacks a respect for basic rights, and shows little regard for nature. The discourse he was attempting to weave was one that constructed a population of social and ecological *savages*—a teeming, brown horde of chaos whose movement had to be forcefully arrested for the good of America.

While extreme, O'Neill's logic is not unique. Indeed, it closely mirrors that expressed by greens like Edward Abbey and Garrett Hardin, prominent geopoliticians like Samuel Huntington and Robert Kaplan, quasi-popular writers like Jean Raspail and Peter Brimelow, and a variety of environmental and nonenvironmental organizations who echo the sentiment that American sovereignty must be secured from the potential flood of Third World invaders who currently lie in wait at the borders. In a seminal contemporary nativist work, *Alien Nation: Common Sense about America's Immigration Disaster* (1996), Peter Brimelow expresses surprise as he relays the following anecdote:

> I have found myself discussing my *National Review* cover story with a group of environmentalists ... who voted for Patrick J. Buchanan in the 1992 presidential primaries because of their fear that immigration-driven population growth is ecologically insupportable. Probably both Buchanan and the professional environmentalist lobby in Washington would be equally astounded by news of this emerging electoral bloc. (19–20)

How is it that this apparently paradoxical alliance emerges? How do nativists weave nature into their calls for a "state of exception" (or, as Pat Buchanan puts it, *State of Emergency: The Third World Invasion and Conquest of America* [2006])? More precisely, how do nativists go about constructing the relationship between nature and sovereignty in their attempts to exclude immigrants?

My analysis suggests that two discourses of nativism are variably deployed by contemporary environmental restrictionists: (1) *social nativism* and (2) *ecological nativism*. These discourses construct nature through a variety of epistemological practices that result in divergent understandings of the relationship between nature and sovereignty, as well as varied efforts to reconfigure this relationship toward a similar end—the strengthening of the white nation. I make the case that the political impact of these two discourses is to provide nativists a flexible set of discursive strategies with which to advance their exclusionary prescriptions, enabling both the broadening and deepening of overtly xenophobic alliances.

### NEW POTIONS IN OLD BOTTLES: SOCIAL NATIVISM AND NATURE

The following statement is useful in beginning to unpack the nature–sovereignty relationship for nativists:

> We believe that the natural environment and resources of a nation are among its most precious, valuable, and irreplaceable treasures. We believe in the protection of the environment from reckless greed as well as from irresponsible government. We support the protection of truly endangered species of wildlife and areas of natural beauty.

The statement sounds commonplace for an environmental organization. If one were to guess who made it, a representative from the Sierra
Club or the Natural Resources Defense Council might come to mind.
Or perhaps even a Democratic Party candidate reciting a line from the
party's platform. In fact, the declaration is part of the mission statement
of the Council of Conservative Citizens (CCC), a white supremacist
organization that, in the same document, also insists that the United
States is a "part of the European Civilization and the European People
and . . . the American people and government should remain European
in their composition and character" (Francis 2005).

The CCC is a fringe organization, but one whose membership is
often active in state- and local-level debates. In 2006, in Fort Collins,
Colorado, the annual Rocky Mountain Sustainable Living Fair was the
site of controversy when the group Northern Coloradoans for Immigration Reduction set up a booth and began distributing fliers detailing
the environmental argument for reducing immigration. Among those
present was Perry Lorenz, a prominent member of the CCC who had
recently caused a stir in his unsuccessful run for the local school board
when he praised *The Bell Curve* and suggested that intelligence might
be biologically rooted in race (Jobling 2004). Lorenz, who describes
his move to Colorado from California as an effort to "get back to the
United States," was also part of a seven-person contingent that infiltrated
a state-level roundtable on urban sprawl to stress the linkages between
environmental degradation and immigration (Williamson 2001).

These examples are reflective of broader efforts by nativist groups to
strategically latch on to nature in their attempts both to broaden their
support by appealing to moderate or leftist organizations and to enhance
the anti-immigrant sentiment of their existing base by highlighting the
traditionally conservative appeal of *conservationism*. The remainder of
this section will unpack the ways that ideals of nature, nation, state,
and race are related to broader efforts to reconsolidate this particular
vision of the "sovereign nation-state," and how immigrants function as
the biopolitical threats against which the nativist self is secured.

## The National Crisis

The nativist group most active in advancing environmental restrictionist
arguments—as part of the America's Leadership Team alliance—is the

American Immigration Control (AIC) Foundation. The AIC Foundation was founded in 1983 by John Vinson, a regular contributor to the CCC's *Citizen's Informer* Newsletter. The Southern Poverty Law Center (2001) notes that Vinson "often speaks at CCC meetings, and is a founding member of the white supremacist League of the South." Vinson argued, in a 1998 article titled "Europhobia: The Racism of Anti-racists," that "multiculturalism which subordinates successful Euro-American culture to dysfunctional Third World cultures, keeps gaining ground against surprisingly weak opposition. . . . White Americans . . . passively accept government-sponsored anti-white discrimination—even that which benefits recently-arrived immigrants" (as cited by Muradian 2006, 209).

The AIC Foundation website is dedicated primarily to selling books, booklets, and pamphlets that put the looming national crisis front and center. Titles include Brimelow's *Alien Nation*; *Immigration out of Control*; *The Coming Anarchy*; *Will America Drown? Immigration and the Third World Population Explosion*; and *Erasing America: The Politics of the Borderless Nation*. Interestingly, however, out of the many publications summarized on the site, there is not a single mention of nature or the environment.

Nonetheless, a closer analysis of the books and pamphlets being pushed by the organization (as well as by the like-minded CCC, *VDARE*, and *American Renaissance*) reveals that "nature" is a frequently employed discursive tool in advancing nativist logics. In fact, nature is used in a way that is consistent with much of traditional conservative thought, as *a source of order* that works to grant nativist tropes of difference epistemological legitimacy. Nature represents (1) a sacred marker of God's Truth, (2) a scientific Truth rooted in Darwin, and/or (3) a political Truth in line with the minimalist state prescribed by Locke or the "Founding Fathers." Woven throughout each of these epistemological strategies, one also sees nature being deployed symbolically as (4) a metaphor of chaos carefully linked with non-European Others, against which the crisis of Western civilization is framed. The sole thread uniting these diverse practices is an instrumental attempt to reconfigure sovereignty so that the *sacred white nation* can be secured.[1]

In the following section, I briefly unpack the ways in which these anthropocentric ideals of nature are deployed to advance nativist politics. Although this discussion may initially seem tangential to my main focus (i.e., the relationship between ecocentric conceptions of nature and restrictionist forms of sovereignty), it provides the comparative context needed to reflect on the similarities and differences between social nativism and other iterations of environmental restrictionism. I then proceed to a more detailed discussion of the role that ecocentric constructions of nature play in advancing nativist politics. I find that, though it is not pervasive, there is a substantial dialogue occurring over the role that a commitment to the nonhuman environment ought to play in white nationalist politics.

### The Christian Nation

The CCC's mission statement begins with a forceful assertion—the group's "first principle"—that America is a "Christian Country," which is carefully linked with its "second principle," that the United States is a "European country" (Francis 2005). Throughout nativist dialogues, Christianity is rhetorically wedded to "traditional" values and social hierarchies, including legality, order, and the cultivation of ostensibly decent personal traits (honesty, virtue, and respect for life, liberty, and property). In contrast to the "naturally Christian" United States, a variety of other religions are differentially marked as self-interested and/or savage.

Following the white supremacist tradition, Judaism is targeted particularly harshly, with "Jews" constructed as a "hostile elite" concerned primarily with furthering the interests of their ethnic group over the broader national public (MacDonald 2011). The vast majority of attention, however, is focused on the "savagery" of Islam. In May 2011, for instance, the American Renaissance approvingly quoted a presentation given by Dutch nativist Geert Wilders, who characterized Islam as a "totalitarian ideology of hate" and alleged that "leaders who talk about immigration without mentioning Islam are blind" (Randall 2011). Immigration from Islamic countries, it is argued, imperils those "natural" Christian values that already face an uphill battle in a liberal multicultural society:

> Far be it from us to tell Arabs or Persians or Pakistanis how to live or what to believe. Conservative Islam holds much promise for men whose lives and cultures have been blighted by Western vulgarity. Many earnest people seek in Islam a refuge from license and

materialism. However, as Europeans are discovering and as we eventually will, Islam is hungry for converts and power. Even worse, in the United States it is poised to join forces with an unstable and violent racial minority. Islam can bring us only trouble. We have every right and every reason to insist that Muslims stay in their own countries. (Boggs 1993)

This seminal nativist essay begins by linking national sovereignty with cultural relativism ("far be it from us" to tell others what to believe)—a connection that is intensified by the universal dominance of "modern" liberal Western ideals that, the author suggests, are incompatible with "traditional" values. However, similar to nativist portrayals of Jews, "Islam" as a whole is asserted to be a power-hungry cult whose practitioners are seeking to advance their "in-group" interests by allying with racial minorities against the traditional, white, Christian majority.

Cementing this narrative, nativists meticulously document instances of violent crimes, alleged acts of terrorism, and supposed attempts to impose Sharia law by "Muslims."[2] Recent headlines on the CCC website include the following: "AWOL Muslim Private Planned to Murder His Fellow Soldiers," "Three Black Muslim Leaders Convicted of Racially Motivated Triple Murder," "Black Panthers Announce Egyptian Style 'Showdown,'" and so on.[3] In each piece, Muslims are constructed as violent, irrational, and antidemocratic. Of particular relevance, the relationship between Islam and African American activism is continually reiterated; the "enemy" is not only external but lives among us. "Islam," *American Renaissance* contributor William Boggs observes, "lies at the dangerous intersection between race and immigration" (Boggs 1993).

Although the views of nativist organizations are typically cloaked in praise of masculinity (see Ferber 1998), gender is also deployed in the nativist defense of Western nationalism and the liberal democratic values that are said to accompany it. After being expelled from the Sierra Club for publicly making numerous racially offensive statements,[4] *VDARE* contributor Brenda Walker makes the case against immigration on the grounds that it imports "groups for whom the social norms include slavery, female genital mutilation, forcibly arranged marriages and other horrors." She continues,

The false ideology of multiculturalism with its accusation of racism against anyone who will not submit has intimidated Americans into

believing it is desirable to welcome millions of immigrants from cultures which consider women inferior. . . . The absurd preference for
third world cultures in our immigration policy amounts to importing
sexism. (Walker 2005)

Through this strategy, whole cultures of migrants are constructed as
misogynistic threats to the universal Western values of equality and freedom. The take-home, in no uncertain terms, is that nonwhite migrants—
particularly non-Christians—are savages, and the further importation of
Islamists threatens to corrode the already weakened linkages between
Christianity and the white nation.

Nativists attempt to justify this discrimination by appealing to divine
constructions of nature, insisting that racial and national preferences
are *natural* according to close biblical readings:

> The Bible supports racial preservation and even separation. The Bible
> teaches that mankind is composed not of an amorphous mass of in-
> dividuals but of nations. It also teaches that the basis of all genuine
> nations is a common ethnic stock, which is more important even
> than a common language, culture, political allegiance, or locale. The
> Bible praises homogeneity as a blessing, and posits it as the basis of
> love, friendship, social peace, and national harmony. The Bible also
> sanctions love of nation and fatherland, a virtue antagonistic to in-
> discriminate and large-scale immigration. (Trask 2001)

It is argued, however, that as mainstream Christianity has become
polluted with liberal, multicultural ideals, it has forgotten this divinely
sanctioned state: "Like the seeds that fell on stony ground which had
no depth of earth, cosmic Christianity was scorched and withered
away because it had no roots. . . . Christianity's roots are in humanity,
in the blood. Sever those roots and Christianity becomes liberalism"
(Council of Conservative Citizens 2010c). The white Christian nation
is a timeless, absolute Truth set in stone by "law of nature and nature's
god," and this relationship between the natural religious order and the
sacred white nation must be reawakened.

### The Natural Scientific Nation

The notion that the white Christian nation is rooted in "nature's God"
is paradoxically buttressed by a stronger and more frequently cited

commitment to social Darwinism. Indeed, though appeals to Christianity are scattered throughout nativist proclamations, they are dwarfed in both quantity and emphasis by "scientific" support for racism and ethnocentrism. For example, Steve Sailer (2004), a frequent contributor to *VDARE* and founder of the Human Biodiversity Institute, articulates a theory of "ethnic nepotism," which he contends "explains the tendency of humans to favor members of their own racial group by postulating that all animals evolve toward being more altruistic toward kin in order to propagate more copies of their common genes."[5]

The concept of ethnic nepotism, Sailer argues, is derived from evolutionary biologist William Hamilton's notions of "kin selection" and "inclusive fitness."[6] It was introduced by Pierre van den Berge, a sociologist and anthropologist who is purported to have found support for the concept in his experiences with ethnic conflict in the Belgian-controlled Congo and Nazi-occupied Belgium. Ethnic nepotism is based on the "gene-centric" sociobiological notion that genes can provide evolutionary explanations for human behavior; in this case, we all have an innate tendency to act with a preference toward those with similar genes.

Sailer argues that the ideas of socio- and evolutionary biologists, such as E. O. Wilson and Richard Dawkins, logically lead to the conclusion that preferences for "our own" races and nationalities are natural and even beneficial— "ethnocentrism, clannishness, xenophobia, nationalism and racism are the almost inevitable flip sides of ethnic nepotism"—but the liberal culture of political correctness creates an epistemic closure where scientists are unable or unwilling to voice such ideas.[7] This claim of political correctness trumping biological Truth is constantly reiterated throughout nativist writings. For example, Kevin MacDonald, an evolutionary psychologist at Cal-State Long Beach and an ardent white nationalist, links these supposed sociobiological Truths to the study of psychology: "All peoples," he writes, "have ethnic interests and all peoples have a legitimate right to assert their interests, to construct societies that reflect their culture, and to define the borders of their kinship group" (*Occidental Observer* 2010). MacDonald employs this linkage in attempts to explore the "self-interested," "in group" behavior of "Jews" and other ethnic minorities, and he uses his social Darwinian explanations to justify his anti-immigrant conclusions:

given that some ethnic groups, especially ones with high levels of ethnocentrism and mobilization, will undoubtedly continue to function
as groups far into the foreseeable future, unilateral renunciation of
ethnic loyalties by other groups means only their surrender and defeat
and disappearance—the Darwinian dead end of extinction. . . . The
future, then, like the past, will inevitably be a Darwinian competition.
And ethnicity will play a crucial role. (MacDonald 2004)

In short, Darwin remains central to white nationalism. In celebration
of the 150th anniversary of *On the Origin of Species*, Cornelius Troost
(2009), a former UCLA professor of science education, reflected on
(what he alleges to be) the distorted contemporary legacy of evolution:

> The truth about Darwin is being submerged in the multicultural
> phantasmagoria enveloping our culture. . . . The mass movement to
> "equalize" society quite simply lacks a scientific basis and, in fact,
> is built upon a premise denied by Darwin. Races not only exist, but
> they are different in very deep ways that may well descend to the
> moral foundation of humankind.[8]

### Sacred Nation, Broken State

This social Darwinian framework is conjoined with a libertarian conception of the state. The nativist argument is that if what are typically
viewed as social categories (i.e., race and nation) are, in fact, naturally
given, and preferential treatment of one's own in-group is a normatively
beneficial evolutionary strategy, then we do not need any state intervention to alleviate social injustices. There is no reason for social programs
to control for poverty, to correct historical forms of discrimination, or
to provide safety nets for the marginalized, if these social inequalities—
racial, class based, and gendered—are natural. In an essay titled "Why
Biology Is the Friend of Liberty—and the Enemy of 'Totalitarian Creep,'"
Robert Weissberg (2011), an emeritus professor of political science at
the University of Illinois–Urbana, contends that "treating race related
biological differences as readily amenable to state intercession virtually
guarantees expanding oppressive (if well-intentioned) state power."

Nativists reconcile such disregard for "the government" with their
constant proclamations of national pride through reanimating a sharp
distinction between "the state" and "the nation." A seminal article on

*VDARE* is ominously titled "When the State Is the Enemy of the Nation" (Francis 2004). The article was written in response to an op-ed in French newspaper *Le Figaro* by Jean Raspail, the author whose novel *The Camp of the Saints* ([1975] 1994) depicts a poor, brown, savage tidal wave of immigration sweeping through France and decimating civilization. Raspail's editorial, titled "La patrie trahie par la république" (The fatherland betrayed by the republic), chronicles the ways in which France's "political class . . . helped destroy the nation by doing nothing to resist the anti-white, anti-Christian invasion" (Francis 2004). The author of the response, Sam Francis, forcefully argues that not only is such a conjuncture possible in the United States, it is already occurring, and it may be too late to stop it. The nation is in peril:

> Like the real France, the real America is also a "country of common blood" (Jefferson used that very phrase in the original Declaration . . .). In fact, every real nation is a country of a common blood. The only nations that claim to be defined by creeds are—come to think of it—totalitarian states. . . . When the common blood dries up and the civilization founded on it withers, all that's left is the state—the government. (Francis 2004)

### Sovereignty, Nature, and White Nationalism

The national crisis spawned by the liberal, multiculturalist state is thus linked with the deterioration of American sovereignty. And the greatest threat to national sovereignty, nativists make clear, comes from the continued immigration of nonwhite populations. "National sovereignty is weakened by open border and lax law enforcement," states Brenda Walker. "The continuing extreme level of immigration, both legal and illegal, will change this country far more than anything else in the coming decades unless it is brought under control soon. . . . And once America has been dismantled from a unitary nation into a grouping of ethnic enclaves, it will be broken forever" (Walker 2007). A recent letter to the editor in the *Citizens Informer* framed the crisis in even starker terms:

> The time has come to division the country into a series of ethno-states. Very few people are comfortable with multiculturalism. Only progressive Whites perceive some kind of sick advantage in it. Mexicans

believe in diversity so much they are ethnically cleansing Los Angeles of its former black neighborhoods. Eventually, they will cleanse the entire Southwestern part of the country, maybe more. Muslims are even less tolerant. The reason for the fall of the world's greatest civilizations is multiculturalism and miscegenation. This will surely be our fate as well unless we act to prevent it. (Alexander 2011)

To secure sovereignty—to revitalize the white nation—nativists employ visceral language to construct the "foreign" threat in terms that will provoke disgust and, ultimately, dehumanization. Central to this narrative is the use of nature as a metaphor for chaos that is carefully layered with racialized imagery. Raspail's *Camp of the Saints,* for example, is replete with images of "flooding," of "waves," of masses "drowning" in chaos and filth:

> Then, after a while, there were too many poor. Altogether too many. Folk you didn't even know. Not even from here. Spreading through cities, and houses and homes. Worming their way by the thousands, in thousands of foolproof ways. Through the slits in your mailboxes, begging for help, with their frightful pictures bursting from envelopes day after day, claiming their due in the name of some organization or other. Slithering in . . . whole countries full, bristling with poignant appeals, please that seemed more like threats, and not begging now for linen but for checks to their account. . . . Soon you saw them on television, hordes of them, churning up, dying by the thousands, and nameless butchery became a feature, a continuous show. . . . The poor had overrun the earth. (15)

Throughout Raspail's novel, the "waves crash" into the motherland and the "wind blows" the vile horde along—natural flows metaphorically accompanying an outside threat that is more animal than human. Immigrants, backed by their nonwhite domestic supporters and well-intentioned multiculturalists, are variously portrayed as maggots, vermin, rapists, and blood-thirsty butchers. Readers are invited to become warriors fighting to save a white nation, which embodies all that is sacred, in peril.

Nature is often deployed as a symbol of savagery, but there is also real debate among nativists over whether the far Right should care about the natural environment. Brimelow (1995, 21) notes, in his introduction to *Alien Nation,* that his analysis of immigration has opened his mind to environmentalism, which he had previously thought of as "just another excuse for government regulation." Similarly, dialogues over environmentalism on nativist websites have led to impassioned exchanges and even a sort-of reflexive thinking on the far right. For example, a 2001 *VDARE* article suggested that conservation was a traditional value of the right, and, more importantly, one that could serve to "shore up the demographic base of the Republican Party without alienating minorities" (Sailer 2001). A respondent to the article made the following argument, drawing a distinction between "environmentalism" and "conservationism":

> I believe the Right is quite correct in distancing itself from so-called "environmentalism." After all, as they say in Europe, "the green tree has red roots." The roots of the environmentalist and conservationist movements are indeed radically different. The former is unquestionably statist, anti-sovereignty, egalitarian, interventionist, irrational. The latter is its approximate antithesis.... I believe this is perfectly consistent with paleoconservatism (and certainly Jeffersonian agrarianism) which is simply the desire to preserve our heritage and our property.... Speaking for myself, an Eagle Scout who loves the pinnacles of civilization and the most remote wilderness alike, I find environmentalism repulsive and conservation a necessity. (Dunaway 2001)

This statement is, in many ways, reflective of nativist attempts to draw nature into efforts to reconfigure sovereignty toward exclusionary ends: an ambivalent, loosely defined nature is being woven into a militarized, nostalgia-laden iteration of sovereignty—one with an idealized vision of a racially and culturally homogeneous "nation," linked to a "state" that is conceptualized in libertarian terms as the *foremost threat to liberty* (while the "wilderness" the state protects is paradoxically ensconced in the national imaginary).

Typically, however, when social nativists express concern over the nonhuman realm, it is clearly bound up in an instrumental effort to advance unambiguously xenophobic, racist ends that portray nonwhites as savage. A recent CCC article typifies this approach:

> An animal preserve in Zimbabwe set up by white charities was destroyed by Zimbabweans who slaughtered over a thousand rare animals.... All of Sub-Saharan Africa's animal preserves were originally

established by white governments and charities. These preserves are financially supported by white charities from the west, but are constantly attacked by Africans. . . . Efforts to preserve wildlife around the world are led and financed by whites. Not that white people are ever given any credit for it. (Council of Conservative Citizens 2010b)

The juxtaposition between civilization and savagery in this discourse would be laughable, were it not taken so seriously by those deploying it.

The white nationalist website Majority Rights also recently initiated a dialogue among its followers on the relationship between American white nationalism and the environment. While there was significant disagreement, the responses from two commenters on the message board were telling (Majority Rights 2008):

> Kind of ironic that White people are the biggest promoters of preserving everything except White people and their environment. . . . Whites will gather, raise money and move in political activist mode to preserve the natural habitat of the Red Crested-Web Footed Lake Loon, yet raise not an eyebrow as Jolly Old England mutates into Eurabia. . . .

> . . . Native Born White Americans need to increase their fertility even if it means more sprawl and paving over state and national parks . . . or [the] expulsion of a majority of post 1965 non-whites. This really is the only choice.

In these responses, it is not population growth or fertility writ large that is the problem; it is the population growth caused by immigrants and the fertility of nonwhite populations. In fact, reminiscent of eugenics-era first wave restrictionism, the white population, according to many nativists, needs to be augmented. "Our" national emergency requires intervention at the level of the population—differentially managing fertility, arresting movement, and imbuing "blood relations" with the appropriate cultural norms needed to restore the natural order. If "the state" is to work in service of the nation, it needs to recognize this biopolitical necessity and take appropriate action.

In sum, social nativists depend on a variety of epistemological strategies that deploy nature as a marker of order supporting white political supremacy; however, they are quite ambivalent in their dealings with nature as an intrinsically valuable entity. There is no logical reason that social nativists cannot be greens, but given today's American political terrain—where environmentalism is perceived to be so intimately bound up in progressive, Democratic politics—a substantive shift among white nationalists in the near future toward environmentalism is not terribly likely, and their muted attempts to instrumentally appropriate nature are so clearly bound up in their racist nationalism that they are not likely to influence many environmentalists (or even, for that matter, moderates who do not consider themselves greens but care about clean water or air). To appeal to such groups, social nativists are being forced to turn to other discourses and to alliances with organizations who aren't so obviously nativist. Hence the AIC Foundation's involvement in America's Leadership Team.

## OLD POTIONS IN NEW BOTTLES: ECOLOGICAL NATIVISM

The following statement is instructive in beginning to unpack ecological nativism:

> It might be wise for us as American citizens to consider calling a halt to the mass influx of even more millions of hungry, ignorant, unskilled, and culturally-morally-genetically impoverished people. At least until we have brought our own affairs into order. Especially when these uninvited millions bring with them an alien mode of life which—let us be honest about this—is not appealing to the majority of Americans. Why not? Because we prefer democratic government, for one thing; because we still hope for an open, spacious, uncrowded, and beautiful—yes, beautiful!—society, for another. The alternative, in the squalor, cruelty, and corruption of Latin America, is plain for all to see.

The statement, with its reference to an uncivilized Latin civilization, sounds eerily similar to that of traditional, social nativism. If one heard it out of context, it would be a safe assumption to link it to the American Immigration Control Foundation or CCC. However, the author quickly conjoins these ethnocentric anxieties to tales of imminent ecological devastation. The passage, written by Edward Abbey (1988, 43) (whose "green" motivations are unimpeachable within contemporary environmentalist imaginaries), is prefaced on the assumption that restricting immigration will prevent "the ongoing destruction of what remains of our forests, fields, mountains, lakes, rivers and seashores."

As several opponents of restrictionism have recognized, it would be a mistake to depict the environmental restrictionist movement as purely nativist (Bhatia 2004; Muradian 2006; King 2007; 2008). Indeed, certain restrictionists have long histories of environmental activism and appear to be genuine in their concern for nature (Reimers 1998). The grouping that I term "eco-nativists" are difficult to make sense of as they express viewpoints that overlap in important ways with the anxieties of social nativists, yet also devote significant attention to environmental concerns and come from backgrounds of environmental activism.

A case in point is John Tanton. An ophthalmologist from northern Michigan, Tanton first emerged as a player in national environmental causes in the 1960s but had already been concerned with overpopulation for some time:

> As early as the '50s, he avidly read reports from the Population Reference Bureau, and by the time Ehrlich's book was published, he and Mary Lou had already started work on the first Northern Michigan chapter of Planned Parenthood. "I believed in the multiplication tables," says Tanton. "Since I was a physician and could do something about birth control, it struck me that this was where I could make my contribution to the conservation movement." (Hayes 2006; see also Rowe 2002, 22)

After becoming active in local- and state-level environmental organizations in the late 1950s—founding the local chapter of the Audubon Society, heading up organizing in northern Michigan for the Sierra Club and League of Conservation Voters, working in support of a variety of state-level land conservation measures—Tanton chaired the Sierra Club's National Population Committee from 1971 to 1974 and founded and served on the board of Zero Population Growth (ZPG) from 1973 to 1978 (including a stretch as president from 1975 to 1977).

Soon, however, his activism veered into more explicitly social territory. In 1979, Tanton formed the Federation for American Immigration Reform (FAIR) to aggressively push for the immigration restrictions that he had been unable to convince the Sierra Club and ZPG to advocate. Over the next decade, he would found the Center for Immigration Studies, NumbersUSA, U.S. Inc., the Immigration Reform Law Institute and Journal, the Social Contract, U.S. English, and ProEnglish, and would provide funding to numerous other restrictionists organizations (including the American Immigration Control Foundation and Californians for Population Stabilization) (Reimers 1998; Southern

Poverty Law Center 2002b). In doing so, he began to cultivate connections with social nativists: holding a series of WITAN (named after Witenagemot, which means "wise council" in Old English) seminars attended by a broad swath of nativists (including Jared Taylor of the white supremacist *American Renaissance*) and environmental restrictionists alike; publishing Raspail's *The Camp of the Saints* through his Social Contract Press;[9] and coauthoring *The Immigration Invasion* with Wayne Lutton, the white nationalist editor of the Social Contract Press.

Judging by numerous statements in the 1980s and 1990s, Tanton's opinions evolved along with these alliances. For example, in one of a series of 1986 memos that were leaked to the mainstream press in 1988,[10] Tanton provided his colleagues a list of queries that were to be discussed at the WITAN seminars, including the following:

> Will Latin American migrants bring with them the tradition of the mordida (bribe), the lack of involvement in public affairs, etc.? What in fact are the characteristics of Latin American culture, versus that of the United States? . . . As Whites see their power and control over their lives declining, will they simply go quietly into the night? Or will there be an explosion? Why don't non-Hispanic Whites have a group identity, as do Blacks, Jews, Hispanics?

Widespread outcries by greens and social justice groups after the release of these controversial remarks do not appear to have provoked a shift in his expressions of nativism. In a 1993 letter to ecologist Garrett Hardin, Tanton wrote, "I've come to the point of view that for European-American society and culture to persist requires a European-American majority, and a clear one at that" (Southern Poverty Law Center 2008). Similarly, in a 1996 letter to Roy Beck of NumbersUSA, Tanton voiced his concerns that current immigrants may prove inassimilable: "I have no doubt that individual minority persons can assimilate to the culture necessary to run an advanced society but if through mass migration, the culture of the homeland is transplanted from Latin America to California, then my guess is we will see the same degree of success with governmental and social institutions that we have seen in Latin America" (Southern Poverty Law Center 2008).

These apparently incongruous positions render Tanton somewhat of an enigma, with observers left struggling to reconcile his commitment to both nature and nativism. A recent *Washington Post* (Huslin 2006) article begins,

> Let's just get this out of the way. John Tanton, mastermind of the modern-day movement to curb immigration, is a tree hugger. Literally. He has a favorite pair of ash trees "this big around," he says, spreading his arms wide. He likes to visit them every so often in the forest just north of here, to see how they're doing.

Similarly, journalist Chris Hayes (2006), writing for *In These Times*, registers his surprise at Tanton's personal politics:

> Given that the movement he helped create now finds its base among conservative Republicans, you might expect John Tanton to be an unapologetic reactionary. You'd be wrong. He's a self-described progressive, ex-Sierra Club member, Planned Parenthood supporter and harsh critic of neoclassical economists. So I wanted to know: How did a whip-smart, mild-mannered farm boy committed to conserving the natural world end up seeding and nurturing a movement that now dispatches gun-toting vigilantes to patrol the border?

The sentiment being communicated here is that these two logics— environmentalism and nativism—are at odds. My analysis, however, finds that they are tied together through a narrative of natural crisis that is meticulously woven into a variety of hypernationalistic tropes. In this sense, Tanton is not simply a former environmentalist-gone-bad; like other econativists, he is an environmentalist wedded to a specific construction of nature that is itself embedded in exclusionary notions of nationalism, race, and culture. These commitments to a nationalized and racialized nature have led him into activism aimed at securing American sovereignty from the supposed threat posed by immigration.

### The Natural–National Population Crisis

Appeals to ecological nativism commence by emphasizing the importance of national wilderness as a part of "our" national heritage, an observation closely followed by a bevy of demographic projections that demonstrate how this ideal is threatened by overcrowding. Frosty Wooldridge, for example, is a restrictionist who was recently featured on the online documentary series *Tomorrow's America* as an "environmental activist" seeking to raise attention to the looming national population crisis: "Overpopulation," he proclaimed, "will become the single greatest issue in 21st century America and we must stabilize population in order to solve it" (Tomorrow's America 2010). This is a message he reiterates weekly in letters to the editor that he submits to local and national media outlets, in his books (titled *America on the Brink* and *Immigration's Unarmed Invasion*), and in the presentation that he delivers around Colorado, titled "The Coming Population Crisis in America."

In my 2011 interview with Wooldridge, he demonstrated passion for the topic of overpopulation and recited statistics at an impressive clip:

> Each time you add one new person, that's 19.4 acres of ecological footprint.... We're adding 100 million more by 2035.... The average American has a ten to thirty times greater ecological impact than people in the Third World.... By 2030 the Chinese will be putting 16,000 new cars on the highway every week.... The Chinese use 98 million barrels of oil per day.... India will be 1.6 billion within forty years.... China will be 1.5 billion by 2050.

Reflective of second wave environmental restrictionism, however, Wooldridge's numerical barrage is contextualized through a constant citation of a chaotic "Third World" that is argued to provide a mirror into "our" futures. Wooldridge, who says he has been involved in environmental issues since attending the first Earth Day celebration in 1970, recounted to me that it wasn't until visiting China and Bangladesh that he became truly aware of the connections between population growth, immigration, and environmental degradation: "It wasn't till '84 when I walked on the wall of China . . . China is wall to wall people . . . India is wall to wall . . . Bangladesh has 157 million in a landmass the size of Colorado" (Wooldridge 2011). In describing his encounters in the "Third World," Wooldridge makes it clear that "we" are not immune from the chaos wrought by the cultural practice of overpopulation:

> I have seen the enemy [and] I know what is coming.... Add 200 million people, and we will be Bangladesh: illiterate, ignorant, especially if you add rituals . . . cockfighting, female genital mutilation, dog fighting.... It gets really nasty when incompatible cultures are brought up in a First World environment. (as quoted in Kohoutek 2004)

And while relying on passionate appeals to secure romantic wilderness from the fate of the anarchy lurking outside "our" bounds, the econativist discourse concurrently employs the rationalism of neo-Malthusian demographic projections to embed these emotional concerns within a more "objective" register. Although population anxieties have been a source of contention within traditional, social nativist organizations, for econativists, population is, in many respects, the end-all be-all of natural and national health. Though the arguments vary in form, the substance is always the same—more people inevitably leads to more environmental degradation, thereby threatening the nation-state.[11]

This is a significant shift from social nativism because the particular framings of nature on which econativists rely enable anxieties over population to be expressed in ways that more directly mesh with the political anxieties of environmentalists. Nonetheless, the state of exception that they urge Americans to recognize has significant overlap with social nativist logics and intense racial and gendered implications for nonwhite immigrant and nonimmigrant populations. Emerging from the post–World War II second wave of restrictionism that I identified in the preceding chapter, the econativist logic employs varied epistemological practices that combine romanticism, demography, fertility rates, sociobiology, and orthodox international relations in articulating connections between nature, nation, state, and race in attempts to imbue sovereignty with an exclusionary ethos.

### The Demographic Steady State

Whatever the genuine feelings and political commitments of some econativists, the discourse moves away from overt nativism through an emphasis on the sheer number of immigrants, an explicit disavowal of racism, and an appeal to environmentalists to take these "facts" seriously:

> Identifying causality is not assigning moral "blame." However, political pressure groups have sought to intimidate those correctly linking environmental degradation, population growth, and immigration by hurling such spiteful epithets as "racists" or "nativists." . . . Demography drives human destiny. David Brower knows this, our politicians discount it.[12] (Burke 2000)

The solution to this politically correct impasse, then, lies in a "demographic steady state" where "replacement rates" are realized; Native Americans have achieved this rate, but growth from immigration has upset the potential equilibrium (Federation for American Immigration Reform 2008). Particularly troubling in this regard are the fertility rates of "foreign" women:

> The foreign-born account for a much larger share of U.S. births than their share of the population. Native-born Americans average roughly 13 births per thousand people; immigrants average roughly 28 births per thousand. As a result, the foreign born have a disproportionate share of the births in the U.S. According to the Census Bureau, in 2000, births to foreign-born mothers accounted for 17 percent of the births in the United States. (Federation for American Immigration Reform 2008)

These high fertility rates are attributed to a number of factors, including American aid and immigration policies. Take, for instance, the position of Virginia Abernethy—a self-described "ethnic separatist" and Vanderbilt professor emeritus who formerly edited the journal *Population and Environment,* currently sits on the Board of Directors of the Carrying Capacity Network, and holds a leadership position with the white nationalist organization American Third Position (A3P). Abernethy exemplifies an econativist approach to fertility in advancing what she terms the "fertility opportunity hypothesis." Her contention is that as perceptions of economic opportunity increase, people have more children; when economic opportunity collapses, people have fewer children. The lesson she aims to drive home is that immigration, foreign aid, and other "redistributive" policies worsen the demographic crisis in developing states. Instead, "letting the population bear the weight of a contracting economy, so that they perceive that opportunity has diminished, is the path to rapid fertility decline and eventual population stabilization" (Abernethy 2006, 229). In other words, inequality is *natural and necessary.* In response to the claim that such a policy would be unethical, she offers a vision of progress: "the present may be painful but the future is not hopeless because prosperity can build from a platform of demographic stability" (229). In an article appearing in *The Social Contract,* Albert Bartlett (2005) approvingly cites "Abernethy's Axiom" in making the case against foreign aid on the grounds that "the perception of improving economic wellbeing . . . is followed by an increase in the fertility of the recipients of the aid."

While this logic itself is hotly contested,[13] such supposedly scientific concerns also often seep into racial anxieties over the growing numbers of brown bodies. John Tanton, for instance, once mused, "Can *homo contraceptivus* compete with *homo progenitiva* if borders aren't controlled?" (Southern Poverty Law Center 2002a).[14] A recent contributor to *The Social Contract* put it more bluntly: "The U.S. is the only industrial country with a growing population. And 80 percent of the growth is due to immigration and the rest to the babies of immigrants . . . their weapon is their babies" (Duncan 2007). Paralleling nativist paranoia over the coming "*reconquista*," econativists foment cultural essentializations in which the very presence of immigrant families is seen as evidence of a conspiratorial form of statecraft from below (see, e.g., Horowitz 2005).[15]

In an interview with the author, Marilyn Chandler DeYoung (2011b), at the time the chair of the Board of Californians for Population Stabilization (CAPS) and a former Nixon appointee to the Rockefeller Commission, echoed these sentiments in linking the allegedly rising birthrates of Muslim populations with post-9/11 national security concerns:

> The Muslims are another group you have to face, because they're trying to control the world by having lots of children. Their women are uneducated and at complete control of the man. . . . We've lost ground with Arab countries in the 40 years we've been working on this. . . . I had an interview with Mubarak when he was Secretary of Home, Health and Welfare, and he was advocating population stabilization.[16]

This securitization of fertility, family practices, and childbirth, though not without historical precedent, is a strategy that has captivated econativists for some time. DeYoung recounted to me how one of the top priorities of CAPS is to challenge the Fourteenth Amendment's birthright citizenship clause—or, at least, conventional interpretations of *jus soli*. "Right now," she explained, "we're working on the birthright visa or 'Birthright tourism.' . . . Many of them are called 'anchor babies.'"

The "anchor baby" terminology was introduced in the late 1980s but has in recent years gone mainstream. According to FAIR (2010), an anchor baby is defined as an offspring of an illegal immigrant or other non-citizen, who under current legal interpretation becomes a United States citizen at birth. These children may instantly qualify for welfare and other state and local benefit programs. Additionally with the passage of the 1965 Immigration and Nationality Act, the child may sponsor other family members for entry into the United States when he or she reaches the age of twenty-one. . . . The sheer numbers are staggering.

The term thus emerged from the observation that children of immigrants root the family into the country. Whereas single male immigrants frequently work abroad for some time before returning home, it is argued that those with families tend to stay in the host country. More importantly, as Lutton (1996) explains, "the citizen-children are automatically entitled to all of the benefits available to Americans, and, upon reaching the age of 21 years, can legally sponsor their parents and siblings for citizenship . . . making it possible for an entire family to gain entry into the United States and its social welfare programs." Frequently, the urgency of the anchor baby crisis is underscored in more essentialized terms. Take, for instance, the line of inquiry exhibited by another former chair of CAPS, Diana Hull:

Did the fourteenth amendment actually establish or even intend to establish that the baby of a Mexican national who swam across the river to get to US soil immediately become entitled to every benefit available to children of citizens? (Hull 2008)

Continued practices of *jus soli*, it is asserted, are threats to the rule of law on which national sovereignty depends: "Granting birthright citizenship to the children of illegal aliens whose first act in coming to the U.S. is to break our laws, cheapens the meaning of our Constitution and denigrates the principle of the rule of law upon which our country was founded" (Elbel 2007). Or, as Wooldridge succinctly put it at an anti-immigrant rally, "we absolutely demand that there are no more allowances for anchor babies. . . . We don't need a bunch of anchor babies." "Name one single advantage," he continued—reciting a line that he had also used during our interview—"of adding 200 million people to America. . . . Can anybody come up with one? Well I can tell ya, China and India haven't figured that out either" (Wooldridge 2006).

The discourse of econativism reinforces what sociologist Leo Chavez terms the "Latino Threat Narrative." Chavez (2008, 90) remarks that, through this narrative, "even with birthright citizenship, the children of Latinas, particularly undocumented Latinas, are cast as illegitimate members of society, as mere anchor babies, whose very existence and purpose in life are reduced to the biopolitics of immigration." This discursive strategy—wedding passionate appeals to save romantic wilderness to the apparently "scientific" rigor of Malthusian-inspired population projections—nonetheless plays a crucial ontological role: in a language laden with racial imagery and cultural essentializations, immigrant populations—particularly Latina/o families, mothers and children—are constructed as ecologically savage (in contrast to the ecological saviors invited to join in advancing the econativist logic). Neo-Malthusianism is by no means a priori nativist, but the constant citation of a "savage" developing world and the essentialization of Latina reproductive practices render this particular manifestation nativist despite its ostensibly ecological focus.

### Cultural Carrying Capacity and Sociobiological Realism

Insofar as the nature conceptualized by econativists appears cleansed of the cultural politics of social nativist groupings, it also plays a role in alliance building. Econativists frequently employ ecological concepts, such as carrying capacity, to legitimize their essentialized notions of the "Third World" or "Latin" culture, while simultaneously working to expand the restrictionist coalition beyond the far right. For example, Garrett Hardin is well known by environmentalists (and international relations scholars) for his 1968 essay "The Tragedy of the Commons," which is influential for its depiction of a collective action problem and Hardin's concomitant assertion that self-interested actors have no rational incentive to conserve resources in the absence of private property or a strong coercive state. Nonetheless, the overarching normative concern of this essay—excessive "breeding"—is often overlooked:

> In a welfare state, how shall we deal with the family, the religion, the race, or the class (or indeed any distinguishable and cohesive group) that adopts over breeding as a policy to secure its own aggrandizement? To couple the concept of freedom to breed with the belief that everyone born has an equal right to the commons is to lock the world into a tragic course of action. (1246)

There is thus a cultural component to Hardin's tragedy. The problem, as he saw it, was not merely that self-interested individuals are bound to breed; it was that certain religions, races, and classes are particularly egregious transgressors of this necessary social norm. Moreover, it was, according to Hardin, the absolute wrong religions, races, and classes who were overbreeding. In fact, Hardin was an adamant eugenicist—a former director of the American Eugenics Society who accepted a $29,000 grant from the racist Pioneer Fund (Miller 1994–95, 60) and viewed infanticide as an "effective population control" (Spencer 1992; Beirich 2007).

The relationship between Hardin's neo-Malthusianism and his eugenicism can be more closely connected by looking to his 1986 speech titled "Cultural Carrying Capacity." Hardin begins by decrying "human exceptionalism"—the promethean idea that humans are not bound to the laws of nature because of our ability to create technology that can overcome ecological limits. Instead, he asserts, "the kinship of man and the animals (meaning other animals) remains a fruitful working hypothesis for biologists. . . . This hypothesis is recommended to scholars of all persuasions as a sovereign remedy against deceptions engendered by exemptionist thinking." Following this line of thought, Hardin notes that all species, humans included, have a carrying capacity. However, he contends that the ethology of humanity has revealed certain differences, and this concept must thereby be amended to add a social dimension:

> For non-human animals it seems reasonable to measure carrying capacity in terms of resources available for survival. In evaluating the human situation, however, we are not satisfied with so simple a metric. We hold that "Man does not live by bread alone." We go beyond the spiritual meaning of the Biblical quotation in distinguishing between mere existence and the good life. This distinction, like so many population-related ideas, was well understood by Malthus, who held that the density of population should be such that people could enjoy meat and a glass of wine with their dinners. Implicitly, Malthus's concept of carrying capacity included cultural factors.

From this almost Aristotelian logic, Hardin derives a simple scientific conclusion: to lead the "good life"—however defined—humans need a minimal amount of energy with which to produce materials. The fewer people in the world, the more energy each can use, and vice versa.

Complicating this scenario, Hardin asserts, is the fact that humans do not—*will not and cannot*—live as "One World":

> Is it wise to hope and plan for One World, a world without borders? Or must our plans assume the continuation of subdivisions something like the nations we now know? This is perhaps the most fundamental political question of our time. The insights of biology are needed to solve it.

Dreams of world government, or "spaceship earth," he insists, suffer from the debilitating effects of collective action problems that he demonstrated in "The Tragedy of the Commons." Self-interested competition for scarce-resources, in Hardin's Darwinian frame, is a natural constant: "if discrete entities (nations, for example) are in reality competing for scarce resources, those entities that follow Marx's ideal [from each according to his ability] . . . will be at a competitive disadvantage competing with more self-seeking entities" (Hardin 1986). Thus Hardin's sociobiological logic arrives at the same point as realist international relations theorists; his is a world driven by Darwin rather than Hobbes or Thucydides, but his political imaginary is founded on the same principles: anarchy, scarcity, self-interest, and competition.

The take-home, as Hardin (1989, 22) would later write, is that "we are not faced with a single global population problem, but, rather, with about 180 separate national population problems." What's more, the solution to these problems does not lie in charity or aid—in providing more resources or even redistributing existing resources (a principle that, he suggests, flies in the face of natural selection)—rather, it lies in population reduction. There must exist a match between a nation's resources and population; "the only legitimate demand that nations can make on one another is this: 'Don't try to solve your population problem by exporting your excess people to us'" (22).

Based on this logic, it is no surprise that Hardin was an early proponent of environmental restrictionism or that his concepts continue to animate econativist discussions. Hardin's notion of carrying capacity is deployed most prominently by the appropriately named Carrying Capacity Network (CCN), which displays the definition on its website: "the number of individuals who can be supported in a given area within natural resource limits and without degrading the *natural, social, cultural and economic environment* for present and future generations"

(Carrying Capacity Network 2010a, emphasis added). Working from this definition, the apparent incommensurability of commitments to both nativism and nature is resolved through the construction of a grand "problem" that is argued to be responsible for environmental and societal declines alike: a sweeping pro-growth ethos that fails to entertain the possibility of cultural, political, economic, and environmental "limits to growth."

Citations of cultural carrying capacity abound in econativist works, often in ways that stray dramatically from the scientific jargon of Hardin. For instance, despite including "resource conservation" as one of its five missions, the Carrying Capacity Network (2010a) dedicates the vast majority of its space to detailing instances of *cultural* pollution:

> Practices which impair or destroy fundamental cultural values impair the sustainability of a nation—as the eminent Garrett Hardin asserted in his classic 1986 essay "Cultural Carrying Capacity"—just as overuse of not-easily replaceable resources is a transgression of long-term ecological carrying capacity.... Among cultural values essential to the sustainability of the United States are, for example, Freedom of Speech, Rule of Law, and Respect for a shared Heritage and English Language—all basic to social cohesion, national unity and national preservation.

Despite voicing positions that verge perilously close to traditional, social nativism, the CCN is considered a respected voice in the restrictionist movement, thanks largely to the fact that prominent ecological economists Robert Costanza and William Rees sit on its board of advisors.[17]

### Think Globally, Act Locally, Exclude Nationally

The potential appeal of the econativist narrative is further enhanced by the deployment of popular environmental terminology. In a 2006 public presentation, Stuart Hurlbert, of CAPS, began by employing a quotation by Rene Dubos, advisor to the 1972 United Nations Conference on the Human Environment: "ecological consciousness should begin at home." Or, as it's more often put, "think globally, act locally."[18] Though such terminology is common among environmentalists, Hurlbert weds this green ideal to a territorially bound national community by turning to Hardin's (1989) insistence that "we will make no progress with population problems ... until we deglobalize them." To reject the counterargument—that population is a global problem and "we" have an ethical obligation to all living beings (immigrants included) by virtue of our common ecological interconnection—Hurlbert turns to Hardin's "lifeboat ethics." The metaphor, from a 1974 essay, is a simple one: there is only so much room on "our" lifeboat, and to sustain any quality of life, "we" simply cannot allow any of those swimming in the waters alongside us on board. Hardin (1989) thus abstracts the social Darwinian notion of survival of the fittest upward to extend to nation-states—a move that he justifies through an appeal to orthodox international relations theory:

> All population controls must be applied locally. ... For one nation to attempt to impose its ethical principles on another is to *violate national sovereignty* and endanger international peace.

Through this logic, the problem of immigration is transformed into a crisis of sovereignty. The population catastrophes on the horizon necessitate "mutual coercion, mutually agreed upon" (Hardin 1968, 1247). In other words, the majority of the people agree to limit population growth, through coercive means if necessary. For econativists, the Anglo-European nation provides the mutual agreement, and "the state," if it is to be legitimate, must deploy its coercive capacity to enforce this agreement. With this, it becomes clear why followers of Hardin link up with followers of social nativists like Pat Buchanan and Peter Brimelow. There is little paradox here at all; their logics converge despite their divergent frames of nature. What these Darwinian, Hobbesian, and conservative discourses have in common is the overriding faith that social and natural order and equilibrium are to be found in the nation-state. And in the evolution of the nation-state, excluding immigrants is natural. In this regard, the use of popular environmental terminology masks the deployment of social Darwinian ideals that work to distance the national environmental subject from any ethical obligation to immigrant populations. Econativism thus continues along a discursive pathway put into place by "second wave" environmental restrictionism; beneath the objective veneer of neo-Malthusian population anxieties lay scientifically and morally dubious commitments to cultural primitivism and lifeboat ethics.

## Sovereignty, Nature, and Lifeboat Ethics

Hurlbert concludes his presentation with a literal scripting of lifeboat ethics. He flips to a slide displaying an image from the film *The Perfect Storm*, with a small boat—which he has titled *U.S.A.*—crashing against a massive tidal wave, which clearly signifies population growth from immigration. In a graphic above the boat, he has placed a large list of organizations that are ostensibly contributing to the wave (Democratic Party, Republican Party, Obama, McCain, Sierra Club, Mexican Government, ACLU, etc.) and, in a graphic below, a much smaller list of organizations who are attempting to save the boat (CAPS, NumbersUSA, FAIR, CCN, NPG, etc.).

Throughout econativism, one finds (1) an abiding sentiment that to defend against the ecological savages, "we" need ecological saviors, and (2) a hardly concealed anger that no one seems to be listening to these saviors. In our conversation, Wooldridge repeatedly bemoaned the fact that he and his colleagues weren't taken more seriously and left me with some cautionary advice:

> What I'm talking about is not politically correct, but the fact is this is what's coming. . . . You're gonna find that everybody wants to avoid and evade this issue. It's the last taboo in 21st century America.

The notion that those who disagree are irrational, or hyperemotional, or too concerned with political correctness is found throughout econativist dialogues. The political battles that they have lost are not evidence of contested truths or failing strategies but proof that they—and the Anglo-European ideals that they represent—are victims of epistemic closure. After observing Tanton's efforts to tap into this politics of resentment, however, Christopher Hayes (2006) suggests that there is hypocrisy at play. His argument is worth quoting at length:

> Though he plays the victim, Tanton wants it both ways: harnessing the political power that comes from tapping into nativist grievances and building bridges with outright racists, while at the same time dismissing any of the negative consequences that might come from such partnerships. . . . The success of US English taught Tanton a crucial lesson. If the immigration restrictionist movement was to succeed, it would have to be rooted in an emotional appeal to those who felt that their country, their language, their identity was under assault.

"Feelings," Tanton says in a tone reminiscent of Spock sharing some hard-won insight on human behavior, "trump facts."

The irony is thus that econativists criticize their opponents for relying on "feelings" rather than "facts," at the same time as they continue to stir the hyperemotional pots of race, culture, and nationalism—at times indirectly through their application of ostensibly ecological ideals. The neo-Malthusian emergency of which they speak is at once natural and national, and both social and ecological concepts are deployed to support the case that "we" are imperiled by the movement, fertility, and cultural practices of migrant bodies. The ties that bind the nation to nature are so thick that one can't possibly untangle the two concepts.

The nationalized constructions of nature that I've outlined play three crucial roles within the econativist discourse. First, *ontologically,* the national environmental subject is constructed by juxtaposing the romantic ideal of "national wilderness" against a chaotic "developing world" whose cultures supposedly militate against the preservation of such national treasures. At the same time, Malthusian concerns over demographics proceed through cultural essentializations that construct Latina/o families, mothers, and children as ecologically uncivilized. Constant references to these symbols of savagery provide the Other in opposition to which the econativist self is secured.

Second, *strategically,* the employment of cultural carrying capacity enables nature to function as a nodal point, linking ecologically minded thinkers with traditional, social nativists through the privilege afforded to "the nation," order, self-interest, and anarchy. While enabling alliances with social nativists, this nature works as a progressive signifier that allows the discourse of econativism to attempt to disassociate itself from nativist groupings in the public psyche.

Third, *ethically,* the use of popular environmental terminology masks the deployment of social Darwinian ideals (lifeboat ethics) that distance the national environmental subject from any ethical obligation to immigrant populations. "Back in '84 when I got to China," Wooldridge tells me, "I literally pledged my life . . . just like Susan B. Anthony or Martin Luther King who I marched with in '63 as a kid." Hurlbert (2006) thinks the same; his presentation repeatedly expresses outrage against those greens who refuse to "speak truth to power."

Through his *Perfect Storm* image, the message is clear: only a small number of people have the Truth that will save the boat and those on it. The patriotic imagery Wooldridge and his colleagues employ is no accident; from their neo-Malthusian vantage point, they are the defenders of American sovereignty and the ecology that undergirds it.

## CONCLUSION

In his seminal discussion of neoracism, Etienne Balibar ([1991] 2005) argued that political efforts imbued with naturalized, biological claims of racial superiority were increasingly being recoded into a cultural discourse of hypernationalism that focuses attention on threats to national sovereignty. Balibar made the case that, operating amid the specters of Nazism, Jim Crow, and colonialism, the discursive transition from overt racism to these slightly more nuanced visions of nationalism rested on the naturalization of the latter as socially acceptable in reference to the former: "the core of the meaning contrasts a 'normal' ideology and politics (nationalism) with an 'excessive' ideology and behavior (racism)" (46). And though these ideologies are popularly imagined as separate from one another, Balibar recognized that the "nature" deployed in biological racism never really went away in hypernationalist projects; rather, the "natural" and "cultural" were being woven together in ways that were nevertheless presented as definitively "cultural." Indeed, though he did not employ the terminology, Balibar was cognizant of early iterations of econativism:

> In classical Social Darwinism, we thus have the paradoxical figure of an evolution which has to extract humanity . . . from animality, but to do so by the means which characterized animality (the "survival of the fittest") or, in other words, by an "animal" competition between the different degrees of humanity. . . . In differentialist culturalism, one might think this theme was totally absent. I believe it does exist, however, in an oblique form: in the frequent coupling of the discourse on cultural difference with that on ecology (as if the isolation of cultures were the precondition for the preservation of the "natural milieu" of the human race), and, especially, in the thoroughgoing metaphorization of cultural categories in terms of individuality, selection, reproduction and interbreeding. (57)

As Balibar highlighted, nature plays a vital role in both the traditional racism that animates the social nativist discourse and the neoracism that animates econativism. In the former, nature functions as a source of order—referring to both God's and Darwin's "laws" of racial difference; a Lockean political ideal that delegitimizes state action to ameliorate these "natural" racial inequalities; and a symbol of anarchy that is attached to those populations located outside of the racialized national norm. At the same time, there is debate among social nativists over whether protecting the national nonhuman realm ought to be a commitment of the far right. Social nativism, however, is plagued by limitations; the fact that their racist nationalism is visible in all its sovereign splendor engenders censures from across the mainstream political spectrum.

In the latter, as I have just discussed, nature functions as a marker of alterity, a nodal point, and a privileged ethical foundation that links the protection of a culturally homogenous nation with that of natural wilderness. Rather than speaking in overtly racist terms, the use of ecological concepts provides a "scientific" language through which a commitment to an Anglo-European national culture is strengthened. In the lifeboat ethics of econativism, nature nonetheless serves to reinforce racial difference. Whereas social nativism proclaims the connection between race and sovereignty for all to see, econativism functions through a biopolitical register in which the "primary" strategy is to save "the nation" from "our" population emergency and any coercive interventions or racialized implications of this strategy are positioned as mere effects of this natural logic. This shift has enabled econativists, such as Hardin and Tanton, to play a crucial role in anti-immigrant alliance building, fostering relationships among conservationists, green followers of Darwin and Malthus, and the American far right, despite their extremism.

The differences between the two nativist logics, though at times slight, are important. The traditional, social nativist constructs "the immigrant" as part of a "wave" or "horde" that lacks specificity. As such, it induces a generalizable image of chaos, violence and impurity, one working at a visceral level, that invites the viewer to relate that image to the omnipresent "threats" surrounding him in his day-to-day life—the new neighbor with an accent, the guy on the street in baggy jeans, the rapper on TV, the brown-skinned janitorial worker, and so on—and it implores him to think, "These fears are *natural*."

The political contribution of econativism is to give an additional, ecological connotation to this horde, which at once introduces a degree of sophistication to the nativist argument and also imbues it with an added intensity; the environment isn't the only level on which "they" are savage, it's another level. The econativist viewer is subject to the same tropes, and is encouraged to think the same things about the same categories of people, but is also encouraged to think to herself, "You're doing this for *Nature*."

These discursive differences are politically productive. Both nativist discourses work as forms of statecraft from below, attempting to reinforce sovereign borders by appealing to ideals of nature that legitimize biopolitical interventions targeting nonwhite and immigrant populations. Nature, then, is not ancillary to the struggles of nativists to reconfigure sovereignty; rather, it is through specific constructions of nature (some anthropocentric and others ecocentric) that nativist visions of sovereignty become intelligible. These natures reflect both ontological and epistemological commitments as well as strategic ones— "cultural" visions of national and racial purity derived, in part, from natural epistemologies as well as "natural" visions of overpopulation, wilderness, and competition derived, in part, from cultural ideals of nationhood, race, and colonialism. The fact that a panel on sustainability could include someone like O'Neill is neither coincidental nor paradoxical; it is a function of contemporary restrictionist strategies and environmentalist ontologies and epistemologies shot through with the exclusionary historical residues of sovereign power.

# 3

# THE CHALLENGE OF ECOCOMMUNITARIAN RESTRICTIONISM

> In what does national integrity consist, what might
> nationhood and belonging mean, what moral and material
> entitlements might it entail, at a time when global
> capitalism seems everywhere to be threatening sovereign
> borders, everywhere to be displacing politics-as-usual?
>
> **JEAN AND JOHN COMAROFF,** "Naturing the Nation:
> Aliens, Apocalypse, and the Post-colonial State"

As Peter O'Neill discussed "culture" at the town hall panel, Philip Cafaro, seated two chairs over, must have been uneasy. Cafaro, professor of environmental ethics at Colorado State University and president of Progressives of Immigration Reform, has dedicated himself to advancing the "liberal" argument for immigration reduction. An ardent environmentalist who identifies as a progressive, the presentation that Cafaro gave eschewed any mention of cultural continuity, instead depicting the precarious state of the Cache la Poudre River, a federally designated Wild and Scenic River that is threatened by the proposed Glade Reservoir. The reservoir, supported by regional business and development interests, is an attempt to provide water for future residential development plans that proponents argue are necessitated by expected population growth. Cafaro, and fellow members of the organization Northern Coloradoans for Immigration Reduction,[1] contend that this expected population growth is being driven by immigration. In a 2010 blog post for NumbersUSA, he expanded on this logic, expressing dismay at the possibility that the reservoir would be built:

> A lovely river flows through my town: the Cache la Poudre.... I've helped the local Audubon Society census its bird populations, and wrote a proposal to have the river corridor designated a state important bird area. I've pointed out kingfishers, osprey and foxes to my sons on our river walks. And when I asked my wife ... to marry me, the "natural" choice was along the banks of the Poudre.... I love the Cache. And I hate plans to siphon off its last unallocated "flows" and pump them into a new storage reservoir. (Cafaro 2010a)

Cafaro's narrative thus commences by aesthetically linking this "lovely" river to a local communal imaginary: Fort Collins is defined by the Cache la Poudre, and through the use of personal history, he suggests that his identity is irrevocably connected to both the city and the river. However, his "nature"—both the nonhuman nature that he "loves" and the human identity that he has internalized—is threatened by the crisis of population growth:

> Of course the reservoir's proponents also get to have their say, and the water district has hired a fetching young woman to tell their side of the story. She begins a fancy power point presentation. And here they are, two slides into the proceedings.... The population projections! Again, looking thirty to fifty years out from the present. Again: low, medium, and high growth projections. And again, it is obvious: we're going to have more people here. They will need water. Etc. The whole rest of the presentation flows from that one slide. And with that one slide on their side, the presentation will be very tough to argue away.... If our population wasn't growing, no one would be proposing this reservoir.

In a personal interview, Cafaro (2011) echoed these sentiments in reflecting on his role working to "Save the Poudre" from damming:

> Over the course of twenty five years, again and again, I've seen that population projections make a big difference in justifying bad projects.... We're trying to make a case for not building this dam, but it's hard when more and more people are moving here.... You take away that population growth, you take away the whole fight about the dam.

Population growth, these examples imply, is the primary driver of environmental degradation. As such, stabilizing population ought to be the ultimate environmental goal—taking priority over diminished consumption, industrial regulations, state water law, national trade policy, or any kind of radical resistance against capitalism. It is the only way to save the local places that "we" care about. And out of this local necessity emerges a national policy prescription:

> I'm no longer willing to keep my mouth shut about population growth, just because most population growth in the U.S. is now caused by immigration and the topic makes a lot of people uncomfortable. Hell, discussing immigration makes me uncomfortable! I would much rather avoid the topic, particularly among my fellow progressives. More than once, I've been called a nativist, a xenophobe, a racist—not because of anything objectionable I've said about any racial or ethnic group, but simply for saying that we should reduce immigration. Who needs it? The answer, I think, is that nature needs it. Nature needs fewer people—globally, but also right here, in the United States. . . . America's rivers, forests and grasslands; the birds and mammals and other species with whom we grudgingly share the landscape; desperately need fewer Americans, not more. (Cafaro 2010a)

In opposition to the econativist discourse, Cafaro makes a point of emphasizing that immigration is not his target, a "growth-first" logic is. Immigrants, he asserts, just so happen to be contributing to the destruction of nature—not because of any "cultural" deficiency but because of their sheer numbers. And to protect "our" communities (local and national), someone has to speak for all of the "rivers, forests, grasslands, birds and mammals" who cannot speak for themselves.

The narrative that Cafaro weaves is reflective of a broader discursive grouping that I refer to as ecocommunitarianism, an emergent variant of environmental restrictionism that differs in obvious respects from that of nativist iterations.[2] While ecocommunitarian restrictionism is not reducible to broader green engagements with communitarianism, I do argue that there exist certain commonalities between this iteration of ecocommunitarianism and ideals on which many American greens rely. Ecocommunitarian restrictionists employ a language of liberal multiculturalism, criticize the neoliberal fetishization of growth, urge America to exercise leadership as a strong global environmental steward, and emphasize the importance of connection to "wild places." Elements of econativism—neo-Malthusianism population anxieties and romantic ideals of national wilderness—remain prominent in this discourse, but these forms of knowing nature are carefully enmeshed in a communitarian ideal rather than a hypernationalist one. Eco-communitarians articulate relations between nature and sovereignty that converge, in important respects, with the "progressive" project of greening the nation-state.

## ECOCOMMUNITARIANISM IN CONTEXT

Ecocommunitarianism plays ontological, epistemological, and strategic roles within the restrictionist alliance. On one hand, this is the lens that many Sierra Club restrictionists, in addition to organizations like Alliance for a Sustainable USA, Californians for Population Stabilization, NumbersUSA, and Cafaro's own Progressives for Immigration Reform, employ to understand the relationship between immigration and environmental degradation. In this sense, examination of the ecocommunitarian discourse gives us insight into the ontologies and epistemologies through which environmental restrictionism advances among mainstream environmentalists and organizations that position themselves on the left of the American political spectrum. But, on the other hand, ecocommunitarianism is also the logic being advanced by a number of organizations that I highlighted in the previous chapter—the Federation for American Immigration Reform (FAIR), the American Immigration Control Foundation, the Social Contract Press, Carrying Capacity Network (CCN), and the Center for Immigration Studies (CIS)—in their materials *geared toward public consumption*. In fact, ecocommunitarianism is the chosen discourse of the America's Leadership Team (ALT) alliance. This suggests that ecocommunitarianism plays a strategic role in the efforts of nativists to expand their anti-immigrant coalition into the ranks of contemporary "progressivism."

The discourse enables nativists and econativists to respond to the critiques of "racism" and "xenophobia" with which their cultural essentializations are increasingly met outside of the far right. For example, after a recent *New York Times* article recounted some of the xenophobic statements and racist allies of John Tanton, he was removed from the FAIR Board of Directors, and the organization attempted to publicly distance itself (Deparle 2011).[3] In a strange twist of fate, as the network that he helped to create has successfully moved into more "mainstream" circles, Tanton's econativism has grown too controversial for several restrictionist organizations who prefer to position themselves as moderate (FAIR), nonpartisan (CIS), or "liberal" (Californians for Population Stabilization, CAPS). In select venues, employing carefully calibrated tones, discourses of restrictionism are moving left, and ecocommunitarianism appears to be central to these efforts.

What has led to this discursive shift? To understand the potential appeal of ecocommunitarianism, one has to understand the broader discursive terrain on which contemporary American debates over immigration and environmental degradation reside. As I have previously discussed, scholars of neoracism observe that since the civil rights and decolonial movements of the 1960s and 1970s, appeals to ostensibly "cultural" discourses of hypernationalism have supplanted appeals to "natural" discourses of biological racism (see, e.g., Balibar [1991] 2005; Bonilla-Silva 2001). As scholars of anti-immigrant movements have shown, these neoracist projects have solidified on the far right since the early 1990s (see, e.g., Perea 1997; Chavez 2008; Jacobson 2008), but their expansion into moderate and leftist circles has been largely blocked by the institutionalization of principles of liberal equality—the mainstreaming of multiculturalism, continued attempts to understand the contemporary implications of historical traditions of racism and colonialism, and renewed attention to structural asymmetries of power provoked by the intensification of neoliberal globalization. In this context, I contend that Balibar's analysis of the role of race in hypernationalist projects has become commonsensical among American "progressives" (as evidenced by the forceful critiques of econativism that I detail in chapter 4). As environmentalism is hedged firmly on the left of American political imaginaries (Dunlap, Xiao, and McCright 2001; Bryner 2008; Anderson 2011), a "cultural" politics of social justice has seeped into the ideals of many mainstream environmentalists. This is reflected in the institutionalization of environmental justice within major environmental organizations (Bernstein 2006) and in much-publicized recent alliances between environmental and social activists (Steele 2008; Jakopovich 2009; Blue-Green Alliance 2012).

At the same time, however, these cultural politics intersect with a "natural" register where the epistemological practices outlined in the previous chapters—Malthusianism, romanticism, and Darwinism—

retain prominent positions. As I alluded to in the introduction, contemporary American environmentalism is characterized by a dichotomous ontology through which apparently contradictory political ideals are filtered: on one side a cultural register where liberal equality is prized (and ideals of social justice are increasingly relevant), on the other a natural register where epistemologies that have a long history of complicity in exclusionary social forms—Darwinism, Malthusianism, romanticism—remain prominent.

This chapter analyzes how these ideals of nature are woven in the efforts of ecocommunitarians to advance restrictionist politics. I contend that ecocommunitarianism represents a "best case scenario"—it is environmental restrictionism at its most logical and persuasive. Theirs is not a crisis of national homogeneity threatened by cultural impurity but one of "natural places" threatened by a hegemonic neoliberal ideology. The ecocommunitarian aim is to reconfigure sovereignty through the construction of a progressive environmental citizenry, in which nonhuman species and future generations are included in a multicultural, social-democratic nation-state. Nowhere in this narrative are *immigrants* deemed "savage"; rather, *immigration* provokes opposition in relation to its alleged complicity with a neoliberal political economic agenda.

My argument, however, is that ecocommunitarians advance an ethical imaginary that is unwilling to recognize the transnational structures through which environmental and social injustices are institutionalized and therefore is unable to provide a satisfactory adjudication of ethical obligation. While the extreme political economic impacts of neoliberalism are recognized, a normative ideal of obligation to others contingent on membership within a sovereign political culture serves to displace blame for environmental (and social) degradation away from the very sovereign structures that produce harm and toward migrant populations. Whether it is driven by ontological and epistemological or strategic commitments, ecocommunitarianism continues to rely on black-boxed notions of "national cultures" and state-centric logics of morality that resonate strongly with contemporary nativists. In this vein, the ecocommunitarians have forged a discourse that is readily appropriable by exclusionary interests who seek to creatively manipulate the aforementioned disjuncture between the generally "progressive" politics of the environmentalist movement and the often conservative epistemologies through which greens continue to know nature. For this reason, the discourse should be forcefully rejected by environmentalists concerned with socioecological justice.

## THE CRISIS OF NEOLIBERAL GLOBALIZATION

In the June 16, 2008, issue of *The Nation,* ALT placed a full-page advertisement depicting a bulldozer plowing through a pristine forest (Figure 2). Linking the destruction of nature with a pro-growth ethos, the headline proclaimed the machine "One of America's Best Selling Vehicles":

> Bulldozer sales in America have been booming. Road builders need them to level rolling hills into concrete interchanges and bypasses. De-velopers need them to turn farmland into housing developments and shopping malls. You can find big earthmoving equipment throughout America, turning our most picturesque land into suburban sprawl, while adding to some of the worst traffic problems in the world. Yet the bulldozers keep on coming, ripping up some of the most beauti-ful farms and forests in the world and turning them into concrete and asphalt suburbs. But with U.S. census projections indicating our population will explode from 300 million today to 400 million in thirty years and 600 million before 2100, bulldozer sales should keep on booming. Unless we take action today.[4]

In a move reflective of broader ecocommunitarian tactics, the imper-iled state of "our" national wilderness is here attributed to the priority placed on economic development—an unfortunate trend that is argued to proceed in direct relation to population growth. More population, the narrative goes, inevitably breeds more environmentally destructive economic growth.

As this ad indicates, the central pillar of ecocommunitarianism remains a familiar neo-Malthusian logic, but this emergent discourse— unlike the libertarian leanings of nativist groupings—couches the crisis of population growth in a forceful critique of neoliberal economic policies. In his 2001 congressional testimony, Bill Elder, of Sierrans for Population Stabilization, echoed this sentiment: "Of course, some economic interests with a short-term outlook welcome population

FIGURE 2. "One of America's Best Selling Vehicles." Advertisement by America's Leadership Team appearing in *The Nation*, June 16, 2008.

growth. . . . Environmentalists do not, because we understand its true environmental quality-of-life and economic costs."

This sharp distinction between "the economic" and "the environmental" animates a zero-sum logic that is a hallmark of ecocommunitarianism. In our interview, William Ryerson (2011), former president of Progressives for Immigration Reform and the Population Media Center, spoke at length about the ways in which supporters of the *Wall Street Journal* and *Forbes* lobby for immigration on the grounds that the influx of cheap labor will drive economic growth. Marilyn Chandler DeYoung (2011b), former chair of CAPS, concurred in remarking to me that the "business community is very reluctant to give up the cheap labor that they've had access to for so long."

However, the self-interested attempts of capital to attract flows of labor from "outside" only tell part of the story. William Rees, cofounder of the ecological footprint and Fellow at the Post-Carbon Institute, puts forth a broader ecological critique of liberal capitalism. Rees (2011) observes that "money enables people in rich countries to appropriate the carrying capacity of people in poor countries." Trade driven by liberal economic models, according to Rees, has created a condition in which rich countries have accumulated ecological footprints that vastly exceed their biophysical capacities:

> Large populations are supported by trade and dumping waste into the global commons, moving people around doesn't solve this. In a marketplace, wealthy countries are still able to purchase biocapacity. . . . Money enables people in rich countries to appropriate the carrying capacity of people in poor countries. People become incapable of providing enough of their own landscape to support themselves. (Rees 2011; see also Rees 2006, 222)

Herman Daly (2006, 187), the founder of steady state economics, extends these concerns over free-market trading practices to a whole-scale critique of "globalization":

> Globalization refers to the global economic integration of many formerly national economies into one global economy, mainly by free trade and free capital mobility, but also by somewhat easier or uncontrolled migration. It is the effective erasure of national boundaries for economic purposes.

Contrasting the boundless telos of *globalization* to the state-centric ideal of *internationalization,* Daly concludes that the emergence of a global economy has wreaked havoc on the national community:

> In the United States we have seen the abrogation of a basic social agreement between labor and capital over how to divide up the value that they jointly add to raw materials (as well as the value of the raw materials themselves, i.e. nature's often-uncounted value-added). That agreement has been reached nationally, not internationally, much less globally. . . . That agreement on which national community and industrial peace depend, is being repudiated in the interests of global integration. That is a very poor trade, even if you call it "free trade." (188)

Ecocommunitarianism thus emerges out of an opposition to neoliberal globalization.[5] But to fully understand the significance of this opposition to neoliberalism, and how it works to attract the sympathies of mainstream greens, it is necessary to momentarily step back from ecocommunitarianism and locate the discourse within the political conjuncture in which it has emerged. The following section seeks to do so by examining recent shifts in the relationship between capitalism, sovereignty, and biopolitics.[6] I then return to my examination of ecocommunitarian restrictionism in exploring how nature fits into this nexus.

### Neoliberalism, Sovereignty, and Bare Life

Daly's argument—that the twentieth-century accord between capital and labor has been severed—mirrors the seminal account offered by political scientist John Gerard Ruggie to explain the decline of twentieth-century social welfare states. Ruggie (2003, 93–94) asserts that in the 1930s through 1970s, capital and labor reached a compromise of sorts, where "all sectors of society agreed to open markets . . . but also to contain and share the social adjustment costs that open markets inevitably produce." Drawing on the work of economic historian Karl Polanyi, Ruggie introduces the concept of "embedded liberalism," which refers to the idea that the gross inequalities and crises produced by capitalism can be, in part, warded off by embedding this system within specific social institutions. Polanyi asserts that capitalism in its laissez-faire variants has a tendency to become disembedded from social norms, mutating into a logic of its own that extends an ethos of economic competition into all dimensions of social life (becoming the proverbial tail that wags the dog). Embedded liberalism (institutionalized in the United States through the New Deal and Great Society programs) provided the white working classes of the United States and Western Europe with social welfare systems, health care, pensions, and, eventually, environmental regulations that insulated them from the ruptures that typically accompany liberal free-market systems.

Starting in the late 1970s and early 1980s, however, the compromise began to crumble. Ruggie observes that through the emergence of a neoliberal international regime—global production chains accompanied by domestic decisions of powerful states and reinforced by World Bank, International Monetary Fund, and General Agreement on Tariffs and Trade (later World Trade Organization) mandates that forced the hands of less powerful states—the "compromise of embedded liberalism," through which nation-states had retained social legitimacy, was replaced by the dominance of the neoliberal rationale to which Daly refers.

Accompanying (and reinforcing) the macropolitical shifts that Ruggie describes—that is, the dramatic scaling back of state intervention into the economy—has been a powerful micropolitical logic that has worked to revamp the terrain of social legitimacy. As Foucault argues, neoliberalism functions not simply as a set of political economic prescriptions but as a new political rationality that actively cultivates specific forms of subjectivity (Foucault [1979] 2008, 241). Anthropologist Aihwa Ong (2006, 13) concurs, asserting,

> Neoliberalism is merely the most recent development of . . . techniques that govern human life, that is, a governmentality that relies on market knowledge and calculations for a politics of subjection and subject-making that continually places in question the political existence of modern human beings.

In this sense, neoliberalism is a technique of "governing through freedom" that aims to construct entrepreneurial, consumptive, efficient subjects who, by internalizing market-based rationalities, come to think of their individual liberty as irrevocably bound up in consumptive choices, self-responsibility, and free markets (Rose 1996). As neoliberal subjectivity becomes more and more prevalent, societal demands are made not only to withdraw the state from the "private sphere" but to infuse the "public sphere" with a market-based logic, thereby redefining the social and environmental purposes of areas of life that had previously been governed by noneconomic logics (e.g., health care, education, environmental protection).

At the same time as this neoliberalization creates dramatic social and environmental effects, the neoliberal political agenda is cast by proponents as natural, commonsensical, and nonpolitical. It is said to be founded in the "autonomous," "expert-driven," "objective" realm of economics or to reflect an attempt to conform to the timeless Truths of sacred national texts (i.e., the Declaration of Independence and Constitution). Neoliberalism thus functions as a subtle form of depoliticization. On one hand, it "hides its ideological scaffolding in the dictates of economic efficiency and capital growth, in the fetishism of the free-market, in the exigencies of science and technology" (Comaroff and Comaroff 2001, 242). On the other, particularly in the American context, its ideology is masked by its conformity to a purportedly universal national historical imaginary.

This *subtle*, apparently nonpolitical form of subject making is increasingly deployed as justification for the *violent* manifestations of sovereign power—the abandonment of certain populations to "bare life"—that Agamben theorizes. In explaining this trend, Ong (2006) introduces the concept of "neoliberalism as exception." Ong recounts how neoliberalism has forced changes in the political economic calculations of Southeast Asian states, which, amid the exceptional conditions of neoliberal globalization, have suspended their normal political economic orders by strategically carving out spaces (export processing zones, high-technology zones, special administrative zones) governed by neoliberal rationales. Such shifts have reconfigured citizenship so that "highly skilled" noncitizens obtain more political protections than many citizens, who increasingly toil in special administrative zones (absent environmental and social regulations, and subject to strict policing) where women and racial or ethnic minorities work alongside "low-skilled" immigrants (Ong 2006). In the American context, a similar process has occurred, where neoliberalism has intersected with Republican "culture wars" in the discursive positioning of racial minorities, poor populations, and immigrants as lazy, lawless, disorderly "threats" to a society purportedly imperiled by the governmental excesses and inefficiencies that their care produces (see Giroux 2006; Chavez 2008). The result has been a dramatic scaling back of the social safety net as well as an explosion in the Border Patrol, prisons, detention centers, and social systems of surveillance.

This violence extends to nonhuman lives as well. The literature detailing neoliberalism's destructive impact on nature is voluminous, with scholars and activists detailing how neoliberal trade regimes have curtailed the power of states to put in place regulations protecting nonhuman lives (McCarthy 2004; Eckersley 2004); how this regulatory environment has rendered environmental disasters—like oil spills—more or less inevitable (Prudham 2004); how the conditionalities employed by international financial institutions have advanced the privatization of natural resources (Goldman 2006); how the same institutions, in coordination with powerful transnational corporations, have pushed forward the commodification of indigenous knowledges (Tsing 2005) and genetic materials (McAfee 2003); and how neoliberal national development strategies have decimated the natural and cultural resources of indigenous and marginalized populations (Sawyer 2004; Goldman 2006).

In this regard, the institutionalization of neoliberalism—which ostensibly rests on the withdrawal of the state—has actually been accompanied by the paradoxical expansion of coercive force aimed at populations who defy or resist attempts to be molded into neoliberal subjects (and thus pose the threats against which the neoliberal state secures its legitimacy). The aforementioned examples make clear that violent incursions are increasingly driven by an intersection between the logics of sovereignty, biopolitics, and neoliberalism. Various populations are valued differently in relation to a logic of neoliberalism and the strategic efforts of states, capital, and social actors to position themselves within flows set into motion by shifts within the global political economy. In different respects, immigrants and nonhumans occupy particularly precarious positions within these struggles.

## Negotiating Exceptions to Neoliberalism

Ong (2006, 4) makes the case that while "neoliberalism as exception" is a powerful force, there are also ways in which states and societal actors can carve out "exceptions to neoliberalism" by excluding "populations and places from neoliberal calculations and choices." Efforts to construct exceptions to neoliberalism take widely divergent forms: from providing social safety nets to marginalized populations to denying particular populations the benefits accrued through their participation in neoliberal regimes.[7] Exceptions to neoliberalism also vary in terms of the political community they aim to invent and the scale and social purpose of governance they seek to achieve. For example, while Ruggie attempts to theorize the emergence of a global public domain that might embed neoliberal reason within a supranational form of governance, Daly is involved in an effort to negotiate an exception to neoliberalism by returning to an ideal of government by nation-states. Complicating this, Daly's restrictionism is not tethered to a Keynesian welfare state but to a "steady state" (albeit with socially democratic tendencies) that institutionalizes strict limits to growth—economic, environmental, and cultural—at the national scale (Daly 1974).[8] Though most eco-communitarians do not frame their project in the technical, political economic terms of Daly, the entire discourse of ecocommunitarianism is organized around an opposition to "free markets," "neoliberalism," "development," or the "growth paradigm" and a parallel sense that the "nation-state" has lost control amid these powerful political economic forces. In this sense, ecocommunitarianism represents an attempt to negotiate an exception to neoliberal globalization premised on the destructive ecological implications that this phenomenon has wrought.

Returning to the ALT advertisement, the bulldozer, it seems, has no driver—the visual does not portray the human actor responsible for the desecration of wilderness. However, the text, through a nuanced path that discursively articulates a connection between a neoliberal model of growth and the inability of the nation-state to protect its nature, displaces the destruction indirectly onto immigrant populations.[9] The ad suggests that "we" face a crisis of sovereignty. The forces of globalization, propelled by ideals of neoliberalism—themselves pushed forward by certain rationales institutionalized within powerful states and interests—have created a conjuncture where nation-states can no longer control the population dynamics that drive environmental degradation and social deterioration. In the remainder of this chapter, I detail how immigration is discursively linked with the economic interests of the actors driving neoliberalism and constructed in opposition to "environmentally responsible" institutions, communities, and citizens. My contention is that ecocommunitarians seek to negotiate this exception to neoliberalism through a declaration of an *ecological state of exception* that is argued to necessitate the suspension of the "normal" social concerns that typify contemporary American progressive political discourse.

### Toward a Green State

This opposition to neoliberalism is itself not unique, as the dominance of neoliberalism is contested by many on both left and right. For opponents on both sides of the political spectrum, the question that emerges is, How do "we" articulate "our" systems of governance and political communities in such a way as to allow beneficial flows passage inside these boundaries, while blocking flows that hamper "our" ability to organize social life toward the end(s) that "we" deem acceptable? For contemporary American progressives, in particular, an additional question necessitates consideration: How do we do so, without harming those populations that are already marginalized? What is novel about ecocommunitarianism is the carefully crafted answer that is provided to this latter question and the ways in which nature is folded into the response.

The ecocommunitarian logic begins by constructing a sharp distinction between "immigrants as humans" and "immigration as policy." Distancing himself from the nativist logic, Daly (2006, 189), a former board member of CCN, remarks, "It is a terrible thing to be 'anti-immigrant.' . . . Immigration, however, is a policy, not a person, and one can be . . . 'pro-immigration limits' without in the least being anti-immigrant." In the same vein, the mission statement of the Center for Immigration Studies (2011) proclaims that the organization is "animated by a 'low-immigration, pro-immigrant' vision of an America that admits fewer immigrants but affords a warmer welcome for those who are admitted." Similarly, in an article titled "'No' to Immigrant Bashing," Roy Beck (1996) of NumbersUSA observes,

> The task before the nation in setting a fair level of immigration is not about race or some vision of a homogeneous white America; it is about protecting and enhancing the United States' unique experiment in democracy for all Americans, including recent immigrants, regardless of their particular ethnicity.

Ecocommunitarians insist, however, that to provide for continuation of this multicultural "experiment in democracy," ecological limits must be respected. In articulating these limits, ecocommunitarians continue to forcefully advance neo-Malthusian critiques, but their population anxieties are increasingly wedded to a national consumptive imaginary. For example, a widely cited CCN study suggests that immigrants' levels of consumption rise dramatically in coming to the United States:

> We need to recognize the simple fact that the last thing this world needs is more Americans. The world just cannot afford what Americans do to the earth, air, and water. And it does not matter whether these Americans are Americans by birth or by border crossing. It does not matter what color their skin is. It does not matter what language they speak or which god they worship. What matters is that they will live like Americans. (Dinalt 1997)

That the CCN study was methodologically dubious[10] did not stop other restrictionists from citing it as empirical fact. In a recent article in *Environmental Ethics,* Cafaro and Staples (2009, 26) echo the same logic in juxtaposing average American ecological footprints with averages from the United States's top ten immigration source countries: "On average, immigrating from nine of these ten countries greatly increases an individual's ecological footprint—and the ecological footprints of his or her descendants—by 100 percent to 1,000 percent or more." In other words, Americans—writ large—are consumers, and more Americans means more consumption. This sentiment both distances itself from the unreflexive nationalism of nativist groupings and taps into the collective consciousness of environmentalists through an appeal to transform America into a responsible *global* environmental steward by limiting "our" consumptive practices.

In fact, concerns over increased consumption are frequently linked with America's "global obligation" to ameliorate the crisis of global climate change.[11] For example, a recent CAPS advertisement appeared in *Roll Call* under the headline "Mass Immigration and Global Warming: Gives the Term Melting Pot a Whole New Meaning" (Figure 3). The text continues,

> America leads the world in many different categories and capacities. Unfortunately, when it comes to global warming, we're leading the world in the wrong direction. The US generates more greenhouse gas emissions and pollution than any country. The root cause? Out of control immigration growth fueled by mass immigration. . . . It's time to lead the world on the right direction in global warming. The first step is setting the right example by rolling back mass immigration to sensible levels that will allow America to begin healing its environment here at home. Then we can truly begin to lead the world in global warming.

The advertisement makes an overt appeal to the external dimension of sovereignty by asserting that the continued presence of America as an international leader is contingent on actions "at home" from which our legitimacy as an international leader is derived. Put differently, nonhuman flows, such as $CO_2$, that originate in the United States have global environmental implications. To decrease these destructive *nonhuman flows,* "we" need to block the incursion of "foreign" *human flows* to secure the approval of an international community that functions through a morality of state centricity. Of course, the transnational political economic flows that drive this movement of bodies, enable these shifts in consumption, and complicate this state-centric morality are never mentioned in these studies, advertisements, and testimonies.

Nonetheless, these "facts" of consumption are continually cited by environmental restrictionists and, among the network of restrictionist organizations, are transformed into veritable truisms.[12] In this respect, they are premised upon a form of *methodological nationalism* (Chernillo 2006) that is significantly more subtle than that deployed by econativists. Ecocommunitarians reinforce the boundaries of the green nation-state by naturalizing territorial borders through the routinized citation of subject positions premised on dichotomies between citizen and immigrant, inside and outside, domestic and foreign. This logic insists that when one steps across a line, one's consumptive practices

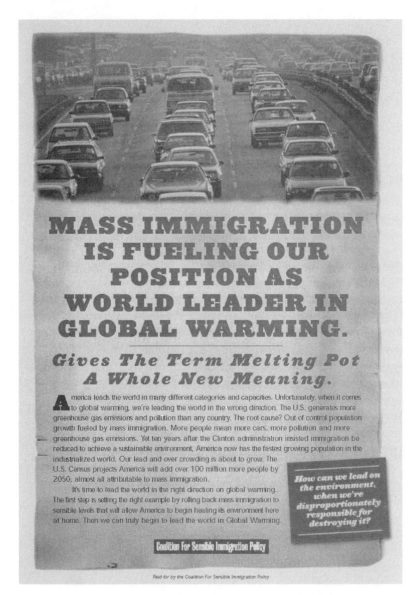

FIGURE 3. "Mass Immigration and Global Warming: Gives the Term Melting Pot a Whole New Meaning." Advertisement by CAPS appearing in *Roll Call*.

immediately begin to adhere to the linear patterns of an Other national culture. With this, "the immigrant" becomes a stable identity in environmental discussions; national membership is *the* referent in relation to which a subject's environmental beneficence or negligence can be gleaned. There are thus normative choices embedded in the ecocommunitarian analysis; it is not an effort simply to "speak for nature." Put differently, the ecocommunitarian nature is rendered intelligible through foundational ontological assumptions about the management of space and subjectivity. Ecocommunitarians employ a nuanced form of methodological nationalism, couching their "objective" claims within an internationalist discourse where global environmental stewardship is dependent on shifts in essentialized national consumptive patterns.

### Natural Places and Ethical Obligations

The ecocommunitarian acknowledgment of the global scope of environmental problems raises the question, If nature is a global concern, why focus on national solutions? In anticipating this critique, ecocommunitarians make it clear that a call for global responsibility is not a call for "globalism." For example, in reinforcing his distinction between "internationalization" and "globalization," Herman Daly asserts that globalization threatens not just the authority of the state but the social purpose on which a sense of national community depends. This is so, according to ecocommunitarians, because of the complicity between global arrangements and the interests of capital. Specifically, ecocommunitarians stress that lax immigration policies are in the interests of transnational elites, lobbied for by neoclassical economists, multinational corporations, and neoliberal interest groups, because they produce a flexible, mobile labor force with no sense of *place*.

The echoes of romantic linkages between national culture and wilderness are readily apparent here. "Place," in the ecocommunitarian narrative, represents "a deep attachment to specific geographies fashioned by repeated interactions that provide both the context and content for the construction of personal and cultural identity" (Chapman 2006, 216). While national communities, according to Robert Chapman, are founded on close interactions with sacred places, globalization destroys these attachments to project onto the earth a capital-friendly landscape of "space," a "mere spatial extension that lacks the capacity to uniquely influence what it contains" (215–16). Following this line of thought, Cafaro (2010b, 192–93) links protection of "place"—specifically, the *natural place*—with patriotism, or love of "the fatherland":

> Environmental activists typically work to protect the places they know and love, whether it is open-space threatened by sprawl, or a downtown threatened by a new Super Wal-mart. . . . They do all this not to make a buck, but because they care about where they live and other special places they have gotten to know, and because they want to preserve them for their children and grandchildren. (192)

In an interview with the author, he further developed this line of thought:

> Objectively, one place is not more important than the other. But for me, I care about particular places. They're the places I know. They are the places that I can engage to protect within the political frame-work. . . . For me, I'm a patriot, I think. I care about my country. I care about the country that my children are going to live in most likely, and my grandchildren. More than I care about other places. And I think that's a very powerful motivator for people. It's been a power-ful motivator in protecting national parks. . . . I think it's good for people to really care more about the places they live in. (Carafo 2011)

Place thus functions as a national environmental and social necessity that is being undone by the deterritorializing impulses of neoliberalism.

Through this narrative, neoliberal hegemony is linked with a "global space," in opposition to progressive environmentalism, which is the product of a "national place." By opening up the nation-state to a variety of economic flows, neoliberalism is argued to diminish the capacity of the state to deal with social and environmental problems that the nation deems legitimate sources of concern—a phenomenon only amplified by heightened immigration. For instance, Cafaro (2010c) wonders how citizens could be convinced to make environmental sacrifices if national projects to, say, decrease carbon dioxide output were countered by population growth from immigration:

> If we want to convince our more skeptical fellow-citizens to fol-low our lead and consume less, we need to get population growth under control. . . . [Saying] "you need to consume less, make these efforts and sacrifices, so that our country can accommodate tens of

millions more Mexicans, tens of millions more Chinese . . . and all their descendants." . . . Even a reasonable and conscientious citizen might well ask why he or she should bother.

Bill Elder (2001, 39) reiterated this position in his aforementioned congressional testimony:

> As environmentalists, we think people are entitled to cleaner air (water that we can swim and fish in, etc.), not just the same quality we have now. We also think that many Americans will make sacrifices to accomplish such goals. But we do not think Americans will respond to the call to conserve—only to see the fruits of their sacrifice eaten up by government sponsored population growth.

For the state to attain the political capital necessary to provide a range of environmental protections for its citizens, the body politic must be prepared to practice and demand sacrifice. And these sacrifices are contingent on the ability and willingness of the state to assert control over its territorial boundaries to stem population growth. In short, environmental sacrifice necessitates correspondence to the historical ideal of a nation-state that possesses an absolute ability to regulate the entrance of external flows.

### Environmental Ethics amid the Ecological State of Exception

The appeal being made to political community here is not one of blatant hypernationalism but a communitarian concern for self-determination wedded to the purported exigencies of a global environmental crisis—a crisis that, ecocommunitarians emphasize, already faces an uphill battle in a period of neoliberal hegemony. Undergirding the narrative is a sharp division between "the economic"—associated with instrumental reasoning, narrow self-interest, private benefit, and the global scale—and "the environmental," associated with intrinsic value, broad conceptions of interest, public benefit, and the national scale. Chapman (2006, 215), for instance, reduces the complex political terrain on which debates over immigration and environmental degradation play out, into two groupings: "One group accepts the current neo-liberal paradigm supporting globalization, the other rejects it." The logical conclusion is that "we" have a moral obligation to "our" nature and "our" future that trumps any responsibility to a populace that enjoys political rights elsewhere. As Cafaro and Staples (2009, 19) argue, "with open borders, the interests of nonhuman nature would be sacrificed completely to the interests of people. . . . The *economic interests* of would-be immigrants would trump the very existence of many nonhuman organisms, endangered species, and wild places in the United States" (emphasis added).

This discursive move, however, brings up a tension in the ecocommunitarian logic. On one hand, it is recognized that, within the existing global political economic system, "our" quality of life is sustained through *ecological debt*. The consumptive practices on which the economy *and environment* of the United States depend are contingent on the importation of goods from outside—and the environmental degradation created through the methods used to extract, produce, and ship these goods. Rees (2011), for example, refers to developed nations' unfair use of the world's natural capital as "appropriated carrying capacity." On the other hand, however, this *transnational* debt doesn't translate into a transnational ethic. While recognizing the spatial reach and force of neoliberal globalization, ecocommunitarians adjudicate ethical obligation through a normative ideal contingent on the nation-state as the dominant (and legitimate) actor in political affairs. Chapman (2006, 215), for example, cites the seminal communitarian, Michael Walzer, in asserting that "sovereign nations have no legal mandate nor moral obligation to accept immigrants; indeed, nations have the legal right and in many cases the moral mandate to control membership" (see also Daly 2006, 189).[13] Thus, although ecocommunitarians recognize the devastating impacts that neoliberal globalization has wrought on nature and society—and the ways in which certain actors have been asymmetrically positioned to benefit from this order—they move from a transnational narrative of political economic linkages to a state-centric narrative of self-responsibility when debating issues of ethical obligation to immigrants:

> It seems wrong to suggest that these achievements,[14] which may provide meaning, secure justice, and contribute substantially to people's quality of life, must be compromised because people in other countries are having too many children, or have failed to create decent societies themselves. . . . Would be immigrants need to take up responsibilities for self-government which they and their leaders have neglected in their own countries. (Cafaro and Staples 2009, 20)

Oftentimes, this narrative of self-responsibility is coupled with the assertion that "we" face an ecological crisis so grave that it trumps the social ethics that would ideally be recognized in times of ecological normalcy. For example, while expressing sympathy for the myriad social and ethical dilemmas involved in immigration debates, Ehrlich and Ehrlich (2004, 108) conclude that significant restrictions are essential for the transformations necessary to ward off ecological apocalypse:

> To the degree that migration as a "safety valve" keeps poor nations from squarely facing their own demographic problems while swelling the numbers of higher-income consumers, migration will have a negative influence on the chances of reaching global sustainability.

Working within this communitarian framework, Chapman (2006, 215) considers the right to a healthy national environment a "subsistence right"—in other words, a "right that is the condition for the possibility of itself and other rights." His contention is that national ecological destruction, caused by neoliberal globalization and the forces propelling it (immigrants included), is a crisis of such epic proportions that it trumps social concerns, and permitting entrance to immigrants would only precipitate the ecological crisis that awaits. ALT concluded a 2009 ad with the following warning:

> If we can all agree on an immigration plan that is fair and workable, we can avoid the projected growth of another 100 million people in just 30 years. If we don't, the demand for fresh, clean water will continue unabated. Until the tap runs dry.

Their entire campaign is geared to convincing American progressives and environmentalists of the need to take a temporary "time out" on immigration, to suspend their "normal" social concerns as a consequence of the crisis facing nature. Negotiating an exception to neoliberalism is thus premised on declaring an ecological exception.

## SOVEREIGNTY, NATURE, AND THE ECOCOMMUNITARIAN CRISIS

To reconfigure sovereignty amid an ecological crisis created by neoliberal globalization, an ethical concern for "the immigrant" is displaced through a communitarian vision of an ecologically flourishing nation-state where obligation to humans and nonhumans alike is a function of inclusion within a bounded territorial and cultural community. In contrast with nativists, the "enemy" tying this communal narrative together is not immigrants or any foreign entity but those amorphous forces of neoliberalism whose incessant flows debilitate the types of ecological sacrifices that could be fashioned by a sovereign ecological state. In an attempt to secure these bounds, the national place of environmentalists is juxtaposed against a homogenous space of difference—the global space—in which transnational capitalists, immigrants, and cosmopolitan idealists all reside. The immigrant is constructed not as a savage who poses a direct threat to the sovereign but as a *delinquent* whose deviation from environmental norms poses a barrier to the development of a sustainable society.[15] In other words, immigrants are not the main problem, global neoliberalism is; attempts to reduce immigrants to "bare life" emerge indirectly through a form of guilt by association.

It should be noted that the rhetoric of ecocommunitarianism—steeped in a liberal language of equality—aims to eschew statements that could be viewed as derogatory, or dehumanizing, or as in any way constructing immigrants as "bare life." At points, sympathy is expressed over the myriad plights faced by immigrants (though this does not match the sympathy extended toward nonhumans), racism is rejected (though reduced to a purely interpersonal construct), and the political economic linkages driving immigration are duly noted (though greater emphasis is placed on internal problems in "sending" countries). Ecocommunitarians generally detest the North American Free Trade Agreement (NAFTA), want the United States to give more humanitarian aid, and accept the necessity of action at the global scale.[16] In fact, many ecocommunitarians are radicals who would welcome the overhaul of the liberal political economic system. For example, when I asked Cafaro about what ought to be done to achieve ecological sustainability, he predictably discussed a national population policy but then laid out several additional steps:

> Within the current system, I'd like to see us put a price on carbon . . . [and] I'd like to see us effectively reduce the impact of corporations on our political process. I think that would do more than anything else in helping to protect the environment. . . . And then, if you really want to get utopian/optimistic about it, it's hard for me to imagine us creating sustainable societies in the context of the endless growth

economy. So I'd like us start figuring out what a very different sort
of economy would look like. (Cafaro 2011)

However, the perceived impossibility of changing the institutions and
structures driving neoliberal globalization creates a selective utopianism
where immigration restriction is somehow seen as the "low-hanging
fruit" in efforts to ameliorate environmental degradation. For example,
Camarota, of the Center for Immigration Studies, argues that it's more
political feasible to restrict immigration than to reduce greenhouse gas
emissions through state regulations (Camarota et al. 2009):

> If you're asking me whether politically it's easier to reduce immi-
> gration—which is generally supported by most of the public when
> asked questions on that—or whether it's easier to cut our greenhouse
> gas emission by 80 percent . . . is it easy to fight that political battle?
> I don't think so. I think that if you wanted to try to make the case
> for less immigration, I think that there are a lot of interest groups in
> Washington that would line up. . . . Trying to reduce our greenhouse
> gases is a very long, difficult battle and so is an immigration policy
> that's environmentally sustainable. But if you ask me which is easier,
> I would say obviously the immigration battle is a lot easier than the
> environmental.

The argument made by ecocommunitarians is that political institutions,
consumptive cultures, and political economic structures are incredibly
difficult to change, but a restrictive national immigration policy is a
realizable goal.

In attempting to legitimize this position as "progressive," ecocommunitarians claim that they are merely seeking to institutionalize the conclusions of two Clinton-era commissions: the U.S. Commission on Immigration Reform (Jordan Commission) and the Council on Sustainable
Development (Beck 2009, 16).[17] But ecocommunitarian prescriptions
go far beyond the relatively ambiguous findings of these exploratory
bodies. In fact, despite their seemingly benign rhetoric, the organizations
deploying the ecocommunitarian discourse have embraced draconian
policies: forcefully rejecting the Dream Act (Brown 2011), supporting
Arizona's SB 1070 (Durant 2010), seeking to repeal the Fourteenth
Amendment's birthright citizenship clause, and calling for a temporary
moratorium on immigration (ostensibly until the ecological crisis abates)
before going back to "normal" levels of around two hundred thousand

to three hundred thousand per year (see, e.g., Beck 2008). Not only are immigrants incapable of speaking or acting on behalf of nature within this discourse but ecocommunitarianism adds weight to growing anti-immigrant sentiment that strips immigrants of any potential for being viewed as national environmental subjects, while simultaneously exposing their day-to-day lives to the ever-present possibility of coercive force.

In sum, there exists a disjuncture between the carefully sculpted, progressive rhetoric of ecocommunitarianism and prescriptions that are overwhelmingly illiberal. I do not mean to imply here that the "liberal" rhetoric is somehow disingenuous; to the contrary, I do not doubt that the humanitarian concerns Rees, Ryerson, Cafaro, and other ecocommunitarians expressed are sincere. But such concerns are always trumped by the perceived necessity of saving a nature that only becomes intelligible through contingent articulations that subtly nationalize it: neo-Malthusian population anxieties are wedded to a national consumptive imaginary; romantic ideals of American "natural places" are opposed to the "global spaces" of neoliberalism; and ethics constructed around "sovereign cultures" elevate a commitment to the nation's nature above any obligation to social Others. The result is a tripartite logic: (1) the diagnosis of an ecological exception created by neoliberal globalization; (2) the conclusion that ecological sustainability, which outweighs all social goals, can only be pursued within the nation-state; and (3) the evangelism with which these Truths are advanced.

As such, despite the humanitarian rhetoric, my analyses have yet to find a single example of an ecocommunitarian prescription driven by an ethos that recognizes "the immigrant" as a political subject worthy of ethical obligation: that echoes more socially attuned deep ecological thinkers in arguing for a gradual and humane decrease in population;[18] that recognizes the value of compromise in attempting to balance the exigencies of protecting nature with the exigencies of correcting for egregious social injustices; that does anything but reduce the lives of immigrants to mere "consuming units" (King 2007, 320); or that focuses on the structural causes of immigration and proposes concrete solutions that would ameliorate these political economic factors. Instead, what I have found is a prescriptive politics organized around the dictates of national ecological emergency, one that attempts to reconfigure sovereignty to insulate America's natural places from the ruptures of globalization and asserts that this is ethical because it will help to protect nonhumans and ameliorate America's ecological debt. The structures that have produced the debt are left unchallenged, and those populations whose lives have already been deleteriously impacted by the debt are left to fend for themselves under the state-centric norms of communitarianism.

## The Biopolitics of a Postracist Racism

Interestingly, despite passionate appeals for saving natural places, and an explicitly stated *normative* preference for a communitarian vision of sovereignty, the ecocommunitarian discourse frequently collapses into a rhetoric of hyperobjectivity when faced with environmentalists who oppose immigration reduction. Anyone who disagrees is accused of not looking at the facts but instead "playing the race card" (Beck 2009), or succumbing to "political correctness" (Beck and Kolankiewicz 2000), or being influenced by their "bleeding heart" rather than reason.[19] The idea is the emotional resonance of the immigration debate is so intense that these dissenters are unwilling to speak the truth and/or are unable to even grasp reality. When anyone dares to accuse ecocommunitarians of racism, the reaction is even stronger; the accusers are "blinded about population concerns by [their] emotions . . . rather than from any interest or knowledge about the environment" (Pasternak 2011) or are engaging "in ad hominem and McCarthyesque attacks of the worst kind" (DeYoung 2011a). As Beck (2009) puts it, "the environmental argument against high immigration is so upsetting and challenging to many liberal Americans that they resort to fabricating a myth that those perpetrating the environmental argument are really just racists hiding behind arguments that are acceptable to mainstream Americans."

In this regard, the ecocommunitarian discourse reflects a shift away from the cultural essentializations characteristic of neoracism and toward a discourse of postracism (or "color-blind racism") that avoids racialized rhetoric and enacts territorial and national boundaries through appeals to "liberal" environmental and social commitments. Ecocommunitarians never discuss race except to disavow any accusation of racism being leveled against them as a form of political correctness. For example, filmmaker Dave Gardner, who produced a 2011 documentary film called *GrowthBusters,* recently responded to a reader of his blog who commented on the historical linkages between population control and racism:

while it is good to know about this history, I don't feel a strong need to bring it up. Frankly, those trying to stifle the conversation bring it up more than enough. That was past and while it is good to be on guard, that history says nothing about current efforts and motives. Nothing. (Gardner 2011)[20]

This vision of a postracial environmentalism is enabled by a post–civil rights era racial terrain in which the overt state racism that guaranteed white Americans systematic privileges over racial minorities was made illegal. Political theorist Joel Olson (2004, 76) argues that in contemporary political life,

> whiteness thus tends to shift from an individualizing to an aggregate form of power. Guaranteed standing is replaced by statistical advantages. Poverty, violence, inferior schooling, poor health, high incarceration and unemployment rates, lack of assets and substandard housing continue to disproportionately affect those who are non-white, while whites continue to disproportionately escape them.

These racialized inequities extend into environmentalism: whites are disproportionately provided environmental goods (e.g., natural resources and access to wilderness), while nonwhites are disproportionately exposed to environmental hazards (pesticides, pollutants, etc.). The discourse of postracism as deployed by ecocommunitarians not only fails to confront these inequalities but actively reinforces them. The ecocommunitarian appeal to a postracial reality reflects both white privilege and what Park and Pellow (2004, 416; see also Pulido 2000) term "environmental privilege":

> immigrants and people of color bear the cost of both environmental destruction (when industry extracts or pollutes natural resources) *and* environmental protection (when white, affluent communities discover that an industry is toxic, they then protect themselves by shifting the burden onto lower income neighborhoods and communities of color).

Environmental restrictionism represents the same process that these environmental justice advocates observe, yet abstracted up from the local neighborhood to the national border. White and affluent populations are insulated from environmental harm not by gated communities but by guarded walls.

Although ecocommunitarians insist that these racial inequalities are purely incidental, there are legitimate reasons to consider both the racialized impacts of restrictionist prescriptions and the ways in which racist logics have broadened the appeal of the current environmental restrictionist coalition. Specifically, the organizations deploying eco-communitarian logics demonstrate a profound capacity to look past the racial implications of the policies they support, like SB1070, and a blatant willingness to ignore the racist and xenophobic positions of their strange bedfellows to forge strategic alliances (a case in point is the inclusion of the AIC Foundation in ALT). As Salazar and Hewitt (2001, 302) note,

> as much as environmentalists take pains to separate immigrants from immigration, the experience of Latinos in the U.S./Mexico border region suggests that enforcement officials often fail to distinguish between (brown) skin color and (illegal) immigration status. Environmentalists' rhetorical distinction does not comfort those who suffer from the border patrol's corporeal conflation.

As the power to enforce anti-immigrant measures is extended from the federal government to a variety of state and level actors, the impacts of restrictionist immigration policies on nonwhite citizens become more severe. Under the ecocommunitarian ethos of sovereignty, racist and nativist policies are explicitly denounced, but their state-centric moral-ity, coupled with a narrative of ecological exception, results in policy prescriptions and coalition building steeped in biopolitical valuations that accept and legitimate the attempted reduction of immigrant (and, increasingly, Latino citizen) populations to lives that can be sacrificed for the good of America's nature.

## CONCLUSION

Comaroff and Comaroff (2001, 240) observe that "imagining the na-tion rarely presumes a deep horizontal fraternity anymore. . . . While most human beings still live as citizens *in* nation-states, they tend only to be conditionally, partially, and situationally citizens *of* nation-states" (italics original). In such a conjuncture, the cultural essentializations on which econativism relies will not resonate with the progressives that American restrictionists need to expand and further legitimize their movement. I thus contend that we are moving toward a third wave of environmental restrictionism that differs in important respects from previous iterations. Third wave restrictionism employs a far more nuanced discourse—that of ecocommunitarianism—that resonates with the ontological and epistemological commitments of mainstream greens and progressives. In attempting to attract these progressive interests, ecocommunitarians articulate an opposition to neoliberalism, appeal to a multicultural (as well as intergenerational and interspecies) nation, emphasize the need for global environmental stewardship, extend their overriding focus on population to consumption, and express concern for the romantic "wild places" that can only be saved through the particularistic attachments of nationhood. All of this is couched within a broader narrative of ecological crisis.

Despite this apparently progressive discursive shift, my critique of ecocommunitarianism has proceeded at two levels. First, ecocommunitarians fail to consider the broader political terrain on which their argument is lodged. For ecocommunitarians, the appeal to a communitarian nationalism is, in part, strategic. For instance, Cafaro (2010b, 195) has argued in favor of linking environmentalism with patriotism: "Environmentalists, who generally skew left politically, might have been able to block some of these assaults on nature, if we could have found common cause with conservatives for whom patriotism themes resonate." But at what cost? As political theorist Robyn Eckersley writes in her own discussion of ecocommunitarianism, whether environmentalists should situate their projects in narratives of nationalism or patriotism depends on careful consideration of the discursive, institutional, and historical contexts. She contends that, "in the absence of an engaged citizenry and a robust public sphere, facilitated and informed by a diverse, independent and critical media, environmentalists may be better advised to challenge and subvert, rather than merely extend, the language of patriotism by calling on us all to become planetary patriots and global ecological citizens" (Eckersley 2007b, 200). In the United States—a national context that not only lacks a critical media but also has a long history of exclusion based on race, culture, *and nature*— hypernationalists can too easily appropriate this patriotic language to serve purposes that are both racist and nativist.

As greens have become aware that nativists are doing just that, environmentalist organizations (including those comprising individuals sympathetic to population concerns, but also concerned with social justice) have become divided—as the splintering of the Sierra Club and Earth First! amid these debates illustrated. For this same reason, the environmental restrictionist position also disables one of the most potentially impactful avenues for environmental progress—further alliance building between traditional environmentalists and other social groupings on the left (labor, civil rights, and social justice organizations) who have been historically undermobilized on environmental issues.

And yet, one could argue that these strategic considerations alone do not make the ecocommunitarians "wrong." My second—and more foundational—critique is that the extant structure of sovereignty that ecocommunitarians recognize in their diagnosis of the crisis of neoliberal globalization does not mesh with the structure of sovereignty that they revert to in their adjudication of ethical obligation. It should be noted that nature is definitively not "sovereign" in the ecocommunitarian logic; as Cafaro, Chapman, Daly, and Rees make clear, it is enmeshed in a nationalist imaginary. Ecocommunitarians recognize that the proper relationship between immigration, environmental degradation, and sovereignty cannot be solved by a simple empirical analysis. Rather, this matter necessitates difficult normative choices over what populations—human and nonhuman—ought to be included in the political community, what the social purpose of the political community ought to be, and what "our" obligation is to those lives outside. However, anytime their position is opposed, ecocommunitarians double down on a sovereign nature, where numbers are all that matter, and biophysical analysis of the nonhuman realm can arrive at the Truth of how we ought to deal with environmental degradation, without mediation from culture.

The result is an environmental imaginary that is unethical, strategically ineffective, and logically inconsistent. In the last analysis, the ecocommunitarian opposition to immigration has less to do with immigrants themselves (and their impacts on the environment) than it does with the impacts of neoliberal globalization on an ideal of nature that is irrevocably bound up in an antiquated conception of an autonomous national culture. As a consequence of its regressive nature, ecocommunitarianism both fails to contest the destructive realities of neoliberalism and reinforces structural patterns of socioecological injustice.

# 4

# RESPONDING TO
# RESTRICTIONISM

Consider also the transformative potential of global ecology.
The human environment is of central importance for future
planetary politics from many perspectives. Central among
them is the potential to comprise a new and very different
social episteme—a new set of spatial, metaphysical and
doctrinal constructs through which the visualization of
collective existence on the planet is shaped.

**JOHN GERARD RUGGIE,** "Territoriality and Beyond:
Problematizing Modernity in International Relations"

Sitting in the audience at the town hall panel and listening to Cafaro's
presentation, I couldn't help but feel a strange ambivalence. Like Cafaro,
I've witnessed how population projections are being used to justify
the damming of the Cache la Poudre River. Like him, I've seen how
population growth has changed Fort Collins, transforming it in the
twenty years that I lived there from a quaint city of 90,000 residents
to an increasingly bustling urban area of 150,000. And like him, I've
grown to love the Poudre River and the community of which it is irrevocably a part. In high school and college, my friends and I would
often inner-tube down the Poudre; in graduate school, I retained my
sanity by running on trails alongside it; and my partner and I have a
favorite backpacking spot up the Poudre Canyon near the source of
the river. So, like him, I hate the plans to dam it.

But, unlike him, I don't view saving the Poudre as in any way
related to restricting immigration. To the contrary, I view immigrants
as vital partners in efforts to resist and reconfigure the deep-seated
structures that produce socioecological injustice. How is it that—out
of this place that we both care deeply about—we could come to such

different conclusions? In the previous chapters, I laid out three discourses of environmental restrictionism: social nativism, econativism,
and ecocommunitarianism. I made the case that the diverse discourses of
environmental restrictionism work to forge relationships between nature
and sovereignty in ways that reflect an array of ontological, epistemological, strategic, and ethical commitments, the end result being that
environmental restrictionists continue to have some success appealing
to individuals across the American political spectrum. The preceding
chapter asserted that many environmental restrictionists, like Cafaro,
have turned away from nativism and toward a far more sophisticated
discourse of ecocommunitarianism that meshes in important respects
with the progressive project of greening sovereignty—appealing to
greens on the political left and thereby posing a unique challenge to
the immigrants' rights and environmental justice advocates who oppose restrictionism.

This chapter is my attempt to think reflexively and honestly about
how opponents of environmental restrictionism conceptualize nature
and weave it into their attempts to reconfigure sovereignty amid the ruptures of neoliberal globalization and the crises—diminishing economic
opportunities, environmental destruction, and the rise of exclusionary
forms of political community—that accompany these ruptures. The
chapter proceeds in two parts. First, I outline an ideal-type discourse
that is employed by many opponents of environmental restrictionism—
the discourse of *global environmental justice.* Proponents of global
environmental justice, namely, environmental justice organizations and
immigrants' rights advocates, argue that nature is an inherently global
concern that reveals the interconnections between humans and nonhumans alike. Like Ruggie, they believe that a commitment to nature
has transformative, deterritorializing potential. From this logic, they
assert that those supporting environmental restrictionism are merely *appropriating* nature to advance alternative, anthropocentric social goals.

Second, I make the case that, although I sympathize with the political commitments of this discourse, it has not focused its energies on
critically analyzing the relationship between the social construction
of nature—that is, how ideals of nature emerge through appeals to
objective knowledge, social norms, and political rationales—and that
of sovereignty. As a consequence, it has not only failed to recognize the

discursive shift to ecocommunitarianism, it is inadvertently complicit in reinforcing several of the foundational assumptions of environmental restrictionism. I conclude by asserting that we (i.e., greens who care about socioecological justice) ought to articulate an alternative discourse; a way of resisting the structures and logics that lead to outcomes like the damming of the Poudre River, without reverting to the insular, exclusionary ethos of sovereignty that is articulated by ecocommunitarians *or* to the supposedly deterritorializing realities of nature in which opponents of restrictionism currently couch their emancipatory hopes.

## THE CRISIS OF SOCIAL EXCLUSION

Spring 2013 was an exciting time for proponents of global environmental justice. Just as environmental restrictionists were readying their annual campaigns to link Earth Day with restrictionist policies, several prominent environmental organizations announced their support for the comprehensive immigration reform that was being debated in the U.S. Congress—one that would have provided a path to citizenship for the roughly 11 million people who are currently forced to "live outside of the prevailing currents of our society" (Brune and Chin 2013). On March 13, Philip Radford (2013), executive director of Greenpeace, published an essay titled "The Environmental Case for a Path to Citizenship" on the liberal website *Huffington Post*. On March 14, the founder of 350.org, Bill McKibben (2013), wrote an op-ed in the *Los Angeles Times* arguing that immigration reform is central to the fight against climate change. And on April 25, the Sierra Club noted the immigrant roots of its founder, John Muir, in offering its "strong support for a pathway to citizenship for undocumented immigrants" (Brune and Chin 2013). It is important to note that these organizations and/or individuals all have historical connections with environmental restrictionism, and yet they are now arguing for collective action that includes immigrants. The "we" of American environmentalism appears to be expanding.

Of course, this opposition to environmental restrictionism is not new. Environmental restrictionism has long met skepticism from those who have found racial, gendered, class-based, and neocolonial undertones in the logics being advanced (Reimers 1998; Lindsley 2001a;

2001b; Salazar and Hewitt 2001; Hartmann 2004; Bhatia 2004; Ruth-erford 2005; Muradian 2006; Urban 2007; King 2007; 2008; Levison et al. 2010; Pearce 2010; Angus and Butler 2011; Park and Pellow 2011). Academic and activist critics alike—the latter including the Center for New Community (CNC), the Southern Poverty Law Center (SPLC), the Committee on Women Population and Environment's Political Ecology Group, the National Network for Immigrant and Refugee Rights, and America's Voice, among others—have been far ahead of the mainstream environmental curve, asserting that the territorialized nature advanced by restrictionists is inadequate in considering the difficult ethical questions stemming from the historical injustices that plague migrant populations and the spatial interconnections that drive both migration and environmental degradation.[1]

Given the range of environmental engagements with both nature and sovereignty, it is no surprise that the critiques opponents level against restrictionists and the alternative forms of community and economy that they propose vary widely: from eco-anarchists to green statists to radical bioregionalists to ecocosmopolitans. However, three common threads unite opponents of restrictionism under the mantle of "global environmental justice" advocates: (1) challenging the environmental restrictionist emphasis on the national scale by emphasizing the global realities of ecological and political economic systems, (2) critiquing the restrictionist focus on population and highlighting the environmental impacts of consumptive asymmetries, and (3) detailing the social goals that motivate certain restrictionists to appropriate the language of na-ture so that they may provide a veil over alternative, anthropocentric social projects.[2]

### Global Flows versus National Borders

For the immigrants' rights and environmental justice organizations opposing environmental restrictionism, the ideal forms of governance and the modes of political community that are best suited to protect-ing nature bear little relation to our current sociopolitical units. As Salazar and Hewitt (2001, 303) note, "a bicyclist pedaling through the Sonoran Desert (covering parts of California, Arizona, Sonora, and Baja California) would have difficulty making ecological or cultural sense of the U.S./Mexico border." In other words, nature does not respect the inviolability of sovereign borders. Echoing this logic, global environmental justice advocates highlight forms of governance and political communities that eschew territorialization, asserting that a real concern for nature exists in opposition to structures of sovereignty. For example, in response to environmental restrictionist sentiment in northern Colorado, Lisa Olivas, a spokesperson for the Fort Collins–based Center for Justice, Peace, and the Environment, argues that "when you look at population control, you have to look at it in a global sense. . . . If you just say 'immigration,' that doesn't help . . . they're still on the planet" (as quoted in Park 2007). Similarly, the CNC concludes that environmental restrictionism is misplaced because "rising temperatures and sea levels don't respect national boundaries, and migration across national boundaries does not change total world population" (Taylor 2014). Summarizing this position, a recent SPLC report emphasized that "most conservationists have come to believe that many of the world's most intractable environmental problems, including global warming, can only be solved by dealing with them on a worldwide, not a nation-by-nation, basis" (Potok 2010, 4–5). These statements all reflect the Sierra Club's (2008) official position on immigration:

> The environmental and social impacts of population growth extend beyond national borders, affecting everyone that shares the earth's natural resources. Population growth increases the demand on natural resources, and impacts the entire global environment.

The logic being advanced here is that there is a functional mismatch between the territorially bound nation-state and the global scope of environmental degradation. Nature exceeds sovereign borders.

The emphasis on the global realities of ecosystems is typically coupled with an emphasis on the spatial reach of contemporary political economic structures. As the Political Ecology Group (2006) observes,

> downsizing, de-industrialization, and the shifting of production overseas by transnational corporations are consequences of the new global economy, where corporations have more freedom than ever to move capital and resources to places with cheaper labor and regulatory costs. At the same time, people are criminalized for moving to find work in areas where natural and economic resources are flowing.

Today's economic, social and environmental woes are only made
worse as opportunistic politicians attack immigrants, workers and
the environment.

The tremendous authority wielded by transnational corporations—
and their role in producing both social inequality and environmental
degradation—is continually emphasized by global environmental justice
activists. Radford (2013), of Greenpeace, argues that "everyone has
an equal right to protection from corporate polluters." Similarly, in
response to the Californians for Population Stabilization's most recent
Earth Day ad, Reshma Shamasunder of the California Immigrant Policy
Center explains that "it is big corporations who are doing the real dam-
age to the environment" (as quoted in O'Connor 2014).

In addition to calling attention to the role corporations play in
producing both immigration and environmental degradation, global
environmental justice activists at times extend this political economic
critique to the forms of free trade pushed forward by a neoliberal
American state. In particular, the North America Free Trade Agreement
(NAFTA) has attracted the ire of opponents. In announcing its support
for comprehensive immigration reform, the Sierra Club reminded its
membership,

> This isn't the first time that the Sierra Club has taken a stand on a
> critical issue. In 1993, the Club opposed the North American Free
> Trade Agreement, a controversial position, but one that has proven
> to be the right choice. . . . NAFTA has been a major driver of undocu-
> mented immigration into the U.S. from Mexico and Central America.
> (Brune and Chin 2013)

A post on the immigrants' rights blog *Imagine2050* similarly rails
against environmental restrictionists for their shortsighted focus on population numbers: "treaties such as NAFTA (North American Free Trade
Agreement) have put Mexican workers in direct competition with their
Northern neighbors. . . . The social and economic conditions in Mexico
causing migration to the Southwest . . . will not be solved by numerical
limits on immigration" (Pskowski 2010). Eric Ward (2009) of the CNC
underscores the ethical implications of this political economic policy:
"It's unfair to blame immigrants who come to the United States because
Washington's policies make it so they can't eek out a living at home."

These critics of environmental restrictionism insist that in a period of globalization, the territorialized nation-state provides an anemic vantage point from which to consider the myriad flows—ecological, political, and economic—that forge patterns of social connection in contemporary life. In this sense, global environmental justice advocates are in agreement with scholars of globalization who argue that contemporary forms of sovereignty exceed the space of the nation-state (see, e.g., Hardt and Negri 2000; Agnew 2009).[3] Even as the United States, in particular, pushes forward neoliberal globalization, the resulting forms of authority backed by coercive force (wielded, at times, by intergovernmental organizations, transnational corporations, and global civil society) are beyond the control of any single nation-state. Given this complex, *transnational* terrain of contemporary sovereign power, critics argue that adjudicating questions of responsibility and obligation by turning to black-boxed "nation-states" or "national cultures" elides the profound spatial connections that are forged by today's dominant political structures and institutions. The case being made is that because environmental restrictionists have not identified the transnational forms of sovereignty producing either immigration or environmental degradation, they cannot possibly formulate an adequate or ethical alternative. Transnational structures require a transnational ethic and, ultimately, transnational resistance.

### Consumption versus Population

This emphasis on transnational political economic structures segues into the second line of defense against the restrictionist logic: an emphasis on the role that consumption plays in comparison with population in producing environmental harms. Regardless of the scale at which one chooses to deal with environmental degradation, the focus on population itself is a source of debate. Global environmental justice activists critique the neo-Malthusian bearings of restrictionists and assert that a more holistic analysis of environmental degradation would place greater emphasis on consumption, thus shifting the burden for ecological restoration from the poor to the wealthy. For instance, the Political Ecology Group (1999, xxiii) observes that "the impact of an immigrant family living in a one-bedroom apartment and taking mass transit pales in comparison to that of a wealthy family living in a single-family home with a swimming pool and two cars." Similarly, the SPLC quotes an expert who concludes that "if everyone in California went to work the way recently arrived immigrants did—by carpooling or using public transportation—that would reduce the number of cars on the road by nearly half" (Scherr 2008, quoting Hayes-Bautista). Frank Sharry, of the immigrants' rights group America's Voice, summed up these sentiments neatly in a recent segment on National Public Radio: "I don't think Americans think that immigrants are the cause of McMansions and SUVs and big oil companies who are ravaging the environment" (Ludden 2008). The underlying sentiment being expressed here is that the "nature" of restrictionism is a bourgeois one. Northern Colorado immigration attorney and immigrants' rights advocate Kim Baker Medina (2012) highlights this point in reflecting on the forces that brought many of her clients to Colorado:

> One of the reasons [many immigrants] are coming here is because they can no longer grow in their countries . . . there's no clean water. How do we tell these people, "Don't come here because you'll spoil our bike paths"?

By paying excessive attention to population, restrictionists define the scope of the problem in ways that artificially inflate the environmental impacts of immigrants, with the blame falling particularly on female immigrants and immigrant families (e.g., the restrictionist move toward ridiculing "anchor babies"). As I detailed in chapters 2 and 3, restrictionists place incredible emphasis on women's fertility; an integral part of demography, they seek to quantify its rates to enable comparisons across populations and projections for the future. Whether done out of genuine environmental concerns or anxieties related to a declining Anglo-European majority, critics point out that this practice ignores the gendered nature of transnational neoliberal structures (Urban 2008). Female workers—many of whom were attracted to manufacturing zones, like the maquiladoras, by free-trade agreements, national development plans, and the prospects of increased autonomy from traditional "domestic" roles—have been subject to low wages and harsh working conditions in a political climate of flexible labor where environmental and social standards may well mean the flight of capital to other locales. Moreover, the securitization of fertility has intense impacts on women's rights and women's perceived role within the nation; it effectively transforms "the bodies of women (especially women of color and working class women) [into] key battlegrounds in defense of a civilized, secure and sustainable American nation" (Urban 2008, 87). Political geographer Stephanie Rutherford (2005, 21) concurs with this viewpoint, arguing that constructing population growth as the primary ecological challenge invites imperialistic interventions abroad:

> The issue can then be discussed in terms of certain kinds of bodies which are the bearers of too much life, shifting the debate and making women's fertility the cause and solution to global environmental problems. What this covers up is the way in which many of the global environmental issues are produced not from the overpopulation of the south but from the overconsumption and exploitation of resources by people and industries of the north.

In addition to her gendered critique of neoliberalism, Rutherford's focus on the exploitation of natural resources calls attention to the mutually constitutive relationship between the ideology of populationism and capitalism. Given these global environmental asymmetries, opponents ask, is population truly the culprit behind environmental degradation, or is it capitalism and militarism? In solidarity with the Occupy Wall Street movement, Angus and Butler (2011, 2) argue that the "real source of environmental destruction . . . [is] not the 7 billion but the 1%, the handful of millionaires and billionaires who own, consume, control and destroy more than all the rest of us put together." Betsy Hartmann (2004, 3) furthers this line of thought:

> In the public consciousness, imposed limits to growth in social welfare expenditures become intertwined with the notion of environmental limits. Missing from the picture, of course, is the role of the rich in gobbling up both economic and natural resources at an ever expanding rate, undermining effective environmental protection, and refusing to invest in new, non-polluting energy sources.

The argument being made here is that, under neoliberal capitalism, sovereignty works not for the people but for the capitalists. And the capitalist logic reduces nature, women, and laborers either to *mere resources* to be employed for the purposes of profit maximization and geopolitical statecraft or to *scapegoats* constructed as threats to draw the attention away from the destructive forces of capitalism. Environmental restrictionism, in this sense, not only enables capitalism (and the modes of sovereignty that support the rule of capital) to advance unabated but often reflects an ideology that views capitalism and environmental protection as compatible with one another (Park and Pellow 2011, 14–15).

## Authenticity versus Appropriation

Operating alongside and reinforcing the capitalistic and gendered nature of environmental restrictionism is, according to global environmental justice advocates, an intense racism that resides just beneath its surface. To underscore the centrality of exclusionary intentions to restrictionist politics, opponents of restrictionism highlight the connections between vocal restrictionist proponents and groups and individuals who have explicitly articulated racist ideologies. For example, John Tanton—the former Sierra Club Population Committee president and so-called father of the contemporary American anti-immigrant movement (discussed in depth in chapter 2)—is an especially controversial figure who has been accused by multiple organizations of maintaining ties with noted hate groups (Southern Poverty Law Center 2002b; Bhatia 2004; Muradian 2006). Numerous restrictionists have also received funding from eugenics advocates, such as the Pioneer Fund, and several—notably Virginia Abernethy, Wayne Lutton, Kevin MacDonald, and John Vinson—have been associated with the white supremacist Council of Conservative Citizens and its *Occidental Quarterly* publication (Bhatia 2004, 211; Muradian 2006, 210).

The primary strategy of organizations advancing the global environmental justice discourse has been to vocally publicize these relationships to demonstrate that even those restrictionists who are well respected in the broader environmental movement—ecocommunitarians like the Ehrlichs, Lester Brown, William Ryerson, and so on—have no qualms about allying with blatant racists and xenophobes.[4] For example, both the SPLC and the CNC have devoted considerable attention to outlining the "John Tanton Network"—a web of interconnection between the various institutions that Tanton created and has been involved with, and the organizations and individuals that currently publicly articulate an opposition to immigration on environmental grounds (see Southern Poverty Law Center 2002b; Center for New Community 2009). Opponents offer this social network mapping as proof that environmental restrictionists are not authentic ecocentrists but rather are "nativists in three-piece suits who are smart enough to figure out how to present a face that looks like they're progressive-minded" (Ludden 2008, quoting Frank Sharry). Restrictionists are said to represent an emerging trend whereby conservatives appropriate nature in their attempts to refashion sovereignty along hypernationalist, blatantly racist lines (Ward 2009; Potok 2010; Ross 2010). At their most nuanced, such appraisals characterize restrictionists into two categories: nativists and neo-Malthusians (Muradian 2006, 208–10; Bhatia 2004, 225). Whatever their differences, both logics are argued to err in failing to recognize that environmentalism is a global struggle that demands cosmopolitan modes of thinking (Potok 2010, 5). Restrictionists are alleged to be engaging in the "greenwashing of nativism" (Ross 2010); they are not real environmentalists but are constructing an elaborate "environmental charade" to veil their actual social desires (Hartmann 2010).

## CONTESTING GLOBAL ENVIRONMENTAL ORTHODOXY

The discourse of global environmental justice reflects ontologies, epistemologies, strategies, and ethics that differ dramatically from those advanced by restrictionists. This dominant response to environmental restrictionism argues that the restrictionist logic fails to identify the transnational structures of sovereignty that produce environmental harm; overstates the role of population, thereby disabling a deeper structural critique of capital that would force northern greens to examine their own practices; and reflects and reinforces the overtly racist and xenophobic intentions of nativists. Global environmental justice activists, thus, reject the environmental restrictionist appeal to green sovereignty as an exclusionary project that instrumentally uses a narrative of natural crisis to advance anthropocentric social ends. Environmental restrictionism, it is argued, perpetuates a variety of social and ecological ills, including climate change, racism, patriarchy, and capitalism.

In the debate between restrictionists and their opponents, it is clear where my sympathies lie: the global environmental justice discourse more accurately identifies the structures of sovereignty producing environmental harm and gestures toward a global ethic that seeks inclusion for human and nonhuman others. However, in the remainder of this chapter, I argue that this dominant response to restrictionism is also flawed in ways that might not be perceptible at first glance. The following section provides a critique of the discourse that has emerged in response to restrictionism, making the case that opponents fail to identify the natural–cultural interconnections through which the ecocommunitarian vision of green sovereignty advances. Specifically, global environmental justice advocates frequently appeal to the very dichotomy between nature and culture on which environmental restrictionism depends. As a consequence, this dominant opposition may unintentionally disable the types of political projects needed to build communities and economies structured around socioecological justice.

## Emancipatory Natures versus Racist Cultures

As I have detailed, proponents of global environmental justice frequently argue that real attention to nature guides "us" toward a liberatory future. An unintended consequence of the equation of a "real" commitment to nature with deterritorialized emancipation is that the ecocommunitarian narrative, which has the most potential to influence progressives, has been widely neglected. The neglect of this discourse is not surprising if one accepts the claim advanced by critics that environmental restrictionists are not ecocentrists; the relative nuances of ecocommunitarianism do not need to be identified and grappled with if all restrictionists are racist xenophobes who are merely appropriating nature. This is worrisome, however, because the ecocommunitarian logic taps into certain ontological and epistemological foundations of mainstream American environmentalism—a rhetorical commitment to a multicultural nation, concern with consumption, attachment to place, emphasis on global stewardship and intergenerational justice, critique of neoliberalism, and so on—and thus needs to be forcefully addressed (an occurrence that is unlikely, given the current strategic trajectory of critical responses).

This failure to address the ontological and epistemological commitments of ecocommunitarianism is all the more troublesome because it leaves opponents of restrictionism in danger of subtly reproducing the modes of exclusion that they seek to resist. The alternative that opponents craft routinely gestures toward the emancipatory, deterritorializing, and mutually constitutive spheres of radical ecology and social justice. Though the counternarratives to restrictionism vary, the relationship between sovereignty, nature, justice, and inclusivity is consistently argued to be straightforward: "immigrants live closer to nature," or "nature thrives on diversity," or "nature heeds no borders."[5] The sovereignty of nature, in other words, provides lessons on which social life can be modeled; the call of the wild and the chants of social justice converge.

It is of course true that, for some opponents, this emphasis on "real environmentalists" (or "a real attachment to nature") is, in part, strategic. They realize that some environmental restrictionists are genuine in their commitments to nature and are making a political argument that those who truly care about the environment ought to recognize the flaws in this logic and embrace human rights and social justice. However, strategic discourses have unintended political effects; one such effect in this case is the absence of a sustained examination of the shifting relationship between racism, nationalism, sovereignty, and ecocentrism. With this in mind, I contend that the primary strategy of social network mapping—of tracing the linkages between environmental restrictionists and overt racists and xenophobes—is a necessary dimension for building opposition, but not a sufficient one.

To be clear, environmental restrictionists need to be called out for engaging in alliances with nativists and for failing to address the racial implications of the policies that they support. However, an overreliance on this strategy unintentionally reinforces a conception of interpersonal racism that fails to address how racial difference is reinforced through concepts and structures that are popularly perceived as color-blind, neutral, objective, or *natural*. To be effective, opponents need to grapple with the ways in which ecocentrism intersects with race, nationalism, class, and gender rather than displacing these exclusionary projects onto ontological terrain of culture. I simply cannot find any evidence that people like Herman Daly or William Rees or Phil Cafaro do not care about nature; rather, it appears more likely that they care so much about a particular, *nationalized* conception of nature that they view efforts to protect it as ethical regardless of the implications on marginalized immigrant populations. I fear that the discourse I have outlined in this chapter, caught up in a twentieth-century struggle against nativists and econativists, misses the strategic leap taken by environmental restrictionists and leaves critics beholden to a strategy that is fundamentally reactive and unable to adequately contest restrictionism's twenty-first-century iterations—increasingly subtle, ecocentric visions that nonetheless reinforce sovereign violence and white privilege.

## Noble Savages and Inclusive Publics

This inability to move beyond an essentialist account of nature impacts the ways in which opponents of restrictionism theorize migrants and/or migration as potential sources of resistance. Although opponents work to deterritorialize environmental thought—detaching issues of consumption and carrying capacity from the nationalistic foundations of environmental restrictionism—they continue to search for a "standpoint linked to finding a space beyond the social" (Sandilands 1999, 69). In other words, the opposing discourse is forged with an eye toward securing immigrants' rights by showing "them" to be an ecologically conscious populace; immigrants are closer to the *real* nature than most middle-class, white environmentalists. Yet the figure of "the immigrant" as model ecocitizen is only sustainable so long as this populace adheres to the consumptive practices of the lower socioeconomic echelon. This construction of "the immigrant" as an ecological steward who consumes less is an ahistorical artifice that does not stand up to the dynamism and difference inherent in actual immigrant populations. Although it may work to momentarily disrupt certain restrictionist positions, it fails to politicize generalizable—often stereotypical—conceptions of "the immigrant." More so, by maintaining a narrow focus on consumption, a private practice, the narrative does nothing to challenge dominant conventions whereby immigrant populations remain situated at the margins of public life. Though "the private" is politicized to reveal the variability of different populations' environmental impacts, the violent exclusion of immigrants from the visible stage of public life remains intact. How can immigrants participate as "environmentalists" in the same way as citizens can, if any appearance in the public sphere is contingent on constructing the immigrant as a noble savage functioning outside of the potentially deleterious impulses of modern civilization?

This is a tension that seeps into recent mainstream environmental engagements with immigration. Environmental organizations have begun contesting the violent exclusion of immigrants from the public sphere, but they have done so by appealing to the supposed environmental beneficence of immigrants. Rebuking the math of neo-Malthusians, McKibben (2013) writes,

> There's a higher math that matters much more. At this point, there's no chance we're going to deal with global warming one household at a time—scientists, policy wonks and economists have concluded it will also require structure change. We may need, for example, things such as a serious tax on carbon; that will require mustering the political will to stand up to the fossil fuel industry. . . . And that's precisely where white America has fallen short.

This critique of white America is powerful, but McKibben couches his argument in a vision that veers dangerously close to reinforcing ahistorical conceptions of immigrants as noble savages:

> Immigrants, by definition, are full of hope. They've come to a new place determined to make a new life, risking much for opportunity. They're confident that new kinds of prosperity are possible. The future beckons them, and so changes of the kind we'll need to deal with climate change are easier to conceive.

Although McKibben's appeal to the immigrant-as-ecological-steward is well intentioned, it reflects an overly universalizing view that erases tremendous heterogeneity among immigrants themselves.

McKibben's narrative is problematic in this regard (for an extensive critique, see Selle 2013), but it is actually consistent with the logic adopted by many opponents of restrictionism. If nature is where liberatory promise lies, then it makes sense to locate immigrants within this ontological zone; emancipatory natures and noble savages go hand in hand. A nuanced recognition of natural–cultural interconnection would potentially unravel the very counterdiscourse to which opponents have strategically hitched their wagon; it would require a systematic assessment of the relationship between ecocentrism and social exclusion rather than a smooth chain of equivalence between commitments to nature and social justice.

## Ecological Futures versus Sovereign Strategies

These ontological and epistemological commitments hamstring the politics of global environmental justice advocates. Specifically, responses to environmental restrictionism are marked by a tension that makes it difficult to formulate strategies working with and against sovereign power: the commitment to a purified nature—a progressive sphere beyond the cultural politics of sovereignty—is mobilized to critique restrictionists, and yet appeals to ecosystems, animals, rivers, and mountain ranges do not provide clear, unmediated guidance into tactics and strategies of resistance. Given the challenges that lie in moving from *what is* (a reality defined by sovereign power) to their discourse of *what ought to be* (a reality defined by nature and those closest to it), it is perhaps not surprising that the strategies of immigrants' rights and environmental groups are marked by a profound uncertainty (and, at times, inconsistency) on the matter of how to effectively engage with sovereign power. On one hand, opponents of restrictionism position the liberatory, global realities of nature in contrast to the exclusionary, violent realities of sovereign power. On the other hand, they disagree on how best to pursue this more inclusive, global vision.

For some opponents, particularly activists who self-identify as leftists or radicals, the global realities of nature point toward a global cosmopolitan alternative—a "planetary patriotism"—toward which we ought to move. As I have detailed throughout the chapter, they argue that because ecosystems and the causal effects of environmental degradation cross borders, so, too, should political responses.[6] The problem is that there is nothing inherently emancipatory about cosmopolitan ideals of governance and/or political community. Cosmopolitan visions (including specific iterations of Christianity, the European Enlightenment, and, more recently, the neoliberal market) are haunted by specters of colonialism and imperialism and are frequently deployed in the pursuit of ends tinged with nationalism (Mignolo 2000). In the case of global environmentalism, in particular, there exists a long history of practitioners motivated by a desire to save a "universal" nature (frequently a Malthusian, romantic, or Darwinian nature) beyond national bounds, paying frustratingly little attention to the historical struggles and social contexts of the populations impacted by their (often well-intentioned) interventions in Latin America, Southeast Asia, and Africa (Peluso and Watts 2001; Tsing 2005).

In fairness, opponents of restrictionism at times recognize this. As Betsy Hartmann (2004, 2) writes,

> from colonial times onwards, wildlife conservation efforts have often involved the violent exclusion of local people from their land by game rangers drawn from the ranks of the police, military and prison guards. To legitimize this exclusion, government officials, conservation agencies and aid donors have frequently invoked narratives of expanding human populations destroying pristine landscapes, obscuring the role of resource extraction by state and corporate interests.

These forms of "coercive conservationism" (Hartmann 2004) have been contested by several opponents who detail how nongovernmental organizations dedicated to population reduction construct poor and foreign people of color as threats to sustainability efforts (Bandarage 1999). Narratives of global overpopulation, for instance, rely on statistical and visual data that "decontextualize bodies and histories, lifting them out of time and space" (Sasser 2014, 12) and rendering them in need of biopolitical intervention. Despite this recognition, opponents of restrictionism frequently turn to a rhetoric of "ecocosmopolitanism" because of its intuitive pull and strategic leverage—out of the knowledge that nonhuman flows do not stop at political boundaries and the hope that images of nature as global might forge more inclusive and ethical political communities. The problem is that political projects founded on the promise of ecocosmopolitanism are ethically risky and strategically anemic. They by and large fail to articulate effectively how their cosmopolitanism will differ from past, exclusionary forms, and they gesture toward a universal global condition rather than constructing strategies built on careful attention to contingent political conjunctures.

For other opponents, particularly mainstream environmental organizations, protecting global ecosystems and responding to the power of transnational capital can be best accomplished by working within the structures of the national sovereignty. Greenpeace's Radford (2013) writes,

> As Americans, we believe all people should be treated fairly, no matter the color of their skin or the country of their birth. This means that everyone has an equal right to protection from corporate polluters, and that no one should be forced into a vulnerable shadow class simply because of paperwork.

In this case, the global ethic that is being advanced is couched within a statist framework; cosmopolitan conceptions of global communities and ethics are folded into efforts to green the nation-state. "Every society," Radford writes, "is judged by how well it embodies its highest aspirations and how it treats its most vulnerable people." He continues, "Only a roadmap to full citizenship will enable all of us, including aspiring Americans, to achieve the safety, sustainability and dignity that everyone in America deserves."

The frame of reference, in this narrative, is the national society (rather than the global), and the goal is to reformulate national popular sovereignty through the inclusion of more voices that can fight against corporate greed. In making the case that immigrants are more likely to be environmentalists than the average American citizen, the Sierra Club similarly observes that "significant numbers of these stakeholders and change agents have been denied their civil rights in the public arena" (Brune and Chin 2013). In these statements, the national public arena is being laudably expanded, but not stretched beyond borders:

> We cannot solve either the climate crisis or our broken immigration system by acting out of fear or by supporting exclusion. One of our nation's greatest strengths is the contribution that generations of immigration have made to our national character. If we are serious about solving the climate crisis and protecting our democracy, then we need to work with the hardworking men and women who want to play by the rules and play a part in building a healthy, safe and prosperous future for our country. (Brune and Chin 2013)

The ethos of sovereignty is being reconfigured in a more inclusive direction, but the constituent parts of sovereignty—the nation, the state, citizenship, liberal democracy, capitalism, and a vision of progress founded on a particularistic "we"—remain intact. The Sierra Club concludes by arguing that to "protect our wild America, defend clean air and water, and win the fight against climate disruption, we must ensure that the people who are the most disenfranchised and the most affected by pollution have the voice to fight polluters and advocate for climate solutions without fear." But what if it is this unexamined commitment to "wild America" that disables a transformative approach to the nature–sovereignty relationship?

## AN ALTERNATIVE DISCOURSE OF NATURE, SOVEREIGNTY, AND MIGRATION?

Throughout the book, I have argued that the nature–culture dualism is contingently produced in ways that legitimate particular forms of sovereign power—that apparently cultural discourses of sovereignty seep into apparently natural discourses of environmentalism, and vice versa. The argument that I am making here is that the continued resonance of the nature–culture dualism among global environmental justice advocates has undermined their ability to respond to environmental restrictionism and to envision strategies geared toward bringing about transformative futures. Opponents of restrictionism—whether they advance an ecocosmopolitan ideal of planetary patriotism or an approach to green sovereignty tethered to a more progressive ideal of econationalism— remain beholden to dichotomous constructions of Nature and Culture as autonomous spheres of life. The foundational assumption driving their opposition is that "real" commitments to nature inevitably lead one to adopt progressive, ecological, and inclusive values. By contrast, the exclusionary forces (i.e., sovereignty, nationalism, racism) in the world are definitively cultural. This is problematic, because the eco-communitarian discourse has been strategically sculpted based on this binary, appealing simultaneously to conceptions of nature (attachment to place, romantic wilderness, cultural consumptive patterns) and ideals of culture (liberal communitarian nationhood, steady states, and social democracy) that resonate with many environmentalists. The opposition to restrictionism both fails to explore how the nature–culture dualism is produced in discourses of environmental restrictionism and unwittingly *adopts and reinforces* the very ontological divide on which restrictionism is dependent.

As Sierra Club director Michael Dorsey (2011) explains, "most environmentalists have no coherent theoretical foundation to which they can articulate their politics, and this is why they are so easily hoodwinked and led astray." To combat ecocommunitarianism, opponents of restrictionism need a discourse that more effectively links a socially inclusive politics to theoretical ideals that break down the sharp nature–culture dichotomy. Such a discourse is much more challenging to articulate, but the strategic rewards are potentially enormous, promoting a reflexive environmentalism that opens the door to new green alliances by elevating the problem of "nature's intelligibility" (Braun 2002) to a place of central concern in dialogues over greening sovereignty. In the following chapter, I attempt to provide insight into what such a discourse would look like. I introduce what I term an *environmental theory of migration* and argue that the construction of truly transformative socioecologies necessitates what might initially seem like a paradox: the abolition of the American environmentalist.

# 5

# TOWARD AN ENVIRONMENTAL POLITICAL THEORY OF MIGRATION

A specter haunts the world and it is the specter of migration.

**MICHAEL HARDT AND ANTONIO NEGRI,** *Empire*

After listening to the town hall panel arguing that immigration is responsible for efforts to dam northern Colorado's Cache la Poudre River, I started to think more about the linkages between transnational migration[1] and this threatened river that I care so much about. But the more I studied this relationship, the more my perspective diverged from that of environmental restrictionists: an emphasis on the sheer number of people in Fort Collins gave way to an emphasis on the political, economic, institutional, and cultural forces that have led people here; the borders separating localities and nations from one another became fragmented amid a tangled web of transnational social relations; and my personal memories of this local place were enlarged by stories that connected it to other places. In engaging with the histories and processes of migration, the temporal and spatial parameters of American sovereignty began to shift, and ideals of nature as inherently deterritorializing were supplanted by a more complex picture of socioecological interconnection. This chapter builds on this engagement, mapping the contours of what I term an *environmental political theory of migration*—an intervention that invites environmentalists to step across the geopolitical, conceptual, and strategic borderlines that, I believe, have disabled their attempts to achieve socioecological justice.

## A MIGRATORY ENVIRONMENTALISM IN CONTEXT

The Poudre River begins high up in Rocky Mountain National Park. It then flows through the canyon bearing its name before spilling out onto Colorado's Front Range. Throughout its 140-mile path, the river is diverted more than twenty times for agricultural, industrial, and municipal uses (American Rivers 2008). In 2008, it was named the third most endangered river in the United States because of the proposal to dam it (American Rivers 2008). In November 2014, the Army Corps of Engineers delayed the planned release of an environmental impact statement related to the Glade Reservoir, but its construction is still very much a possibility (Handy 2014).

The plight of the Poudre is, of course, not unique; its current state of overuse is, unfortunately, common to rivers across the western United States. The most well known example of this is the Colorado River, the dismal state of which is constantly emphasized in the *New York Times*, PBS specials, and academic studies. Photographer Brian Frank's recent project "Downstream: Death of the Mighty Colorado" (2010) details how the river's flows into northern Mexico have been decimated by American consumptive patterns, historical ideologies aimed at "taming nature," flawed political institutions (the Colorado River Compact, the 1944 Water Treaty, etc.), and industrial practices. The caption of one powerful image reads, "[An] eleven year old Cucapá Indian fisherman . . . retrieves an empty net from the receding waters that were once abundant with fish in his village's traditional fishing grounds" (Frank 2010, Image 2). In recent years, the community has been denied fishing rights by the Mexican state, as the little remaining water that trickles into the country is diverted to industry and a biosphere reserve (Muehlman 2013, 3). As a consequence of the lack of water for fishing, farming, and drinking, the very survival of the indigenous community is threatened (Wilken-Robertson 2004). In the surrounding communities of Mexico's Colorado River Basin, the lack of water has led many to migrate north, leading several commentators to categorize these migrants as "water refugees" (see, e.g., Yang 2008).

At first glance, the stories of these two rivers appear unrelated. In fact, the fate of the Colorado and that of the Poudre are intimately entwined. The source of the Colorado River is at La Poudre Pass, which spans the Continental Divide and separates the Colorado from La Poudre Pass Creek—a two-mile-long stream that flows into the Cache la Poudre River. An early transbasin diversion, the Grand Ditch, carries water from the headwaters of the Colorado to those of the Poudre. It was constructed in 1890, as dreams of Manifest Destiny were being realized, to feed the needs of a growing Anglo population in Fort Collins and the neighboring eastern plains. Estimates suggest that the ditch intercepts around 40 percent of the runoff of the upper Colorado (Tweit 2009). It was built by Chinese, Swedish, and Mexican migrant laborers (Waterman 2010, 17).

The water provided by the Grand Ditch not only gave rise to the Poudre River as we now know it but also enabled the construction of an economic system that laid the foundations for the Fort Collins community. The reassembled waters of the Poudre were diverted into agriculture, constructing a flourishing sugar beet industry around which "local business hinged" (Swanson, as cited in Fort Collins History Connection, n.d.). According to a recent analysis, "the impact of the sugar factory on Fort Collins was so substantial that historian Evadene Swanson judged that much of Fort Collins' 'prosperity for the next forty years revolved around the cultivation of beets'" (Fort Collins History Connection, n.d.). To provide labor for the industry, the Great Western Sugar Company recruited German Russian and Mexican immigrants. In fact, "Great Western was so aggressive in their campaign to recruit Mexican labor after 1920 that they traveled to small towns across the Southwest and Mexico with 'moving picture shows'" that depicted an idyllic life in northern Colorado (Donato 2003, 70). Ultimately, Colorado became "one of the world's most important beet producing regions," with Colorado's Front Range leading the way (Twitty 2003, 59).[2]

This brief illustration points toward a system of flows (water, labor, capital) and blockages (borders, dams, connection to place) that asymmetrically link the socionatural realities of Mexican immigrants and American environmentalists. It alludes to structures of authority backed by coercive force that do not mesh with the spatial or temporal parameters of dominant scholarly and environmentalist narratives of the nature–sovereignty relationship.[3] Throughout the book, I have suggested that the divisiveness of debates over the environmental impacts of immigration reveals an American environmental movement struggling to come to terms with complexities that dominant articulations between nature, political community, political economy, race, class, and gender are unable to adequately represent. They illustrate a disconnect between the models of sovereign power that inform ecological action and the actually existing structures of authority that any effective and ethical socioecological resistance must engage.

I have thus far demonstrated that environmental restrictionists, though a heterogeneous coalition, attempt to infuse sovereignty with an ethos that *naturalizes* the "nation-state" and, through reliance on a variety of distinct discourses, works to legitimate the exclusion of immigrants. I have also argued that opponents of restrictionism tend to appeal to a cosmopolitan ethos that conceives of nature as an inherently deterritorializing force existing in contrast to the bounded political communities and forms of governance that constitute traditional ideals and practices of sovereignty. While I am in agreement with much of this global environmental justice discourse, I have made the case that it remains committed to the very ontological divide between nature and culture on which environmental restrictionism depends. In viewing environmental restrictionism as a mere means of appropriating nature to advance exclusionary cultural goals, opponents fail to consider the ways in which ecocentric epistemologies are themselves imbued with the residues of cultural exclusion.

This chapter is my attempt at developing a theoretical alternative that provides insight into how environmentalists might better understand and respond to the complexities of contemporary forms of sovereign power—and their relationships to nature—through a different lens than extant scholarship on this topic has employed. Returning to my opening examples, environmentalists of all stripes share Frank's dismay about the state of the Colorado River. And yet, as the town hall panel shows, the politics of nature have also led many greens *not to share* his dismay over the socioecological conditions that lead many in the delta to migrate north. Through a theoretical and empirical engagement with the realities of transnational migration, this chapter aims to tell a different story about the nature–sovereignty relationship—a story that highlights what environmental restrictionism obfuscates: *contemporary socioecological interconnection* and the ethics and modes of resistance that could potentially flow from it.[4]

## RETHINKING GREEN SOVEREIGNTY THROUGH
## TRANSNATIONAL MIGRATION

In 2013, there were more than 230 million transnational migrants in the world, which amounts to 3.2 percent of the world's population, or roughly one in every thirty-five people (International Labor Organization 2014). The number of transnational migrants is increasing as well; from 2000 to 2010, "4.6 million migrants were added annually, compared to an average of 2 million per annum during the period 1990–2000" (United Nations Economic and Social Affairs 2013). And if global climate change projections are even remotely accurate, these numbers are likely to continue increasing over the course of the twenty-first century.[5] The scope and intensity of contemporary transnational (or international) migration have engendered a resurgence of philosophical interest in the topic, with social commentators analyzing migration as an empirical phenomenon or "the migrant" as a theoretical figure to critically examine a number of foundational political constructs, including sovereignty.

This engagement with transnational migration has, surprisingly, been absent from the attempts of environmental scholars to theorize sovereignty (Conca 1994; Kuehls 1996; Litfin 1998; Deudney 1998; Eckersley 2004; Smith 2011). Transnational migration has, however, attracted the attention of environmental scholars in two respects. First, driven by the realities of climate change, recent years have witnessed an upsurge in attention to environmental migrants (also referred to as environmental refugees or climate refugees). Analysts working primarily (though not exclusively) from liberal institutionalist[6] perspectives have focused on the causes of this migration (Hugo 1996; Hunter 2005), the transnational and global institutions that might govern environmental migration (Warner 2010; Biermann and Boas 2010), and the ethical implications of admitting or excluding environmental migrants (Pevnick 2008; Risse 2008). This body of scholarship has also begun to identify the myriad ways that environmental degradation and scarcity are potential push factors both directly and indirectly causing migration. With few exceptions, the goal of this work is to consider how state self-interest might be recalculated in forging international institutions that could either treat environmental migrants as refugees (e.g., providing rights of relocation) or construct effective international agreements that might lessen the pull of environmental migration by allowing state mitigation and adaptation to climate change.

Second, scholars and activists working from the perspective of orthodox geopolitics have analyzed the relationship between immigration and environmental (and social) degradation, often expressing concern over "floods" or "waves" of migrants that could potentially create geopolitical instability or even overwhelm developed countries like the United States as climate change and resource shortages intensify (see, e.g., Kaplan 1994; Myers 1993; Brown 2008; Department of Defense 2010, 8; for a critique, see Dalby 2002; Bettini 2013). This approach has obvious parallels to environmental restrictionism and is often deployed by restrictionists in attempts to securitize the issue of migration, thus inviting state intervention aimed at reinforcing sovereign boundaries and identities (Urban 2008; Parenti 2011).

Both of these environmental approaches to migration continue to focus on the nation-state as the primary terrain of politics and, in doing so, reinforce dubious binaries between inside–outside, order–anarchy, domestic–foreign, and ethics–self-interest. The realities of transnational migration complicate these ways of thinking, suggesting that struggles over sovereignty occur above, below, and beyond the sphere of the territorialized nation-state (Dalby 2004, 1–2; Shaw 2004, 373–74). In the remainder of this chapter, I turn to transnational migration in attempting to develop a theoretical alternative to these extant engagements. I begin developing this lens by engaging with the work of social theorists who have focused on transnational migration in their efforts to rethink sovereignty. These theorists have (1) used migration as an epistemological lens into the political economic contours of sovereignty, (2) employed "the migrant" as a theoretical figure providing insight into the ontological foundations of sovereign violence, and (3) highlighted migrants as political agents who are revealing new pathways toward resistance against dominant iterations of sovereignty.

In the following section, I examine these interventions and consider how these insights of social theory might be brought to bear on American debates over the environmental impacts of immigration. In outlining this environmental theory of migration, I weave together the statements, ideas, and practices of various environmental justice activists, scholars, and organizations—particularly those working at the intersection of immigrants' rights and environmental justice in the United States–Mexico border region—in attempting to formulate an alternative discourse of the nature–sovereignty relationship that I believe is potentially transformative.

## Migration and Neoliberal Natures: Entering and Exiting Empire

For a variety of social theorists, the lived experiences of migrants provide unique perspectives from which to critically analyze transnational "assemblages" or "regimes" of sovereignty driven by neoliberalism (Agnew 2009). Michael Hardt and Antonio Negri (2000), for example, argue that sovereignty has been dispersed within a deterritorialized "Empire"—a networked juridical order consisting of U.S. military might, powerful industrialized states, transnational corporations, international financial institutions, and a variety of other powers—pushed forward, at points, by all of these actors but fully under the control of none. The juridical order is dependent on a biopolitical foundation that often legitimates the rule of Empire but that also has the ability to unravel it. In a political economic system dominated by post-Fordist production, the very immaterial labor—the production of information, ideas, and forms of communication—that provides the ideological justification for Empire has the potential to create a deterritorialized resistance.[7]

Migrants, according to Hardt and Negri, occupy a unique position within this sovereign assemblage in that their lives speak to political economic trends that prefigure an increasingly common condition of the mobility of labor, and the "cultural mixture" that accompanies this mobility (133–34). In this sense, the migrant plays a pedagogical role:

> Migrations . . . teach us about the geographical divisions and hierarchies of the global system of command. Migrants understand and illuminate the gradients of danger and security, poverty and wealth, the markets of higher and lower wages, and the situations of more or less free forms of life. (134)

The migrant is a liminal figure who operates on the fringes of Empire but understands its cracks and fissures better than the wealthier, more "powerful" individuals and institutions that hold the formal levers of authority. This is not to envision the migrant as a noble savage who holds the Truth; rather, it is to carefully consider the perspectives to which migrants have access because of their unique positions within the order of Empire.

What these social theorists frequently allude to, but leave under-explored, is that the deterritorialized system of sovereignty that they describe rests on a particular socioecological order that produces im-migration. Analysis of Mexican–U.S. migration suggests that rapidly changing relationships to nature play a role in both *pushing* Mexican migrants out of their local communities and *pulling* them into the United States. This is true in two respects. First, in the past thirty years, not only was a process of primitive accumulation set into motion that concentrated landholdings in fewer and fewer hands (often the hands of U.S. agribusiness) but a radical libertarian ideal of property rights came to curtail the ability of Mexican citizens to put in place environmental (and social) laws and regulations (McCarthy 2004; Sparke 2006). Specifically, chapter 11 of the North American Free Trade Agreement (NAFTA) institutionalized a logic of "regulatory takings" whereby states and localities were potentially subject to legal action for any policy that might impact the property value or expected return on invest-ment of transnational corporations (McCarthy 2004). In other words, NAFTA "involved giving corporations the quasi-constitutional right to sue national and local governments if such governments ever sought to re-nationalise or otherwise provide as public services privatized utility, healthcare or welfare services" (Sparke 2006, 158). Sparke concludes that this serves as a form of "new constitutionalism" (Gill 1995) that locks in neoliberal reforms by institutionalizing them in venues (e.g., the International Monetary Fund, the World Trade Organization, national banks, binational trade agreements) that operate at a distance from democratic rule. Control over nature, in this respect, was wrested from the hands of Mexican citizens and moved into those of transnational entities without clear lines of accountability to democratic processes.

As this process has proceeded, natural resources have been com-modified and subject to the forces of the global market—a phenomenon that has left many Mexican farmers unable to compete with corporate largesse and, in many cases, unable to afford basic goods. In the years since the passage of NAFTA, trade among the three North American countries has more than tripled (Villarreal and Fergusson 2014, 10), and Mexican exports to the United States have risen dramatically—which has not translated into job growth or wage increases for Mexican workers (Hing 2010, 12; Villarreal and Fergusson 2014, 20). In agricultural sectors, the situation is particularly dire, as Mexican farmers struggle to compete with subsidized American wheat, corn, and pork imports (Bacon 2012; Council on Hemispheric Affairs 2012). A transnational sovereign assemblage has projected corporate power across borders in a way that makes (sustainable) subsistence farming more difficult to maintain. In such a context, the pull of migration is strong. The form of sovereignty reinforced by NAFTA, then, perpetuates a form of "ecologically unequal exchange" (Hornborg 1998); as manufacturing industries moved south after the passage of NAFTA, environmental harms emerging from their ecologically intensive practices were displaced across the border (at the same time as nonhuman flows, like the Colorado River, continued to be consumed, degraded, and obstructed before they reached Mexico).

Second, the economic realities of the American economy, coupled with the sociocultural stigma attached to jobs that involve *untidy* relations with nature, have resulted in a consistently high demand for immigrant labor—a pull factor for migration. The post-Fordist mode of production is dependent on continued consumption that fulfills imperatives of both the neoliberal political economy and social status. This has created a demand for low-cost goods, food, and services that necessitate low-wage jobs—jobs that have historically been filled by migrant workers and are thus seen as "undesirable" to American citizens (Massey, Durand, and Malone 2003, 41, 145). Jobs, in this sense, are viewed as status symbols depending, in part, on their relationship to nationalized ideals of nature. It is not so much that migrants occupy jobs that are "closer to nature"; to the contrary, certain jobs close to national ideals of nature—parks and forest service workers protecting wilderness, ranchers and farmers "working the land," expedition leaders guiding tourists through hikes and down rivers—remain integral to the American national imaginary. But where workers interact with very different natures—ones that do not fit romanticized ideals of wilderness or small-scale agrarianism but involve killing (industrial meat workers)

or exposure to toxic chemicals (agricultural, technological, and clean-
ing workers)—their jobs have been systematically denationalized and
deemed unfit for most American laborers. Jeffrey Passel (2006) of the
Pew Hispanic Center reports that

> about 7.2 million unauthorized migrants were employed in March
> 2005, accounting for about 4.9% of the civilian labor force. They
> made up a large share of all workers in a few more detailed occupa-
> tional categories, including 24% of all workers employed in farming
> occupations, 17% in cleaning, 14% in construction and 12% in food
> preparation.

Passel also notes that in 2005, 27 percent of workers in the meatpacking industry were immigrants (12) who daily grappled with what Eric
Schlosser (2001) terms "the most dangerous job in America" (see also
Apostolidis 2010; Pachirat 2011). David Pellow (2002, 12) adds that
"in Silicon Valley's high-tech sector, 70 percent of production workers
are Asian and Latino immigrants and sixty percent are women." The
environmental injustices facing these largely immigrant workforces—
exposure to chemicals, pesticides, toxic waste, industrial pollutants,
and occupational hazards—add weight to the claim that neoliberalism
depends on ideals of nature that are nationalized and racialized (Pulido
1996; 2000; Park and Pellow 2004, 416–18).

The approach of ecocommunitarian restrictionists—to contest neoliberalism by reinforcing borders and strengthening the state—then
seems misplaced; as opponents of restrictionism point out, it plays into
the hands of Empire by providing a precarious workforce for whom it
is dangerous to organize to fight against these injustices.[8] Though it is
true that neoliberalism and sovereignty at times function as competing
logics (i.e., neoliberalism breaks down boundaries through the incessant
flows of capital, while sovereignty builds them up through appeals to
national identity), they also produce mutually reinforcing outcomes.[9]
Neoliberalism does not require a strong state to counterbalance it;
neoliberalism has actually strengthened particular institutions within
the state (e.g., Border Patrol, Department of Defense) while channel-
ing its competencies and the forms of biopolitics that accompany it in
directions that further perpetuate the rule of Empire. The relationship
between sovereignty, neoliberalism, and militarism becomes clear in
further examining the plight of transnational migrants.

## Migration, Nature, and Militarization: Of Borders and Bare Life

A transnational mode of sovereignty operating through a logic of neoliberalism changes existing socioecologies in ways that produce migration. The migrants' arrival then challenges traditional communal imaginaries in ways that create resistance in the "host" society—a backlash that often seeks to resist neoliberal sovereignty by reconsolidating "traditional" forms of community, governance, and culture through the exclusion of immigrants. For this reason, scholars have also turned to migrants to understand the ontological violence of contemporary sovereign power—and how it comes to be targeted at particular populations. Most prominently, Giorgio Agamben has built on the work of Hannah Arendt in viewing "the immigrant" as a contemporary manifestation of "bare life"—that life stripped of all political qualifications, included in the juridical order solely through its exclusion. Agamben (1995, 117) writes,

> What the industrialized states are faced with today is a permanently resident mass of noncitizens, who neither can be nor want to be naturalized or repatriated. Often these noncitizens have a nationality of origin, but inasmuch as they prefer not to make use of their state's protection they are, like refugees, "stateless de facto."

Agamben explains that the reaction to the recent increase in migration—a reaction that Arendt noted was also present when nation-states were faced with refugees during World War I and World War II—has been an upsurge in hypernationalism and a forceful rejection of migrant or refugee rights, illustrating a tension between the purportedly universal suppositions of liberal rights and protections and the particularism manifested most clearly in the linkage being articulated between nativity and nationalism. Whereas refugees and immigrants were once phenomena associated with periods of crisis, Agamben suggests that, amid the imperatives of neoliberal globalization—flexible labor forces, the continued de- and reterritorialization that occurs as capital seeks lower production costs, the increased privatization of land and natural resources, looming resource shortages, worsening natural disasters, and a resurgence of exclusionary nationalism—this status is increasingly the reality, rather than the exception, for a growing number of the world's inhabitants. "The immigrant" thus represents an emergent human condition where the potential violence of sovereign politics and life itself are irrevocably entwined. The immigrant functions as a limit situated at the nexus between sovereignty and biopolitics—the life whose violent management is argued to be the condition of possibility for the freedom of the territorially bound nation.

Agamben's work has engendered a variety of efforts to flesh out the relationships between the logic(s) of sovereignty and the almost totalitarian tendencies that the most ostensibly democratic states (e.g., the United States and Western Europe) display in their efforts to restrict immigration. Wendy Brown (2010, 24), for instance, argues that the construction of border walls is a widespread response to the "waning of sovereignty." These spectacular efforts to keep migrants out reflect a new theatrical regime of state power that attempts to project the image of sovereignty to its populace at the same time as it welcomes forces of global integration that limit its actually existing authority and control. Contra Brown, the argument that I have made throughout the book is that border walls do not emerge primarily out of the calculations of a nation-state attempting to project an image of sovereign power to its populace; rather, they emerge out of the demands of a segment of society that perceives an idealized vision of national sovereignty as threatened by the myriad flows characterizing neoliberal globalization (and the new, transnational modes of sovereignty that reinforce and give rise to these flows). However, her broader point—that threats to various conceptions of sovereignty engender the construction of border walls—still holds true. The securitization and concomitant militarization of national immigration policies are attempts by the state to respond to forms of statecraft from below, and thereby to build legitimacy among a fearful, angry, and vocal portion of the populace. These policies increasingly render borderlands "spaces of exception" where prized democratic political protections—due process, equal rights under the law, and so on—no longer apply, and where racialized and nationalized logics of enmity reign.

In the case of the United States–Mexico borderlands, the production of the border as a space of exception is directly related to socio-ecological injustices plaguing migrant populations. This relationship quickly becomes apparent in exploring the struggles of the Sierra Club Borderlands Campaign (SCBC), which has worked to detail how a variety of actors—American environmentalists, social justice advocates, transnational migrants, Mexican farmers, Mexican American citizens, rivers, animals, plant species, and so on—have been impacted by the construction of the United States–Mexico border wall. The example of Dan Millis is particularly illustrative:

> Dan Millis, born and raised in Arizona, has a daily connection to some of the cruelest realities of our border policy. While hiking along a canyon just north of the Arizona/Mexico border with a group of volunteers, Dan stumbled across the corpse of a girl. At only 14, the Salvadoran girl Joseline was the youngest of the 183 recovered bodies along the Arizona border in 2008. (Sierra Club Borderlands Campaign 2012a)

Only weeks later, Millis, who has worked with both the Sierra Club Borderlands Campaign and No More Deaths (a humanitarian organization that attempts to prevent migrant deaths in the border region), was out distributing water jugs and picking up trash in the same area (in the Buenos Aires National Wildlife Refuge near the border) when he was "stopped by federal authorities and issued a citation":

> The ticket was written for "littering" despite the boxes full of trash that he and a group of No More Deaths Volunteers had been cleaning up from the area. Dan refused to pay the ticket, and was later convicted in federal court. (Sierra Club Borderlands Campaign 2012a)

The harassment of humanitarian and environmental volunteers, the SCBC suggests, is reflective of the extent to which national security has been redefined in the post-9/11 era in a manner that effectively overrides any alternative legal and normative rationales. To illustrate this tendency, the campaign details the myriad environmental and social travesties stemming from the border wall and the concomitant suspension of the normal ethical–juridical order: the closing of binational Friendship Park where families split by the border would meet on weekends; the Department of Homeland Security's (DHS) seizure of ancestral land from an Apache nurse whose family settled in southern Texas more than two hundred years ago; the inability of mountain lions, mule deer, and a variety of other species to follow seasonal migration patterns; and the destruction of prized riparian areas (Sierra Club Borderlands Campaign 2012a).

Of specific concern is the fact that section 102 of the 2005 Real ID Act grants the DHS a waiver to the Endangered Species Act, the National Environmental Policy Act, the Safe Drinking Water Act, and thirty-three other federal laws (Sierra Club Borderlands Campaign 2012b). Thus, both the construction of the wall and the thousands of miles of border patrol roads (as well as towers and lights) built along these areas are not governed by the environmental or social regulations present in areas of the country removed from the physical border. In addition to creating profound insecurity for migrants, the wall cuts through ecologically sensitive areas. In 2009, the Borderlands campaign produced the film *Wild versus Wall*, which describes instances of ecological devastation stemming from 650 miles of wall along the United States–Mexico border:

> The international border crosses some of the most biologically rich lands in the world. . . . Some of the plant and wildlife species that call the borderlands home can be found nowhere else on Earth. And many of the migrating species of North America cross this line at some point in their lives. . . . But these vital wild places have been under assault by a border policy that can operate above the law, building walls along the border at any cost. (Sierra Club Borderlands Campaign 2009)

Of note, border wall construction has impacted the Tijuana estuary, which "serves as a filtration system for the Tijuana river valley and provides a rare patch of coastal habitat"; the migration of jaguars in and out of the "sky island" region; and the numerous protected spaces surrounding the Rio Grande (Sierra Club Borderlands Campaign 2009). Existing environmental laws, which recognize the necessity of these protected areas, have been undone by Real ID, "cast aside by costly, ineffective, environmentally destructive and inhumane attempts to 'secure the border'" (Sierra Club Borderlands Campaign 2009).

In this sense, the secretary of Homeland Security—a political appointee—effectively has the capacity to declare a state of exception. *Wild versus Wall* explains that the first three times the exception was invoked was to allow for the construction of walls in (1) the San Diego Estuary, (2) the habitat of the endangered Sonoran pronghorn, and (3) the San Pedro Riparian National Conservation Areas. The fourth instance, however, was a much more sweeping declaration:

On April 1st 2008, the use of the waiver provided a green light for 500 miles of infrastructure projects in all four border states. This waiver swept aside more than 30 important laws created to protect clean water, clean air, wildlife habitat, important historical sites and specific wilderness areas. (Sierra Club Borderlands Campaign 2009)

In the daily enforcement of these exceptional rules, the Border Patrol and other federal authorities are—by performing tasks like the citation of Millis for "littering"—reinforcing a configuration of sovereignty in which the dictates of hypernational security surpass the importance of saving the lives of marginalized human and nonhuman populations. The result, as Millis (2011) explained to me, is a humanitarian and ecological crisis: "the scale of the tragedy of border death boggles the mind." Recent statistics suggest that in the past fifteen years, more than fifty-five hundred human migrants have died in attempting to cross into the United States (Anderson 2013). The death toll on nonhuman life remains unquantified.

As a wide variety of environmental organizations have recognized, in the border region, migrants—human and "non-human"[10]—are frequently reduced to bare life. However, nature also plays a second, less recognized role in the process of border militarization. At the same time as the socioecological shifts created by neoliberalism intensify the push and pull factors driving Mexican immigration to the United States, nature—as both a social construction and a network of material flows—is being deployed to prevent migration. In terms of the former, I have argued throughout the book that environmental restrictionism functions as a form of statecraft from below that reinforces modes of sovereign violence. This logic increasingly animates the efforts of anti-immigrant groups and, at times, extends into institutional justifications for the construction of "new and improved" border walls. In response to allegations that border walls harmed the environment, former DHS secretary Michael Chertoff has argued that "illegal immigrants" are the real environmental culprits, leaving "human waste, garbage, discarded bottles and other human artifacts in pristine areas" (Sullivan 2007). Concerns over a "threatened" American sovereignty thus result in the selective tightening of borders (and the deployment of coercive force aimed at migrant populations)—with nature serving as a justification.[11]

In terms of the latter, the explicit strategy of the Border Patrol over the past twenty years has been to use walls and a massive increase in boots on the ground to force migrants away from traditional ports of entry and into the Sonoran Desert; a strategy that John Fife, founder of the humanitarian organization No More Deaths, refers to as "deterrence through death." The forms of statecraft from below to which environmental restrictionists contribute enable the desert to be deployed as a tool of official statecraft.

### Resisting the Exception: Socioecologies and Strategies

Through these examples, the shape and social purpose of this dominant, arguably hegemonic, iteration of sovereign power begin to become clear. A focus on migration shows how vital particular nature–culture relations are in enabling and advancing a transnational form of sovereignty driven by a logic of militarized neoliberalism.[12] To resist this form of sovereign power, scholars have recognized the importance of integrating the realities and perspectives of migrants into theories and (counter) practices of sovereignty. In this vein, a variety of thinkers—from critical ethnographers to labor historians to social activists—have argued for viewing migration as an act of political resistance (see Apostolodis 2010, xxxii–xxxv). The geographic mobility of migrants enables a unique perspective that, when coupled with their refusal of the existing order, produces a powerful foundation on which a counterhegemonic movement can be constructed. For example, Luis Fernandez and Joel Olson (2011) contend that migration speaks to an overwhelming desire of people to "live, love and work wherever they please." Observing that the freedom of movement is more important for many migrants than obtaining formal American citizenship, their slogan recognizes the inability of de jure logics of national sovereignty to address the de facto realities of actually existing sovereignty in an ethically satisfactory manner (413–14). "This demand for global mobility and local participation," they write, "flatly contradicts the national sovereignty underpinning liberal citizenship" (417). In this respect, Fernandez and Olson argue that the actions of migrants—and even acts of migrating themselves—are forms of resistance that reconfigure sovereignty toward alternative ends, or that seek to reject it entirely.

To what extent can migration function as a form of resistance against dominant forms of sovereignty? Ecocommunitarians view im-migration as complicit in the neoliberal structures that undermine national sovereignty (and thus national environmental protection), asserting that capital desires uncontrolled migration. My argument is that they are mistaken; capitalism flourishes through a "controlled illegality" (Foucault [1979] 2008, 279)—particular forms of labor that flow to particular locales under particular normative and juridi-cal circumstances. A policy that simply opened borders while granting immigrants legal protections would be a nightmare for capital, open-ing the door to political organizing and collective action aimed at obtaining health and safety regulations, higher wages, and protections from environmental hazards, as well as creating opportunity for alli-ance building with other social actors. In constructing immigrants as environmental "savages" or "delinquents," environmental restriction-ists effectively reinforce the pervasive form of social surveillance—the modes of statecraft from below—needed to prevent resistance.[13] In doing so, despite their stated opposition to neoliberalism, they actually provide the disciplinary foundations that stabilize neoliberal rule; they not only produce a social antagonism that disables coalition building against capital, they also reinforce the precarious labor conditions—for example, migrants afraid to speak out against atrocious living and working conditions—on which capital accumulation depends. On one hand, neoliberalism provides the migrant workers that a consumption-based national economy needs to function. On the other, restrictionism (and the resulting securitization of immigration policy) works to ensure that the migrants are not a threat to the global neoliberal order.[14]

Restrictionist responses to militarized neoliberalism thus uninten-tionally create the social antagonisms and precarity that sustain this form of sovereignty—increasingly drawing on ecocentric constructions of nature to do so. The nationalized ideals of nature mobilized by ecocommunitarian restrictionists add fuel to the fire of Empire.[15] The social connections, counterdiscourses, and practices that could breed an effective opposition are marginalized and reduced to "forms of illegality that are less dangerous: maintained by the pressure of controls on the fringes of society, reduced to precarious conditions of existence, lacking links with the population that would be able to sustain it" (Foucault [1979] 2008, 278).

Thus, while acts of migrating themselves reveal cracks and fissures in the machinations of contemporary sovereignty, to confront the institutional and discursive powers of this mode of sovereignty driven by an ethos of militarized neoliberalism, a broad-based transnational coalition forged around a very different normative vision is needed. What should this resistance look like? A growing body of work emerging from both scholars and activists suggests that migrants reconfigure sovereignty in a variety of ways: challenging dominant ideals of national identity through a variety of local, transnational, and cosmopolitan imaginaries; struggling to expand the public sphere by organizing for improved working conditions and opportunities for political participation; and highlighting the disconnect between actually existing social connections that traverse boundaries and theories, practices, and norms of sovereignty dependent on territorially bounded social contracts (see, e.g., De Genova 2005; Walia 2013).

The grounded actions of environmental justice and immigrants' rights groups gesture toward alternative readings of the sovereignty–nature relationship and modes of resistance against its dominant articulations. Indeed, even a cursory look at alliances between immigrants and environmental justice organizations reveals the emergence of transnational environmental publics that are constructed with regard to the localized manifestations of particular forms of sovereign power. Salazar and Hewitt (2001, 305), for instance, observe that "in the rural counties of southwest Oregon, immigrant forest floor workers have organized to improve their working conditions and protect forest resources." In the San Diego–Tijuana region, the Environmental Health Coalition has a long-standing Border Environmental Justice Campaign through which environmental justice advocates and workers in the border zone combat the social and environmental consequences of NAFTA (Environmental Health Coalition 2012). And in Fort Collins, Colorado, the Fort Collins Community Action Network provides a venue to unite otherwise independent local organizations—including the Fort Collins Sustainability Group, the immigrant support group Fuerza Latina, and the Open Communities Collective—to fight for the protection of marginalized human and nonhuman populations.

The strategies of these organizations contest the borders both between nature and culture and between one sovereign nation-state and another. For example, the social and environmental justice organization Center for New Community (CNC) has launched the most in-depth critique and analysis of the environmental restrictionist movement to date through its campaign Race, Migration, and the Environment and its *Imagine2050* blog. And while frequently employing the global environmental justice discourse that I reviewed last chapter, its activism, at times, veers toward a more politically astute response:

> By the year 2050, one out of five Americans will be foreign born. Latino and Asian communities will increase significantly. There will be no clear racial or ethnic majority. We will become a nation of minorities. Today's perceptions of foreignness will challenge how Americans identify themselves over the coming decades. In light of these challenges, Imagine 2050 believes igniting candid conversations around race, immigration, and environment will become increasingly necessary to American democracy. (*Imagine2050* 2012)

Within this project, the collective idea of "America" is not rejected but is retooled by a critical ethos that seeks to nurture respect for difference. Yet this is not the only communal imaginary being conjured; subaltern, local, transnational, and cosmopolitan forms of identity are also embraced at particular moments to strategically push and pull the contours of nationhood away from the hypernationalist terrain on which it is so often lodged.[16] Similarly, for the CNC and its allies, the state is not rejected but is targeted so that it might work with a renewed sense of legitimacy. In those venues that provide strategic leverage, the organization urges federal and state governments to regulate and redistribute to construct a more transparent and participatory democracy (see, e.g., Rich 2011a, 2011b). The state, however, is not a sacred site but a strategic one, and where appealing to this juridical form risks reinforcing an exclusionary ethos, critique replaces engagement and alternative arrangements of governance are advanced. Attempts to work "within" the state are thus supplemented by a variety of actions "outside," including a "Biking beyond Bigotry" tour, a newsletter that satirizes restrictionist claims, and the organization of protests against entities funding restrictionist organizations.

Through this strategy, an alternative nature emerges, one that is carefully coded across these variable social registers to protect and enhance the lives of marginalized population—human and nonhuman—

by way of localized interventions that seek to detach nature from its exclusionary social bases and re-embed it in forms of community and governance that might work toward an inclusive ethos of sovereignty. In a report titled "Race, Migration, and the Environment," the CNC opens by stating, "In order to tackle the serious crises at hand, environmental movements need to reject the historically dangerous understanding that nature is something separate from society, and examine the ways they are interconnected" (McMahon and Sanes 2011). The report proceeds by examining how migrant populations encounter the nonhuman realm and argues that the American environmental movement would benefit from the inclusion of these unique socionatural perspectives. Overall, a commitment to nature is entwined in a commitment to this inclusive, outward-oriented ethos of sovereignty. The radically democratic impetus of such a strategy works to decenter claims of legitimacy away from the traditional state authorities and hypernationalist sympathizers who might work to invoke an exception, while rechanneling the discursive pathways through which commitments to nature might be complicit in reducing marginalized populations to bare life.

By drawing migrants into the center of their environmental practice, organizations like *Imagine2050* are able to tactically resist militarized neoliberalism, breaking down borders, racial boundaries, and the ontological divide between nature and culture. This approach, it should be noted, avoids the two dominant environmental approaches that I reviewed in the introduction—that embrace the greening of the nation-state or reject it in favor of the deterritorializing impulses of nature. Instead, it meshes more clearly with the experiences and strategies of historically marginalized groups, such as indigenous populations, who struggle with and against sovereign power by articulating forms of natural–cultural interconnection that challenge the spatial and temporal assumptions on which dominant iterations depend (Deloria 1984; Bruyneel 2007; Shaw 2008).[17]

## BEYOND GREEN SOVEREIGNTY? MIGRATING TO REBELLION

And yet these extant modes of resistance—while often impactful and always instructive—remain localized, fragmented, and, all too often, reactive to the violences of sovereign power (i.e., protesting detention centers, workplace crackdowns, or border militarization after egregious acts of social coercion and environmental destruction). They offer tactics for differently situated organizations but few strategies for long-range structural change. What would a more unified, revolutionary mode of resistance look like? In the first chapter, I laid out an approach to analyzing sovereignty by focusing on the forms of statecraft from below through which authority backed by coercive force is constituted and legitimated. This approach has enabled me to provide a grounded account of how sovereign power is being reconfigured through a heated social struggle—American debates over the environmental impacts of immigration—but it provides little strategic direction for those socioecological activists enmeshed in daily struggles against sovereignty. For this, a more refined normative vision is needed.

The remainder of this chapter attempts to provide the normative vision that would guide an environmental theory of migration. I sketch this out in two parts. First, I turn to political theorist Enrique Dussel's (2008) provocative call for a revolutionary mode of sovereignty constituted and legitimated through a "state of rebellion"—a mode of resistance in which, I argue, migrants would play a crucial role. Second, I consider how this alternative mode of sovereignty would reconfigure the boundaries between nature and culture, environmentalism and social movements, and one sovereign nation-state and another in pursuit of socioecological justice and sustainability.

### The (Socio)Natural State of Rebellion

Dussel argues that the potential power of the masses in its virtual form, what he terms *potentia,* becomes corrupted as it is institutionalized in the form of sovereign power; it is captured and ultimately employed to serve the political elite's quest for domination (14–17). He suggests, however, that out of frustration with myriad forms of socioecological domination, a mode of resistance founded on *hyperpotentia* could emerge—an untimely eruption of power driven by a political community founded by and for the excluded and suffering (81). Through hyperpotentia, a "state of rebellion" begins to take shape, a counterpoint to the current state of exception produced under militarized neoliberalism, through which "the people"—albeit a radically reformulated people—can capture sovereignty (75).

Thus, contra Hardt and Negri, Mick Smith, and the many greens who reject sovereignty altogether, the goal is not a world without sovereignty. Too often, such a position reverts to naturalism (e.g., bioregions or cosmopolitan governance guided by the "inherently emancipatory" realities of nature) or metaphysics (e.g., Agamben's [2005, 88] "word that does not bind, that neither commands nor prohibits anything, but says only itself"), envisioning a world without power relations that offers little strategic insight for those besieged by sovereign power in the here and now. However, contra those embracing a "green nation-state" (Eckersley 2004) or a "green New Deal" (Jones 2008; Stein 2012), Dussel also rejects a more progressive, inclusive form of state sovereignty. Such a move fails to confront the global power of capital and, I would argue, threatens to reinforce exclusionary modes of political community. The case of ecocommunitarian restrictionism, for instance, illustrates how well-intentioned nationalist modes of resistance are easily overcoded by hegemonic hypernational forms. The nation-state, even in its green guises, is premised on an exclusive mode of community forged through power (and often violence) rather than the realities of contemporary social connection. In this sense, efforts to green the nation-state have subtly reproduced societal divisions (e.g., racialized notions of inside–outside, domestic–foreign, self–other veiled beneath neo-Malthusian or romantic epistemologies) that have contributed to the marginalization of migrant communities—human and nonhuman.

The goal, for Dussel, is not a more inclusive form of sovereignty but a transformational one, built by the "social bloc of the oppressed" and constructed on an ethos of radical socioecological justice (76).[18] The "state of rebellion" unifies all of the diverse actors struggling against dominant forms of sovereignty—immigrants, indigenous activists, the working poor, racial minorities, the homeless, and so on—producing new social antagonisms organized around an opposition to hegemonic structures of rule. Dussel recognizes the complexities and potential blockages to what he is calling for; counterhegemonic opposition might first unite around a shared struggle against militarized neoliberalism, but a substantive normative project is needed to solidify the coalition and hold it together. The challenge is that beneath their opposition to militarized neoliberalism, movements of the left have different, at times conflicting, demands. Here Dussel asserts that these diverse actors can forge articulations that, even if initially tactical, could result in a gradual convergence of strategies and ultimately normative visions; "the demands of movements progressively incorporate those of other movements into their own" (72). Greens, for instance, discover that their struggles to bring about sustainable modes of production align with those of workers, that their internal struggles against racism and patriarchy link up with those of civil rights activists and feminists, and that their struggles to end border militarization bring them into solidarity with the struggles of undocumented migrants. Environmental organizations are already moving in this direction, as evidenced by the Blue-Green Alliance, the effort to bridge the environmental and civil rights movements reflected in "The Soul of Environmentalism" (Gelobter 2005), coalitions between the Sierra Club Borderlands Campaign and human rights organizations, and the Climate Justice and Idle No More movements. What they are frequently lacking is a revolutionary political agenda that offers a structural critique of hegemonic modes of sovereignty, a path toward deconstructing the nature–culture dualism and a comprehensive vision for change. My argument is that one way to advance such a politics would be for environmentalists to situate migration at the center of their ontologies, epistemologies, strategies, and ethics. How would this environmental theory of migration translate into practice? Briefly returning to contentious environmental debates over *population, place,* and *political community* provides a useful illustration.

## Population

In adjudicating disputes over population, there currently exists a tension within environmentalism between steady statists—who attempt to imbue territorial institutions with a respect for ecological limits and view population reduction as central to this end (see, e.g., Daly 2006)—and eco-Marxists and environmental justice advocates, who, at times, eschew (or reject) the issue of ecological limits in favor of emphasizing mutually supportive relations between social and ecological resistance (see, e.g., Hartmann 2004). For steady statists, the continual growth of the human population closely correlates with the growth of human-caused ecological destruction—a relationship that social justice activists, at times, ignore. For the eco-Marxists and environmental justice advocates, such analyses are not only overly universalizing, they also fail to recognize that the numerical power of the global masses is one of the few advantages possessed against the economic and institutional largesse of capital.

Analysis of migration suggests, with eco-Marxists, that a transnational "state of rebellion" is necessary to confront the powerful institutional sedimentation of militarized neoliberalism. As Angus and Butler (2011, 189–202) assert, what is needed is "ecological revolution," not populationism. However, engagement with migrants also suggests, with steady statists, that overstepping ecological limits can reinforce patterns of social marginalization and, in many cases, forced migration. Population reduction, then, can potentially be a laudable normative ideal (particularly in arid urban centers that simply cannot sustain large populations without massive captures of natural resources from elsewhere). But this goal must be severed from the national, racial, and gendered roots in which it is so strongly entwined.

It should be noted that, in contrast with the arguments of environmental restrictionists, a number of opponents of restrictionism do recognize this: Angus and Butler, for instance, frequently emphasize that population is an important issue (see, e.g., Angus and Butler 2011, 3, 191); the Political Ecology Group (1999) contends that "global demographic issues should be addressed in a serious manner"; and an Earth First! activist recently argued for a socially just approach to population in noting that "it is clearly impossible to [sustainably support seven billion people] without severely degrading the biodiversity of the planet and pushing countless species into extinction" (Simmons 2012). In this sense, an environmental political theory of migration aligns with the philosophy of degrowth, asserting that attention to ecological limits must be grounded in a structural critique of social injustice and a commitment to deep democratic practice (Schneider, Kallis, and Martinez-Alier 2010). The state of rebellion, then, rests not on global population control but what Dussel (2008, 121) terms "the fertility of solidarity"—a form of *positive biopolitics* that seeks to harness and multiply the power of the suffering while minimizing the collective environmental impact of social systems of (re)production and consumption. The result would be an (historical, cultural, political, economic) analysis of and dialogue over ecological limits structured around an ethos of socioecological justice (see Silliman and King 1999; Simmons 2012).[19]

## Place

In addition to population, one of the foundational concepts that environmentalists—proponents and opponents of restrictionism alike—continue to emphasize is place. Progressive journalist and activist Naomi Klein, for instance, has recently called for deep structural reform to combat climate change and its resulting injustices. Klein (2014) concludes her provocative call to action by asserting that migration cuts off "our" connection to place:

> We tend to abandon our homes lightly—for a new job, a new school, a new love. And as we do so, we are severed from whatever knowledge of place we managed to accumulate at the previous stop, as well as from the knowledge amassed by our ancestors (who, at least in my case, migrated repeatedly themselves).

Klein then draws on Wendell Berry in concluding that the best step toward resisting climate change is cultivating rootedness:

> After listening to the great farmer-poet Wendell Berry deliver a lecture on how we each have a duty to love our "homeplace" more than any other, I asked him if he had any advice for rootless people like me and my friends, who live in our computers and always seem to be shopping for a home. "Stop somewhere," he replied. "And begin the thousand-year-long process of knowing that place."

While Klein's commitment to place is well intentioned, not only does it reflect the very logic of ecocommunitarian restrictionism but ethnographic scholarship on migrants suggests that this vision of migration as placelessness is not accurate. Contrary to arguments adopted by deep ecologists, "mad farmers," and immigration restrictionists alike, migration is not a placeless phenomenon that unhinges all attachment to prized natural or cultural places. Migrants express deep cares about particular places but often also develop an ability to see how one place connects to another—something that many greens seem unable to do. While scholarship routinely emphasizes the ways in which "precarious immigration status and low socio-economic status" constrain the environmental activism of immigrants (see, e.g., Gibson-Wood and Wakefield 2013, 651), there are also myriad ways that the transnational perspective of immigrants enables unique environmental action. A recent survey of Mexican immigrants in Iowa, for example, found that they "are readily accepting of some U.S. norms around environmental thought and behavior but critical of others" (Carter, Silva, and Guzman 2013, 130). Specifically, "they are wary of the excesses of American consumerism and paint a contrast with their own frugal habits, shaped by life histories that often include rural upbringings, material deprivation, delayed gratification and saving for the needs of extended family" (130–31). Similarly, Laura Minkoff Zern (2012) details how immigrants from Oaxaca—many of whom were farmworkers forced from the fields and to the United States after NAFTA—formed the Oahaxan Children's Garden in a California city in an attempt to provide sustainable and healthy food for their communities. She writes, "Eating food that was freshly harvested was the main way that participants connected their diets from the garden to their diets in Oaxaca" (8). A migratory politics of place draws knowledge from one locale into environmental attitudes and actions in another.

This ethnographic insight meshes with the interventions of social theorists. For example, in discussing the importance of freedom of movement, Fernandez and Olson (2011, 417) develop the concept of *locomotion,* which "implies being of multiple places and moving among them." An environmental theory of migration does not reify movement or dismiss attachment to place. In fact, it finds resonance with Native American approaches to sovereignty that emphasize the relationship between particular socioecological places and subaltern political autonomy. Contra Berry, however, it does call for critical scrutiny of how one place connects to others. Despite the tendency of environmental restrictionists to draw false equivalences between their own deep ecological or agrarian conceptions of place and Indigenous ideals, the Navajo appealing to place to protect "the confluence" because of its sacred location in her culture is far different from a restrictionist in northern Colorado working to save the Poudre River by restricting immigrants.[20] A migratory perspective on place works to recognize these differences by fleshing out the social connections forged through colonial encounters, political economic structures, political institutions, and ecosystems.[21]

A migratory conception of place thus reinforces what American environmental scholar Robert Gottlieb (2001) terms a "locational strategy without borders." Gottlieb recognizes that a "global ethic of place" . . . "exists when immigrant communities maintain a connection, through a linked exchange or development process, to strengthen the community of origin and/or recreate the new community, drawing on the identity and needs of the community of origin" (276–77). Despite the noble intentions of many progressive greens, constructing an environmentalism on an insular conception of the "wild place" is dangerous. In its best forms, it reverts to NIMBYism—often a self-congratulatory NIMBYism[22]—and at its worst, it reinforces border walls. By contrast, an environmentalism of migration has the potential to epitomize the green slogan "think global, act local." In opposition to the arguments of environmental restrictionists who continually assert that population reduction ought to be applied at all scales and that wild places must be closely guarded from outsiders, a migratory conception of "think global, act local" calls attention to contemporary structures of social connection.

Such a view of place-in-relation also has the potential to avoid what Gregory Albo calls "the limits of eco-localism," ensuring that the efforts to protect one place do not merely displace ecological degradation to more vulnerable locales. Albo (2007, 13) asserts that "in the existing neoliberal context, the various forms of 'alternative economic spaces' . . . have added significant dimensions to eco-localist practice, but they have remained quite marginal in terms of total activity and subordinate to the larger valorization processes of the formal economy affecting the city as whole." A migratory vision of place could give rise to translocal alliances that could work to contest the mobility of capital. In Flagstaff, Arizona, for example, the Mercado de los Sueños is an alliance between a mostly immigrant community and local socioecological justice activists (Zacarias 2014). Beyond working to cultivate a local place—an alternative community, economy, and socioecology in Flagstaff's low-income Sunnyside neighborhood—the Mercado has engaged with coffee growers from Chiapas to provide a good that cannot be sustainably produced in northern Arizona, bypassing transnational circuits of capital that usually monopolize these translocal linkages and enriching both communities. These translocal alliances are only beginning to emerge; the networks remain sporadic and thin, but they have great potential for forging the linkages that could help stimulate a state of rebellion.

## Political Community

An emphasis on translocal alliances starts to push the contours of American environmentalism outward, challenging the national "we" that has historically driven it. Who, then, is the "we" of an environmentalism of migration? Before answering this question, it is necessary to discuss who this "we" isn't. And it isn't American environmentalists. In fact, an environmentalism of migration necessitates the *abolition of American environmentalism*. Arguments relating abolitionism to environmentalism are beginning to emerge across the world. Writing in *The Nation*, journalist Chris Hayes (2014) recently compared the abolition of fossil fuels to the abolition of slavery, while actors from the Global South, like Bolivian president Evo Morales, have emphasized climate debt and even climate reparations (Chavkin 2009). My aim, in calling for the abolition of American environmentalism, is to extend calls for "the abolition of white democracy" (Olson 2004) to environmental thought, which—as I have detailed throughout the book—remains racialized and nationalized in ways that produce exclusionary, inequitable, and, increasingly, violent outcomes.

In calling for the abolition of American environmentalism, I do not mean that those who have been socially and juridically constructed as "American" should stop caring about more-than-human lives. Rather, the abolition would occur at two interrelated levels. First, the signifier *American* would be challenged by environmental scholars and activists. Contemporary forms of social connection—chains of production and consumption, entangled histories and cultures, ecosystems, ethics, and strategies—arise from spatial and temporal trajectories to which the conceptions of sovereignty informing environmental thought and practice are unable to do justice. In the American context, connections to national wilderness, population politics, and Darwinian natural science must be disembedded from their racial, gendered, classed, and national foundations. A definitively American environmentalism reinforces sovereignty in ways that disable resistance against neoliberalism. By contrast, the most effective environmental efforts in existence today—the Climate Justice and Idle No More movements—are transnational in scope and scale. To be clear, this would not mean that action at local and national scales ceases to exist but rather that local and national activists employ a migratory lens in formulating their strategies. Giovanna Di Chiro (2008, 279) advocates such an approach in arguing for "transcommunal alliances and communities of practices forged in the knowledge that survival depends not on the retreat to the comfort of 'home' . . . but on the worldly and laborious engagements with the fleshy realities of socio-ecological interdependence."

Second, the signifier *environmentalist*, resting as it does on a commitment to nature, has to be abolished in favor of a politics grounded in socioecological activism. Again, I am not suggesting that existing environmental organizations, like the Sierra Club and Earth First!, should be disbanded; I am suggesting that their practice be imbued with an alternative ontology. Environmentalism, as it is often practiced, remains predicated on an ontological separation that fails to consider the modes of natural–cultural connection that can lead us to sustainability. We need less Edward Abbey (militantly reinforcing borderlines) and more Judi Bari (transgressing them); less attachment to localized places and more attention to the social connections that weave places together; less apprehension about the end of nature and more attention to ending nature (as a universal ontological zone). This very clearly echoes Gottlieb's (2001, 287) call for an unbounded environmentalism in which "the social and the ecological are joined together." Paraphrasing Gloria Anzaldúa (1999, 108), American greens need to "accept the doppelganger in their psyche." The "nature" of American environmentalism depends on a nonenvironmental Immigrant Other; it has since its inception—from the savage pot hunter of the turn of the twentieth century to the chaotic and culturally deficient "Third Worlder" of econativism to the placeless wanderer and neoliberal ally of ecocommunitarianism. Strategies leading to transformative resistance require deconstructing these linkages between immigrant and environmentalist, nature and culture, one sovereign nation-state and another, and rebuilding a migratory environmentalism that unites a multitude of subjects around a struggle against militarized neoliberalism and a deep commitment to socioecological justice without borders.

## CONCLUSION

My contention is that "the migrant" ought to be seen as the environmental subject par excellence. By this I do not mean that migrants should be viewed as "noble savages" at one with nature. Rather, I contend that engagement with migration should sit at the ontological, epistemological, strategic, and ethical foundations of socioecological thought. This emphasis on migration gives rise to an alternative reading of the relationship between nature and sovereignty—one emphasizing the contingent contours of sovereign power and detailing how these modes of authority draw on (and give rise to) particular socioecological interconnections.

Though I have primarily focused on human migration in these examples, an environmental theory of migration will also call attention to the relationship between nonhuman migrants, ideals of nature, and structures of sovereignty. Take, for instance, the case of La Ciénega de Santa Clara. As I have previously alluded to, the Colorado River has, since the golden era of American dam building, often dried up before reaching its terminus in the Sea of Cortez. The 1944 Water Treaty mandated the United States provide some Colorado River water to Mexico, but the water that was delivered had high levels of salinity that threatened Mexican agriculture (Carrillo-Guerrero et al. 2013). In 1972, minute 242 of the Treaty was signed, which required the United States to deliver water to Mexico that met certain salinity requirements. To meet these requirements, the United States constructed the sixty-mile-long Wellton–Mohawk Canal, which dumps high-salinity agricultural wastewater onto the Santa Clara Slough in Sonoro, Mexico.

The more-than-human was but an afterthought in this self-interested iteration of sovereign power, but a flourishing socioecological community began to develop. This "accidental wetland," as National Geographic recently put it, is today a forty-thousand-acre "maze of marshes and lagoons" (Postel 2013) that provides habitat for more than 266 species of birds (Carrillo-Guerrero et al. 2013, 86). Every winter, more than two hundred thousand migratory waterbirds descend on the largest wetland of the Colorado River Delta (Carrillo-Guerrero et al. 2013, 92). It has become a spot for the local community to "picnic, boat and catch fish" (Postel 2013).

Though our access to nature is mediated by discourse, the realities of the more-than-human world should certainly imbue any resistance with a dose of humility and a reverence for our diverse socioecological surroundings. Sovereign power—despite its enormous reach into contemporary economic structures, political institutions, concepts, and systems of meaning—continually confronts forces, processes, and flows that exceed its grasp. In this regard, migrants reveal the limits of even the most seemingly inescapable forms of power, and they point toward strategies of resistance. These resistances appear to be multiplying and have begun to influence environmentalism, but they require radical interventions to cultivate the state of rebellion needed to bring about socioecological justice. An environmental theory of migration builds on the migratory flows that enter and exit La Cienega de Santa Clara, fleshing out their relationship to other threatened flows such as those of the Cache La Poudre River, examining the structures and processes that endanger both socioecological communities, and creating resistance tethered to the realities of social connection.

# TEAR DOWN
# THOSE WALLS

The title of this book draws from a passage by Édouard Glissant, the Martinican poet, theorist, and activist and one of my major theoretical influences. He begins his seminal work, *Poetics of Relation* ([1990] 1997), with a description of forced migration. He invites the reader to imagine the terror felt by slaves as they were loaded onto ships—"the swirling red of mounting to the deck, the ramp they climbed, the black sun on the horizon, vertigo, the dizzying sky plastered to the waves"— headed toward an abyss they could not comprehend. This initial terror was only the beginning:

> The next abyss was the depths of the sea. Whenever a fleet of ships gave chase to slave ships, it was easiest just to lighten the boat by throwing cargo overboard, weighing it down with balls and chains. These underground signposts mark the course between the Gold Coast and the Leeward Islands. Navigating the green splendor of the sea . . . still brings to mind, coming to light like seaweed, these lowest depths, these deeps, with their punctuation of scarcely corroded balls and chains. In actual fact the abyss is a tautology: the entire ocean, the entire sea gently collapsing in the end into the pleasures of sand, make one vast beginning, but a beginning whose time is marked by these balls and chains gone green. (6)

In this passage, Glissant begins to underscore the relations between knowledge (the slave confronting a reality that is unintelligible), the violences of sovereign power (the reduction of African populations to mere cargo), the exclusionary historical residues that continue to haunt the present (the "balls and chains gone green"), and the potentialities that lie in new political conjunctures (the "vast beginning"). His poetics of relation is both a critique of ethnocentric epistemologies that reduce subaltern populations to objects to be grasped in their essence and a normative project that seeks to harness the creative potential of global encounters.

Today's migrants confront a far different reality, are subject to different modes of sovereign violence, and struggle under the weight of different histories than Glissant's description of the forced migration of African slaves. Nonetheless, his project is, I would argue, as relevant to the struggles for migrants' rights and socioecological justice as it is to the struggle for autonomy and authority in the Antilles. To extend Glissant's poetics of relations to these unique experiences, though, the divergent pathways through which sovereign violence, exclusion, and abandonment proceed must be considered. Critically, this book has suggested that "nature"—constructed as a source of intrinsic value—is today emerging as a prominent site of discursive struggle that is deployed by societal interests of many stripes. Some of these interests have violent, exclusionary goals. Others do not but are nonetheless persuaded by the epistemological influence of nationalized ideals of nature or the progressive connotation that a commitment to nature entails. Glissant's *balls and chains gone green* have morphed into *border walls gone green*.

## ENVIRONMENTAL RESTRICTIONISM AS STATECRAFT FROM BELOW

One of the fundamental challenges for scholars and activists who value socioecological justice is to be cognizant of how discourses of ecological exception interweave with exclusionary configurations of sovereignty in ways that attempt to reduce marginalized populations to "bare life." American debates over the environmental impacts of immigration provide a unique lens into this discursive struggle. Each of the environmental restrictionist discourses that I have outlined relies on a construction of crisis, and yet each conceptualizes and works to reconfigure the relationship between nature and sovereignty in ways that differ dramatically.

In teasing out these relationships, I have identified three discourses of environmental restrictionism that variably attempt to reconfigure American sovereignty. First, the discourse of *social nativism* is employed by xenophobic and/or white nationalist groups who are either engaged in environmental restrictionist alliances or are debating the role that a commitment to nature might play in the philosophy of the far right.

Although there appears to be genuine discussion among social nativists over the possibility of committing to protecting nature, they have typically deployed nature instrumentally to advance their xenophobic, racist agendas. Nonetheless, nature plays two central roles in the efforts of social nativists to construct a vision of the Anglo-European Nation in peril: functioning (1) as a marker of order—designating a natural law (declared by God, Science, or the Founding Fathers)—that is linked with the Anglo-European nation and (2) as a symbol of anarchy that is attached to non-European cultures. Within the social nativist discourse, the ethos of sovereignty is overtly racialized, and nonwhite bodies are constructed as biopolitical threats to the vitality of the white nation. As the resonance of this overtly exclusionary discourse is limited to the far right, social nativists seek out alliances with more moderate immigration-reduction organizations and turn to alternative discourses.

Second, the discourse of *ecological nativism* is employed by anti-immigrant organizations such as the Carrying Capacity Network and Social Contract Press and, at times, also appears in the publications of mainstream immigration-reduction organizations, such as the Federation for American Immigration Reform. The crisis constructed by econativists is simultaneously national and natural; the econativist nature becomes intelligible through a combination of Darwinian, Malthusian, and romantic epistemological practices that are all intricately woven into culturally essentialist ideals of nationhood. The notion of "cultural carrying capacity," in particular, serves to project ecological concerns over population growth onto the social register—providing natural scientific legitimation for projects seeking cultural homogeneity. Since the 1980s, econativism has provided a crucial institutional and discursive bridge that—by appealing to both nativists and environmentalists—has served to expand the ranks of the American anti-immigrant movement.

Today, however, the ethos of sovereignty sculpted by econativists, influenced by the lifeboat ethics of Hardin, relies too heavily on cultural essentializations to effectively persuade mainstream American progressives and environmentalists (who have grown cognizant of how cultural discourses can further neoracist logics). As a consequence, I contend that restrictionist organizations in the United States are currently transitioning to a third discourse—that of *ecocommunitarian restrictionism*. Ecocommunitarianism plays ontological, epistemological, and strategic roles within the current environmental restrictionist movement. On one hand, this is the lens through which many environmentalists who are sympathetic to the restrictionist argument view the immigration–environment connection.[1] On the other hand, this is the discourse that the broader environmental restrictionist coalition (i.e., social and ecological nativists) strategically turns to in its efforts to expand its support by appealing to American greens and progressives.

Ecocommunitarians articulate a narrative of socially and ecologically "progressive" communities under attack by neoliberal globalization. Their attempt to reconfigure sovereignty resonates in many ways with progressive attempts to "green sovereignty": explicitly disavowing interpersonal racism; embracing a multicultural, interspecies, intergenerational nation; cultivating attachments to "wild places"; and seeking to construct a socially democratic "steady state." Their *direct* target is not immigrants but the deterritorializing impulses of neoliberal globalization—with which they carefully link immigrants. The ethos of sovereignty articulated by ecocommunitarians is far more nuanced and socially acceptable than those of the other two discourses of restrictionism. And yet, the transnational political economic linkages that ecocommunitarians recognize in their description of how sovereignty has been reconfigured by neoliberal globalization are cleansed from the analytic slate as they move into their consideration of ethical obligation. This conception of ethical obligation is driven by an overarching narrative of ecological exception—an assertion that at the current political conjuncture, the natural crisis facing "us" is so grave that the normal social concerns that drive American progressives' desire to be inclusive must be suspended.

As a consequence, despite their apparently sensible rhetoric, the prescriptions that many organizations employing ecocommunitarian logics advocate remain draconian, and the postracial terrain that they invoke is overshadowed by the racialized realities of the environmental injustices that they perpetuate. For this reason, I contend that although ecocommunitarianism might initially appear a kinder, gentler restrictionism, it is, in fact, a more dangerous, insidious restrictionism. Although my analysis of the relationship between nature and sovereignty is focused on the American case, the ecocommunitarian logic is visible in several national-level organizations, including England's Population

Matters (formally the Optimum Population Trust, and endorsed by James Lovelock and David Attenborough) and Australia's Sustainable Population Party (which recently fielded a full slate of candidates in parliamentary elections).[2] Ecocommunitarianism is *the* environmental restrictionist logic of the twenty-first century.

## SOVEREIGNTY, MIGRATION, AND RESISTANCE

The vast majority of responses to restrictionism—by academics, activists, and the media—have missed this shift to ecocommunitarianism. Responses have relied on a discourse of global environmental justice that clings to an ideal of nature that is cleansed of cultural pollution and provides a clear pathway to deterritorialized emancipation. Some of these opponents mobilize visions of ecocosmopolitanism (or "planetary patriotism"), rejecting any attempt to green sovereignty as inherently ecologically and socially destructive, and asserting that a real commitment to the facts of nature leads "us" toward global modes of governance and cosmopolitan communities. Others embed their commitment to the global realities of ecosystemic interconnection in an attempt to reconfigure sovereign nation-states in more inclusive, ecological directions.

While I am broadly sympathetic to the aims of these opponents of restrictionism, I have argued that the overarching discourse that immigrants' rights and environmental justice activists have sculpted is political disabling on several grounds. First, it does not reflexively consider how genuine commitments to nature may actually intersect with socially exclusionary projects. As a consequence, it has failed to identify and respond to the most sophisticated iterations of environmental restrictionism—those most likely to influence American environmentalists (i.e., ecocommunitarianism). Second, in continuing to forcefully articulate a distinction between (emancipatory) nature and (exclusionary) culture, the ecocosmopolitan discourse unwittingly reinforces the very binary that environmental restrictionism depends on. More precisely, the discourse displaces racism and nationalism onto the terrain of culture rather than considering the ways in which these social constructs might be woven into the very foundations of environmental thought.

Despite these general deficiencies, however, the efforts of a number of environmental justice organizations, activists, and scholars provide insight into a potentially transformative alternative that enables a different reading of the relationship between nature and sovereignty—one structured around the realities of contemporary transnational migration. Engaging with insights from both social theorists and environmental justice advocates who analyze Mexico–United States migration, I made the case that a transnational mode of sovereignty driven by a logic of militarized neoliberalism has created socioecological injustices that both drive migration from Mexico and ensure that the lives of migrants in transit and in the United States are precarious. Effectively responding to injustices produced by this dominant form of sovereignty necessitates what Enrique Dussel terms a state of rebellion—a transnational form of popular sovereignty guided by the suffering and excluded. I have argued that in tearing down the border walls that constrain their practice—in abolishing the national and natural boundaries that define American environmentalism—socioecological activists engaged with the realities of migration could work to further this state of rebellion and ensure that it is guided by an ethos of socioecological justice.

## FINAL THOUGHTS

In the American context, recent immigration debates have revealed a schism among the political right. While American conservatism has, in recent years, been dominated by calls for border securitization and anti-immigrant rhetoric, the demographic realities of a growing Latino base, coupled with capital's call for cheap labor, have resulted in a sizeable portion of the right embracing comprehensive immigration reform (albeit in an incredibly flawed form). Among the conservatives favoring immigration reform, the groups who have successfully forged the anti-immigrant consensus on the political right are now being written off as "population-control groups" controlled by "radical environmentalists" (Bier 2013; Johnson 2013). Coupled with the general shift of American labor and environmental groups away from restrictionist positions, one thing is becoming clear: environmental restrictionists are losing.

But the struggle is far from over. As the realities of climate change become ever more apparent, climactic shifts will begin to disrupt geo-politics and profit making as usual, and migrants seeking refuge from areas that are increasingly difficult to inhabit will foster social animus in their receiving communities. If the status quo continues, immigration restriction may again emerge as the low-hanging fruit in climate politics—a "simple" solution that temporarily displaces environmental and social problems without confronting the deep-seated structures that produce them. Absent a massive resistance, more border walls are in our future.

To counter the drive for border walls gone green, environmental politics requires a radical reformulated "we." Who, then, will be the "we" of an environmentalism of migration? The answer is that it depends. The "we" of environmentalism ought to be a project-in-motion cultivated through engagement with a range of human and more-than-human others. The we at a particular time and place depends on careful consideration of the political conjuncture (perhaps, at times, this *we* won't include *me*). Interestingly, toward the end of the *Poetics of Relation*, Glissant ([1990] 1997) recognizes the appeal of a community formed around ecology. In discussing this potentiality, he distinguishes between "ecological mysticism," which represents "mankind's drive to extend to the planet Earth the former sacred thought of Territory," and a "politics of ecology," which "will bear the germ of criticism of territorial thought" and serve as "a driving force for the relational interdependence of all lands" (146). The latter alternative—far from signaling an abstract embrace of globalism or cosmopolitanism—moves toward a more nuanced reading of socionatural interconnection that is worthy of critical reflection. It is this "we" that an environmentalism of migration must embrace:

> I am doing the same thing in the way I say *we*—organizing this work around it. Is this some community *we* rhizome into fragile connection to a place? Or a total *we* involved in the activity of the planet? Or an ideal *we* drawn into the swirls of poetics? Who is this intervening *they*? *They* that is Other? Or *they* the neighbors? Or *they* whom I imagine when I try to speak? The *we*s and *they*s are an evolving. . . . They find full sense in the extension of discourse, in which peremptory abstract notions gain full force only through force of accumulation, since they cannot burn in the bodies charcoal live. The word mass burns, from its amassing. They find full sense in the echo of the land, where *morne*

meets beach, where the motifs are entwined in a single vegetation, like words off the page. (206–7, italics original)

The "wes" of an environmentalism of migration "are an evolving," but the immediate challenge is to confront the power of a dominant mode of sovereignty that operates through militarized neoliberalism, a form of power that depends on the continued construction of border walls. Resistance, then, requires a global alliance geared toward tearing down border walls of all sorts—including the green variety.

# ACKNOWLEDGMENTS

This book, like most, was a long time in the making, and I owe many people thanks. The project began in 2008 in a conversation with my PhD advisor, Dimitris Stevis, about an ongoing debate in northern Colorado related to the environmental impacts of immigration. It then took root over the course of my dissertation research from 2008 to 2012 in the Department of Political Science at Colorado State University—a process helped along by a fantastic group of professors and grad school colleagues. My dissertation committee—Dimitris, Bill Chaloupka, Brad MacDonald, Eric Ishiwata, and Kate Browne—frequently went above and beyond the call of duty in guiding me through the research and writing process. Several other professors at CSU, including Jared Orsi and Steve Mumme, offered helpful feedback along the way. Cheryl Distaso and Rebecca Poswolsky helped me make sense of the contemporary American immigration restriction movement. Keith Lindner, whom I first met in an environmental politics class at CSU in 2007, has been a continual source of ideas and constructive criticism. Keith read over most of the chapters—several of them multiple times—and offered feedback that dramatically improved their intellectual rigor.

After finishing my PhD in 2012, I took a teaching position at Northern Arizona University in the Department of Politics and International Affairs. Here in Flagstaff, I've been fortunate enough to be surrounded by a supportive group of colleagues. There are too many to name individually, but a few warrant specific mention. As department chairs, Geeta Chowdhry (who exuded kindness and warmth), Fred Solop, and Lori Poloni-Staudinger all did what they could to provide me with the flexibility to write in a teaching-intensive position. Rom Coles, Luis Fernandez, Emily Howard, and Sean Parson each read over multiple chapters of the book and offered constructive comments and critiques. And although I didn't know him personally, as a political theorist involved in immigrants' rights activism in Flagstaff, it's been impossible not to be influenced by the legacy of Joel Olson. In addition to my indebtedness to his excellent analyses of contemporary racism, working with the Repeal Coalition—which Joel cofounded—has been a constant reminder that this book represents more than a theoretical puzzle. Anti-immigrant sentiment continues to have very real (unjust, dehumanizing, and often horrifying) impacts on the lives of many—a reality that needs to be resisted and, ultimately, transformed.

Through the process of turning what began as a dissertation into a book, the editorial team at the University of Minnesota Press has been a pleasure to work with: Pieter Martin continually provided useful feedback and guidance (which I very much needed as a first-time author); the editorial board offered engaged and helpful comments; and the two reviewers, John Meyer and Chad Lavin, were tough but incredibly constructive (exactly what one hopes for in reviewers). The book is much stronger for their suggestions.

Last, but not least, I thank my friends and family. My mom and dad, sisters Julia and Laura, brother-in-law Ken, and niece Olivia have been supportive throughout all of my academic endeavors. More importantly, though, being around my family serves as a wonderful reminder that there are more important things in life than work. Finally, my partner Mary has been everything that one could ask for in a companion; her kindness, understanding, and encouragement have kept me going through the ups and downs of life in the neoliberal academy.

Any errors in spelling or grammar can be attributed to my cat, Copernicus, and his constant desire to lie on the keyboard while I'm attempting to type. All other errors are mine alone.

# NOTES

## INTRODUCTION

1 *Colbert Report,* April 25, 2012.

2 For instance, in introducing a 1994 immigration bill, Harry Reid observed that "our resources are being used up, and our environment is being significantly harmed by the rapidly growing population in the United States.... Fully half of this population growth is a result of immigration" (Reimers 1998, 62). Former Democratic congressman Anthony Beilenson has also been a vocal environmental restrictionist, going so far as to introduce the Population Stabilization and Reproductive Health Act (U.S. Congress 1995; Beilenson 1996).

3 I define *environmental restrictionism*—referred to by others as *anti-immigrant environmentalism* or *immigration-reduction environmentalism*—as the argument that immigration poses a threat to the natural environment of a given, territorially bounded area (in this case, the United States) and, for this reason, ought to be curtailed.

4 The term *liberal* has a varied history, and in the American context, its mainstream usage is not consistent with the general historical meaning of the term. Thus the liberal of contemporary American politics differs from the liberal of classical political economy or contemporary international relations theory. To avoid confusion, I generally use the term *progressive* to refer to the mainstream American left; however, there are several points where an interviewee or text that I am analyzing uses the term *liberal* in reference to contemporary American politics. I employ footnotes to clarify, when necessary.

5 This certainly was not always the case—environmentalism was once a bipartisan commitment among both political elites and the broader American public. This began to change as the Reagan administration worked to extend the "culture war" into environmentalism, and it has only worsened in recent years as global warming has been successfully transformed into a matter of identity politics on the right. Today, as

Anderson (2011, 551) observes, "members of environmental groups belong almost exclusively (and increasingly) to the traditional constituency of the Democrats, not the Republicans."

6  For example, a recent article in the *Washington Post* expresses surprise that Michael Hethmon, one of the architects of Arizona's draconian anti-immigrant bill (SB1070), came to the anti-immigrant movement as "a bookish lawyer afraid that immigrants would overburden the environment" (Fahrenthold 2012).

7  Ecocentrists believe that nature has intrinsic value above and beyond any use humans can derive from it. I use the scare quotes to indicate my position that all attempts to "speak for" or "represent" nature are influenced by cultural norms (although, as I detail later, the more-than-human realm retains a material autonomy from human projects).

8  As Cynthia Weber (1995, 3) writes, "sovereignty marks not the location of the foundational entity of international relations theory but a site of political struggle. This struggle is the struggle to fix the meaning of sovereignty in such a way as to constitute a particular state . . . with particular boundaries, competencies and legitimacies available to it. This is not a one-time occurrence which fixes the meaning of sovereignty and statehood for all time in all places; rather, this struggle is repeated in various forms at numerous spatial and temporal locales."

9  Stuart Hall (as cited by Nelson 1999, 3) explains the concept of "articulation" as follows: "a connection or link which is not necessarily given in all cases, as a law or a fact of life, but which requires particular conditions of existence to appear at all, which has to be positively sustained by specific processes. . . . It is also important that an articulation between different practices does not mean that they become identical or that the one is dissolved into the other. Each retains its distinct determinations and conditions of existence. However, once an articulation is made, the two practices can function together, not as an 'immediate entity' . . . but as 'distinctions within a unity.'"

10  My analysis of sovereignty, it should be noted, does not focus sustained attention on concrete instances of this coercive force being deployed; rather, it examines the discursive processes through which authority backed by coercive force is constituted and legitimated. The coercive force itself is carried out by a range of state and societal actors, but my argument is that discursive struggles over the shape and content of sovereignty create the conditions of existence for these violent actions. The actors performing sovereign power on a day-to-day basis—for example, the Border Patrol dumping out jugs of water left in the desert

by humanitarian volunteers, the local police making Latinos "show their papers" when they appear in public, the anti-immigrant politicians calling for policies that will force "illegal aliens" to self-deport—simply do not exist in the same form without the restrictionist activists and the discourses that they have deployed to foment so much anger against immigrant populations.

11 Foucault ([1978] 1990, 142–43) writes, "For the first time in history . . . biological existence was reflected in political existence; the fact of living was no longer an inaccessible substrate that only emerged from time to time, amid the randomness of death and its fatality; part of it passed into knowledge's field of control and power's sphere of intervention. Power would no longer be dealing simply with legal subjects over whom the ultimate dominion was death, but with living beings, and the mastery it would be able to exercise over them would have to be applied at the level of life itself; it was the taking charge of life, more than the threat of death, that gave power its access even to the body."

12 Contrary to many readings, bare life is not what the Greeks called *zoē* (mere biological life) but a "zone of indistinction" between *zoē* and *bios* (politically qualified life). As Vaughan-Williams (2009, 738) argues, "sovereign power depends upon creating and exploiting zones of indistinction in which subjects' recourse to conventional legal and political protection is curtailed" (see also Ziarek 2008, 90–91).

13 For example, immigration scholar Radhika Mongia (2007) asserts that the conventional account of sovereignty as a universal principle formulated in "the West" and spread throughout the world effectively erases the violence of a colonial encounter that remains constitutive of contemporary structures of authority.

14 In this sense, my approach to sovereignty employs what might be termed a Foucauldian reading of Agamben. As Belcher et al. (2008, 499–500) argue, the areas of convergence between the two thinkers are often lost in comparisons that overstate Agamben's Schmittian roots. These differences are further augmented by simplistic readings of Foucault that draw rigid distinctions between his micropolitical (i.e., disciplinary, biopolitical) emphasis and the supposed macropolitics of sovereignty. As Lazzarato (2006, 13) argues, "Foucault does not neglect his analysis of sovereignty, he merely asserts that the grounding force will not be found on the side of power, since power is 'blind and weak' but on the side of the forces that constitute the 'social body' or 'society.' Sovereign power is blind and weak but that does not signify, by any means, that it lacks efficacy: its impotence is ontological."

15  As political theorist Ronnie Lipschutz (1998, 112) observes, "on one
    hand, nature—the material world—imposes constraints on human
    activities and, in a sense, limits what can be freely and autonomously
    done. On the other hand, Nature—the reified construction that seeks to
    account for power and hierarchy—is invoked to naturalize the control,
    autonomy, and authority exercised by some human beings."

16  The ecological efficacy of nationalism is debated by many greens. In
    making the case for a greener sovereignty, James Meadowcroft (2005,
    12) nonetheless contends that "a nationally oriented eco-state seems
    almost a contradiction in terms." Eckersley (2007a) disagrees, asserting
    that until cosmopolitan ideals become more widespread, the sense of
    solidarity necessary for a flourishing international political community
    will be lacking, and a form of "cosmopolitan nationalism" is the best
    hope for greens.

17  In fairness, at several points, Smith does assert the need to reject these
    simplistic assertions of Nature's sovereignty (see, e.g., Smith 2008, 13),
    but he continues to maintain that a particular iteration of radical eco-
    politics evades sovereign power. Whereas Agamben (2005, 88) attempts
    to escape the logic of sovereignty through metaphysics (the search for
    "a word that does not bind, that neither commands nor prohibits any-
    thing, but says only itself"), Smith (2011, 95) reverts to naturalism. The
    alternative that he privileges is an "anarcho-primitivism," articulated
    around a call to "wildness," that "is a life affirming negativity with no
    use that resists totalizing attempts to impose authority and order on
    life itself."

18  I am referring to Foucault's (1980, 121) famous observation that "what
    we need is a political philosophy that isn't erected around the problem
    of sovereignty, nor therefore around the problems of law and prohibi-
    tion. We need to cut off the King's head: in political theory that has still
    to be done." Smith ostensibly turns to biopolitics to provide insight into
    the micropolitical practices through which populations are abandoned
    to bare life, and yet his final depiction of sovereignty looks strangely like
    that of realist international relations theorists. The sovereign nation-
    state operates according to a logic of its own, insulated from all social
    forces, except those reinforcing anarchy, self-interest, and (for Smith)
    capitalism.

19  Take, for instance, biologist and environmental activist John Cairns
    Jr. In a 2003 article, he argues that the "sovereignty of both individu-
    als and nation states is destructive of the interdependent web of life
    of which humans are a part" (71). The following year, he wrote an

article in the *Social Contract Press* arguing that the United States should exclude immigrants on the grounds that "each nation-state has the responsibility to ensure that its citizens are not compelled to leave it to become a burden on another nation-state" (Cairns 2004). Similarly, George Sessions, whose seminal work of deep ecology makes the case for bioregional thought (Devall and Sessions 1985, 148–49), remains a member of CAPS's advisory board and has spoken out against immigration. Another member of the CAPS advisory board is Dave Foreman, who currently runs the Rewilding Institute. These are but three of many examples of bioregionalist or primitivist thinkers who reject sovereignty (in the abstract) while embracing the use of sovereign power (in practice) to limit immigration.

20  It might be objected that gender or capitalism would also be an appropriate area of emphasis. Though these concepts do frequently enter into my analysis, I chose to focus more sustained theoretical attention on race, in part because there are already excellent analyses of the role of gender (Silliman and King 1999; Hartmann 2004; Urban 2008) and capitalism (Angus and Butler 2011) in environmental restrictionism.

21  These racial divisions between white and nonwhite have been reinforced through discourses of sovereignty imbued with conceptual dichotomies—for example, domestic–foreign, friend–enemy, civilized–savage—through which nonwhite groups have been constructed as deviant, backward, and/or dangerous (thus rendering them in need of normalization, civilization, coercive socialization, or outright exclusion). That national immigration policies have reflected these racialized modes of sovereignty is not surprising. Radhika Mongia (1999, 528), for instance, contends that the national border is not a natural component of sovereignty but a sociopolitical barrier that actually emerges, and is continually reproduced, out of racialized anxieties over migration. Analyses of twentieth-century nativism support this reading, demonstrating how dominant racial imaginaries reduced Mexican immigrants, in particular, to "aliens" and "illegals," while facilitating ethical sympathy and legal tolerance for migrant communities deemed white (see, e.g., Ngai 2003, 58).

22  Neoracism works through historical erasure—for example, arguing against immigration on the grounds of a "traditional national culture" rather than a biological race (ignoring the fact that the "traditional national culture" was constructed in opposition to specific races) or arguing against affirmative action on the grounds of "equality under the law" (forgetting that the law has historically been deployed to

subordinate specific races). Thus certain signifiers have been *historically imbued* with racial assumptions but have been *historically disconnected* from dominant perceptions of racism (as overt, violent, interpersonal, dependent on biological arguments, etc.). Sovereignty and nature are two such signifiers.

## 1. WE HAVE ALWAYS BEEN RESTRICTIONISTS

1  Malthus (1826) approvingly cites Franklin in his second *Essay on the Principle of Population.*

2  I use the "we" here to denote that there have always been varieties of environmentalism that have intersected with restrictionism. I fully recognize that the environmental movement has a complex, heterogeneous history. That said, there is an overwhelming tendency among "progressive" or "radical" greens to assert that there exists a reformist environmental tradition (going back to the capital-friendly conservationist ethic of Pinchot) that has been bound up in social exclusion and a radical ecological tradition (going back to the antigrowth preservationist ethic of Muir) that is emancipatory. As my analysis shows, the reality is more complex.

3  Adam Rome (2008, 433) writes that from "1880 until 1924, when immigration was restricted, almost 25 million people came to the United States from other nations."

4  Hornaday was a member of the Audubon Society and the Boone and Crockett Club. He was also director of the New York Zoological Park, where he famously displayed Congolese pygmy Ota Benga in a cage (Spiro 2009).

5  I detail Grant's environmentalist, eugenicist, and nativist credentials in what follows (see Spiro 2009; Allen 2013).

6  Although ideals of romanticism (where nature is plentiful, intrinsically valuable, and sublime) exist, in many respects, in opposition to Darwinism (where nature is scarce, violent, and rendered intelligible through science), the two came to intersect in the writings of certain greens (such as Grant and Goethe) through a shared commitment to *purity*—both national and natural.

7  Darwin's cousin Francis Galton coined the term *eugenics* in his 1883 work *Inheritance of Human Faculties*. Ross (1998, 60) writes that Galton "conceived it as the means by which the physical and moral attributes of a population might be improved by selective breeding which favoured the increased genetic representation of those who were

considered to possess more of what he variously called 'natural ability' and 'civic worth.'"

8 To be clear, I am referring here to the Progressive movement (which, in today's terminology, would not be considered "progressive" in many respects).

9 For example, during the famous debate over the damming of Hetch Hetchy, Grant and Hornaday split with Gifford Pinchot. Grant and Pinchot reportedly "never spoke to each other again" (Spiro 2009, 61).

10 Davenport, a prominent naturalist, was a member of the American Bison Society and the American Society of Mammalogists (Spiro 2009, 392–93).

11 The quarantine—which Stern implies resulted from racialized anxieties far more than from the real threat of typhus or smallpox—was a process where migrants were stripped naked; checked for lice and typhus; showered in a mixture of soap, kerosene, and water; vaccinated for small pox; and given a general medical examination. Additionally, their clothes were "disinfected" and returned wrinkled or ruined (Stern 2005, 62–63).

12 Mounted Quarantine Guards were charged with vaccinating migrants they found or bringing migrants who appeared sick in to quarantine plants (Stern 2005, 71).

13 Despite this economic need for labor, anti-immigrant sentiment remained high throughout the period. The overtly racist Operation Wetback was a compromise between nativists and industry, with Mexican workers often deported and then immediately enrolled as Braceros (Massey, Durand, and Malone 2003, 37; Ngai 2004, 155–56; Nevins [2002] 2010, 39).

14 Specifically, the Immigration and Nationality Act of 1952 (McCarran–Walter) and the Immigration and Nationality Act of 1965 (Hart–Cellar).

15 The law put into place a twenty thousand per country quota in the western hemisphere. Ngai notes that, by contrast, in the early 1960s, annual "legal" Mexican migration comprised some 200,000 braceros and 35,000 regular admissions for permanent residency. The fact that "illegal" immigration increased dramatically after Hart–Cellar should surprise no one.

16 It is worth noting here that the United States was restricting immigration from Mexico at the same time as neo-Malthusianism was being used to justify policies that significantly increased immigration. Eric Ross (1998, 176–77) observes that "during the 1960's, as foreign investment in Mexico more than doubled, Mexican immigration increased."

As foreign agricultural firms—Campbells, Del Monte, Green Giant, Ralston Purina, and so on—acquired land in Mexico, they "introduced new commercial crops that were heavily dependent on irrigation and mechanized methods of cultivation and harvesting and required far less human labor than traditional rain-fed agriculture" (176–77).

17  Ehrlich's *Population Bomb* contains three fictional scenarios. Scenario 1 discusses a state of emergency that occurs because of resource shortages caused by overpopulation (eventually leading to nuclear war). At several points during the scenario, the issue of urban riots emerges in ways that contain (scarcely veiled) racial coding: "Margaret Andrews had had very few choices in her life since Richard had been killed in the riots. He had died because of the things she had loved him for; his refusal to knuckle under to the dominant white society and, especially, his feeling of community with the oppressed people of the Third World. . . . The clarity with which the Population Control Law was aimed at the blacks and the poor had been the last straw. Even though they had carefully planned their two children, Richard had refused to speak out against the cries of revolution in the ghetto high school where he taught history. His patience was at an end, and his life soon ended also, snuffed out by a random bullet fired in the worst civil disorder in the history of the United States" (Ehrlich 1968, 54). Ehrlich's overarching point seems to be that a politically correct desire for social justice was the downfall of Richard Andrews. His "liberal" racial commitments were ultimately misplaced, rendered meaningless amid the inevitable racial chaos provoked by the population bomb.

18  For example, Abbey's anti-immigrant screeds led a faction called the Biotic Baking Brigade to publish a letter in the *Earth First!* journal expressing regret that they'd never delivered a "lovely refried-bean pie unto the venerated visage of the late lamented author [Ed Abbey]" (Park and Pellow 2011, 159).

19  *VDARE* is a white nationalist webzine named after Virginia Dare, allegedly the first European child born in the new world.

20  As I detail in chapter 4, however, both the Sierra Club and Earth First! have, in recent years, shifted their positions dramatically.

## 2. NATURALIZING NATIVISM

1  It should be noted that many analyses of the far right differentiate nativism from white nationalism. Although there is certainly variability among the individuals and organizations who I categorize as

social nativists, their statements all suggest a commitment to a country dominated by Anglo-Europeans. Some draw on more "cultural" logics, and some on overt racism, but the line dividing nativism from white nationalism is tenuous at best.

2 See, for instance, Brenda Walker's site, Immigration's Human Cost, http://www.immigrationshumancost.org/.

3 The original content analysis was done in spring 2011, but the articles highlighted in November 2014 were virtually identical: "Black St. Louis Street Gang Issues Video Threatening to Murder White People," "75 Year Old Woman Killed in Racial Hate Crime," "Two White Females Attacked in Racially Motivated Hate Crime in Saint Paul, MN," "UAE Denounces Obama Backed Muslim Group as a Terrorist Organization."

4 Walker reports, "My letter from the Sierra Club opened with the accusatory, 'It is reported that your public statements, your website, your postings to VDARE.com, and your reactions to the immigration debate in the Sierra Club are replete with examples of ethnically and racially derogatory language. We do not welcome members in the Club who engage in this behavior.'" Walker's reaction—an attempt to "rebut" these accusations—continues to provide ample support for them (2004).

5 Sailer writes, "The Ethnic Phenomenon is the book Karl Marx should have written. Rather than focusing on the relatively minor phenomenon of class, he should have explored the global importance of kinship" (1–2).

6 According to Eberhard (1975, 1–2), kin selection "explains how aid that is self-sacrificing (in terms of classical individual fitness) . . . can evolve if sufficiently beneficial to relatives." Similarly, inclusive fitness is a concept that rationalizes kin selection by taking "into account the individual's total lifetime effect on the gene pool of the succeeding generation(s), both through the production of the individual's own offspring and through effects on the reproduction of other individuals." Ethnic nepotism stretches these concepts, moving away from familial relations to suggest that altruistic behavior toward one's own race makes evolutionary sense if it furthers the vitality of that race.

7 Dawkins's reply is astute: "The National Front was saying something like this, 'kin selection provides the basis for favoring your own race as distinct from other races, as a kind of generalization of favoring your own close family as opposed to other individuals.' Kin selection doesn't do that! Kin selection favors nepotism toward your own immediate close family. It does not favor a generalization of nepotism towards millions of other people who happen to be the same color as you. Even

if it did, I would oppose any suggestion from any group such as the National Front, that whatever occurs in natural selection is therefore morally good and desirable" (as quoted in Miele 1995, para. 52).

8  In illustrating the intersection between nativism and mainstream conservatism, the author approvingly cites John McGinnis's (1997) article "The Origin of Conservatism," from *National Review,* as a "powerful argument for Darwinian biology as a foundation for conservatism."

9  In doing so, he effectively popularized the book within the United States.

10  Volumes of Tanton's writings are archived in the Bentley Historical Library at the University of Michigan. However, some of the more controversial subject matter—including the WITAN memos—is closed to access until April 2035.

11  The following example is illustrative of the logic: "If the nation's drinking water is endangered by contaminated water with 275 million Americans, what will it be like with 400 million? If our national parks are loved to death with 275 million Americans, what will it be like with many more clamoring for admission? If 40% of Americans are breathing air unfit for human consumption with 275 million Americans, what will it be like with a 50% population increase in 50 years?" (Rowe 2002, 60).

12  This article shows just how strange the environmental restrictionist appeal can be: it appeared on the popular leftist site Common Dreams, but Burke has written for *VDARE* (see Brimelow 2000).

13  Eric Neumayer (2006) tests Abernethy's fertility opportunity hypothesis in all non-OECD countries and finds that "the results clearly fail to support the theoretical predictions" (335).

14  He is riffing here, on a speech by Charles Galton Darwin, Darwin's grandson, that is cited in Hardin's "Tragedy of the Commons." Charles Galton Darwin wrote an influential eugenics tract, *The Next Million Years,* in 1952.

15  As Tanton put it, "perhaps this is the first instance in which those with their pants up are going to get caught by those with their pants down" (as quoted by Southern Poverty Law Center 2002a).

16  I do not know whether Mubarak ever held this exact position. Representative Louie Gohmert was recently skewered by John Stewart for articulating a similar position on a live TV interview. As Stewart sarcastically noted, "even Lou Dobbs thinks this viewpoint is extreme." http://www.politicususa.com/en/jon-stewart-anchor-babies.

17  Rees explained to me in a personal interview that he was unaware of

the connections between the CCN (specifically Virginia Abernethy) and white supremacism when he agreed to join the board. He said that he has had no contact with them since, and he repudiated support for any racist project (Rees 2011). As of May 2014, however, his name remains on the CCN website. One wonders if Costanza is aware of the CCN's agenda or if he was similarly duped by the organization's environmentalist-sounding name.

18 Hurlbert's presentation was publicly available through the CAPS website but has since been removed. However, a similar presentation that he gave can be accessed through the Progressives for Immigration Reform website: http://progressivesforimmigrationreform.org/pdf/PFIR_talk_Sept2013Slides.pdf.

## 3. THE CHALLENGE OF ECOCOMMUNITARIAN RESTRICTIONISM

1 Although it is unclear if Northern Coloradoans for Immigration Reduction remains active today, Cafaro was, at the time, a prominent member.

2 I want to emphasize, again, that my analysis of ecocommunitarianism in this chapter applies to ecocommunitarian restrictionists only. There are many iterations of ecocommunitarianism in environmental thought. As I detail in chapter 5, the normative desirability of various ecocommunitarian logics depends on careful consideration of the contexts in which they have developed and are being deployed.

3 Tanton was removed from the board of directors immediately after the article appeared—purportedly for health reasons—but three months later, he reemerged as a member of the board of advisors (Piggott 2011).

4 The ad can be publicly accessed through the Californians for Population Stabilization website: http://www.capsweb.org/about/our-tv-ads/bulldozer-one-americas-best-selling-vehicles.

5 It is here where the divergent meanings of liberalism can be confusing for those not familiar with the specific context. In this case, ecocommunitarian restrictionism appeals to American liberals—that is, the mainstream American left—through a rejection of neoliberal political economics (the extreme free-market ideology that I unpack in the next few pages).

6 To be clear, the authors discussed in the following section (Polanyi, Ruggie, Ong, etc.) are not ecocommunitarians. Rather, they provide a reading of neoliberalism that helps to explain the emergence of ecocommunitarian restrictionism and the discursive strategy that ecocommunitarians have adopted.

7 According to Ong (2006, 4), "in Russia . . . subsidized housing and social rights are preserved even when neoliberal techniques are introduced in urban budgetary practices. At the same time, in Southeast Asia, exceptions to neoliberalism exclude migrant workers from the living standards created by market-driven policies." The same phenomenon is occurring in the United States; the free-market ethos of NAFTA produces more migrants, while hypernationalist sentiment has resulted in policies that have made both the act of migrating and the ability of migrants to live securely once they arrive far more precarious (I discuss this in more detail in chapter 4).

8 Daly is one of many theorists to note that Keynesian, social welfare states are not necessarily environmentally benign. Indeed, the Keynesian state, founded on heavy industrial production and the continued stimulation of consumer demand, has been quite destructive ecologically (see also Eckersley 2004).

9 This is significant. On one hand, a portrayal of "the immigrant"—to effectively mark any human figure as an immigrant—would have to be racialized to be made intelligible to popular imaginaries. Such a racialized depiction, however, would be forcefully critiqued by the progressive audience that ecocommunitarians seek to target. Instead, ALT indicates the destructive force textually; in this medium, one can make the race of the perpetrator clear without even gesturing toward it. The popular perception of immigration in the United States is always already racialized. The term *illegal immigrant,* in particular, immediately conjures up an image of "a Mexican" for many Americans (see Ngai 2003; Chavez 2008).

10 Dinalt simply compares the per capita consumption patterns of different countries with those of the United States and concludes that in moving to the United States, immigrants will adopt "our" consumptive patterns. For example, he asserts that the average American's energy consumption is 508 percent that of the average Mexican's and then concludes that in moving to the United States, this immigrant increases his consumption by 508 percent. This obviously fails to take into account asymmetries in consumption, assumes a static level of consumption in developing states, and presupposes that immigrants will assimilate to this "American" cultural pattern. No empirical evidence is offered for any of these assumptions.

11 In the most polished restrictionist analysis to date, Kolankiewicz and Camarota (2008) begin with these per capita national consumptive statistics but attempt to control for vast asymmetries in consumption

by including per capita income as a variable. The authors use this simple univariate comparison to come to the conclusion that while "$CO_2$ emissions of the average immigrant . . . in the United States are 18% less than those of the average native-born American . . . immigrants in the United States produce an estimated four times more $CO_2$ . . . as they would have in their countries of origin" (1). On this basis, they conclude that immigration to the United States further contributes to global warming. Although this method is no doubt an improvement over the CCN study, it fails to unpack the myriad intervening variables that impact $CO_2$ emissions and assumes a static level of consumption in developing states. While growth in consumption is an ethical imperative for many in the developing world, the study depicts continued poverty for would-be immigrant populations as the de facto "solution" to the crisis of global warming. Indeed, if income alone is the driver of $CO_2$ emissions, then one wonders why immigration would even be brought into the mix? Why not attempt to stop economic growth or upward mobility instead? Immigration is emphasized because the other solutions are not politically viable as a consequence of the undesirable social impacts that would accompany them.

12  For example, despite their shortcomings, Camarota, of the Center of Immigration Studies, recently cited his aforementioned findings in a prepared statement to the House Judiciary Committee's Subcommittee on Immigration and Claims, asserting that "immigration has the effect of transferring population from the less-polluting parts of the world to the more-polluting parts of the world. . . . Thus even if the highest priority is placed on reducing the emission of greenhouse gases worldwide, immigration is still counterproductive" (U.S. Congress 2001, 32).

13  Iris Marion Young (2006, 104–5) critiques the communitarian logic as follows: "critics of the position that limits the scope of obligations of justice to members of a common political order are right to argue that it is arbitrary to consider nation-state membership as a source of obligations of justice. Political communities have evolved in contingent and arbitrary ways that are more connected to power than to moral right. People often stand in dense relationships with others prior to, apart from, or outside political communities."

14  Cafaro is speaking here of domestic environmental laws and regulations and of shifts in consumption.

15  The delinquent, according to Foucault ([1977] 1995, 251), "is distinguished from the offender by the fact that it is not so much his act as his life that is relevant to characterizing him." The delinquent emerges

as a target of power not because of a transgression against the law but a deviation from the norm (252). Whereas nativist groupings target immigrants for their overt "savagery" and call for demonstrations of sovereign force to atone for the immigrant's acts of illegality, ecocommunitarians target immigrants as a consequence of their supposed adoption of unsustainable environmental practices. The immigrant is not an affront to sovereign power but a barrier to the construction of a sustainable society (which thereby necessitates a sovereign intervention).

16 William Ryerson, for example, is former president of the Population Media Center (PMC). Among other strategies, the PMC focuses on voluntary family planning for women in the developing world.

17 Although I would contest the idea that these Clinton-era panels are "progressive," both commissions did conclude that population growth from immigration impacted ecological sustainability. However, neither came remotely close to calling for the concrete proposals that contemporary ecocommunitarians support. Moreover, in a study undertaken as part of the U.S. Commission on Immigration Reform, Ellen Percy Kraly (1995, i) noted that significant data limitations exist and asserted that despite a great deal of "popular commentary" on the matter, "the direct or causal effects of U.S. immigration on the environment have not been established . . . through scientific study." Given the more recent findings of Squalli (2010; 2011) and Price and Feldmeyer (2012), these linkages are even more dubious today.

18 Reflecting on the Deep Ecology Platform, Michael Zimmerman (1994, 26) contends that "done humanely, as deep ecologists insist, reducing population to a desirable level . . . might take up to one thousand years."

19 The working title of Cafaro's upcoming book was originally "Bleeding Hearts and Empty Promises: A Liberal Rethinks American Immigration." http://www.applythebrakes.org/leader_philipcafaro.htm.

20 Gardner's film *GrowthBusters*—a look at the linkages between economic growth and population growth—has attracted a great deal of positive press among environmentalists. Interestingly enough, the nativist webzine *VDARE* also liked the film (Collins 2011). While there is nothing ecocommunitarians can do to stop nativists from promoting their material, they could do much more to demonstrate an awareness of the historical intersections between population control, racism, and nativism. Instead, they explicitly promote a language of color-blindness that doesn't do justice to the way in which population control plays out, even today. For example, Gardner's film does not deal with immigration, but a quick review of the website found links to restrictionist

organizations such as FAIR. The legal arm of FAIR, it should be noted, is headed by Kris Kobach, who was the main author of the Alabama and Arizona laws. In yet another example of the link between racism and contemporary ecocommunitarianism, Progressives for Immigration Reform links to the CCN on its "Resources" page. The CCN, as I detailed in the last chapter, is directed by self-described ethnic separatist Virginia Abernethy. The dark side of population control is readily apparent even on the websites of groups that are so quick to deny it exists. http://www.progressivesforimmigrationreform.org/about-pfir/resources/.

## 4. RESPONDING TO RESTRICTIONISM

1  It is also worth noting that Earth First! has fundamentally changed its tone on immigration over the past ten years. In fact, a whole series of antiborder articles has appeared in the *Earth First!* journal.

2  In laying out this ideal-type discourse, I am identifying general tendencies among opponents of restrictionism; that is, the major thrust of the argument as it has emerged from textual analysis and interviews. There is significant variability, however, and there are opponents who (in different ways) do not fit squarely into this discourse. As I detail in the next chapter, a number of opponents drawing on postcolonial and eco-Marxist logics provide insight into a potentially transformative alternative.

3  Hardt and Negri (2000), for instance, argue that sovereignty is hedged within a global Empire—a networked form of power institutionalized through the actions of the U.S. military, wealthy nation-states, a variety of intergovernmental organizations and agreements (e.g., the World Trade Organization, the International Monetary Fund, the World Bank), transnational corporations, and some civil society organizations.

4  For example, in a document titled *Nativists and Environmentalists: A Timeline,* the SPLC (2010) details how Paul and Anne Erhlich served on the board of advisors of the Federation for American Immigration Reform until 2003. The report continues detailing the linkages between organizations such as Apply the Brakes and individuals with more questionable motives. Apply the Brakes—according to the SPLC—includes greens Roderick Nash and Lester Brown, but also Don Weeden, whose family foundation bankrolls both nativist and environmental groups.

5  The idea that immigrants are "closer to nature" is expressed by an activist depicted in the CNC's recent film *The Green War on Immigrants*

(2010). The notion that nature "thrives on diversity" was advanced by a well-intentioned audience member at a public presentation in which I recently took part (Center for Justice, Peace, and the Environment, October 12, 2009). The sentiment that nature "heeds no borders" is common but can be found in Potok (2010) and Earth First! (2011).

6 Some activists—particularly those influenced by ecoanarchism—wed a cosmopolitan vision of political community to a local or bioregional mode of governance. A recent *Earth First!* editorial, for example, argued against environmental politics constrained by national borders: "Solidarity with immigrants against borders is one of the most practical and relevant places for the biocentrist—deep ecologist, eco-anarchist, Earth First!er . . . or whatever you may call yourself—to present our vision of the world beyond civilization. The border is not just a line between two places. It's a scar on the earth, and in our lives, where empire and ecocide have met" (Earth First! 2011). This call to action and solidarity is powerful and reflects a laudable, ongoing attempt within Earth First! to integrate commitments to environmental protection and social justice. But what of this borderless world "beyond civilization" to which biocentrism supposedly leads us? Such a logic provides little guidance, instead continuing to project emancipation onto the ontological terrain of nature (which is asserted to provide unmediated direction into the actions that should guide ecological resistance).

## 5. TOWARD AN ENVIRONMENTAL POLITICAL THEORY OF MIGRATION

1 In this chapter, I use the term *transnational migration* rather than *immigration*. I do so because immigrants only exist from the perspective of the nation-state, and I am trying to move discussion of the migration beyond a statist framework.

2 The vital role played by immigrants in building Fort Collins did not mean that they were welcomed with open arms. While a shifting racial terrain enabled the German Russian immigrants to rapidly integrate into the broader Fort Collins community, the Mexican community faced intense and sustained discrimination (Donato 2003). Instead of the social inclusion, free time, and wealth promised by the films, the new immigrants encountered a world littered with admonitions of "white trade only" and "no dogs or Mexicans" (Donato 2003; Thomas 2003, iii). Today the signs are gone, but the forms of sovereign power localized in this place continue to produce displacement, exclusion, and environmental injustice. Unlike the town hall meetings of the past, however, these unjust practices are legitimated not by the overt racism

and sovereign violence that sustained Jim Crow but, in part, on the ostensibly progressive commitments to wilderness and place.

3 Spatially, it reveals patterns of transnational interconnection that constructed the community of Fort Collins (and the "wild" river that sustains it), while, temporally, the history of these transnational interconnections shatters the nationalistic "we" invoked by environmental restrictionists.

4 My approach to analyzing social (inter)connection is heavily influenced by Iris Marion Young's (2006) "social connection model of global justice." Building on Young, this chapter aims to parse out how contemporary social connection is embedded in structures of sovereignty that are dependent on particular natural–cultural relations.

5 Just how many migrants climate change will likely produce is hotly debated. The most recent Intergovernmental Panel on Climate Change report downplayed "alarmist predictions" (i.e., predictions from groups like Christian Aid that had projected up to 1 billion climate refugees) but still warned that climate change would increase displacement (Christian Aid 2007; Tacoli 2009; Intergovernmental Panel on Climate Change 2014).

6 Liberal institutionalists argue that it is possible for sovereign nation-states to create international institutions (or "regimes") that lessen the pull of international anarchy by providing states a venue in which to share information, communicate, and ultimately discover areas of mutually beneficial cooperation.

7 In contrast with a Fordist mode of production (operating through assembly lines, mass production, and wages high enough to buy the material products one produced), a post-Fordist economy functions through just-in-time production, increased mechanization, reliance on flexible labor forces, and the production of immaterial goods (e.g., knowledge, ideas, forms of communication).

8 In this sense, the ability to negotiate an "exception to neoliberalism" (Ong 2006)—to carve out spaces protected from market encroachment or to promote social and environmental protections for specific human and nonhuman populations—is a product not only of one's position within the global division of labor but also of how the social status of one's labor meshes with privileged national conceptions of nature. Put differently, the ability of diverse populations to reconfigure this sovereign assemblage dominated by militarized neoliberalism is dependent on their location within nationalized *natural imaginaries*.

9 This apparent contradiction between free trade and the restricted flow of labor has long marked border policy (stretching back to at least the

1920s). To give one more recent example, 1994 marked both the passage of NAFTA and a reformulated border control policy. At the same time that NAFTA was implemented, the Immigration and Naturalization Service was launching a new policy initiative that focused on securitizing traditional ports of entry and pushing migrants into more sparsely populated, rural areas. In 1996, Congress passed the Illegal Immigration Reform and Immigrant Responsibility Act, which doubled the size of the Border Patrol and funded the construction of initial stretches of border fencing. Since then, the militarization has been furthered by the Patriot Act, the Enhanced Border Security Act, and the Real ID Act (for more detailed analyses, see Andreas 1996, 1998–99; Massey, Durand, and Malone 2003; Coleman 2005; 2007).

10  It might be objected that my use of the terms *human* and *nonhuman* reinforces the very binary between nature and culture that I am trying to disturb. My position here is that the natural and cultural are intimately connected; the materiality of the nonhuman is continually reshaped by a range of cultural projects, while our cultural ideals and institutions (like sovereignty) are imbued with conceptions of nature and shaped by natural forces. And yet, while I avoid the term *Nature* as a universal signifier employed to capture the vast multiplicity of the nonhuman realm (without mediation from culture), I think that it makes sense to speak of particular nonhuman flows, objects, and forces. Within an ontology founded on socionatures, my reference to the nonhuman is a way of recognizing difference within the fraught constraints of our language. As posthumanists remind us, the line between nonhuman and human is continually blurred; however, a description of a "post-human assemblage"—like the United States–Mexico border region or La Cienega de Santa Clara—need also to recognize the specificity of its constituent parts if it is to avoid the pitfall of reducing nature to a purely social construction. Our access to the nonhuman (or "more than human") may be mediated by discourse, but that is not to deny that there exist lives that exceed human control.

11  Thus, at the same time as economic integration was driving migration, for many—particularly "low-skilled" Mexican workers—cross-border movement was growing both more difficult and dangerous. From 1998 to 2012, more than fifty-five hundred migrants died trying to cross the border (Anderson 2013). Making matters worse, a successful crossing, today more than ever, far from guarantees a peaceful existence on the other side: American deportations doubled, from roughly two hundred thousand per year to nearly four hundred thousand per year, between 2000 and 2010 (U.S. Department of Homeland Security 2011), while

American subnational entities produced a variety of laws explicitly designed to make migrant living conditions difficult.

12 I am arguing here that although sovereign power is continually being reconfigured through discursive struggles, it has become sedimented within a powerful set of transnational institutions that are bolstered by the ideological pull of neoliberalism, nationalism, and—in this case—a particular conception of nature.

13 This resonates with Foucault's ([1977] 1995, 280) description of the emergence of disciplinary power after the French Revolution: "the infiltration of political parties and workers' associations, the recruitment of thugs against strikers and rioters, the organization of a sub-police—working directly with the legal police and capable if necessary of becoming a parallel army—a whole extra-legal functioning of power was partly assured by the mass of reserve labour constituted by the delinquents: a clandestine police force and standby army at the disposal of the state."

14 There is a tendency to view the apparent contradictions between neoliberalism and sovereignty as emerging from a uniform logic of neoliberal capitalism. The Foucauldian insight here is that there is no grand logic; as Matthew Coleman (2005, 188) argues, in terms of immigration and U.S. border policy, U.S. statecraft is "composed of the 'collision of mutually opposed tactics.'" The disciplinary and biopolitical tactics that stabilize neoliberalism do not simply emerge from a neoliberal state or from capitalists—in fact, they often emerge from those, like ecocommunitarian restrictionists, who are adamantly opposed to neoliberalism.

15 In his analysis of disciplinary power, Foucault asserts that "the prison has succeeded extremely well in producing delinquency, a specific type, a politically or economically less dangerous—and, on occasion, usable—form of illegality." Similarly, immigration restrictionists produce a form of delinquency that serves the purposes of the neoliberal state perfectly—facilitating the development of a mass of surplus labor that can be inserted into the production apparatus but that also demands intense scrutiny and surveillance from society at large. Environmental restrictionists further this project by reinforcing the brandings of delinquency through a progressive discourse that nonetheless produces a national environmental subject whose opposition to immigration immobilizes any real resistance to neoliberalism.

16 A search of CNC's *Imagine2050* blog highlights a variety of communal forms being advanced, including national and transnational alliances of youths concerned with environmental justice, coalitions between first nations and migrants, and various instances of local community activism.

17  Indigenous cosmologies, for instance, frequently draw nature into origin stories and the cultural traditions that spring from them. The natural–cultural interconnections of these cosmologies are deployed to challenge the *temporal* and *spatial* dimensions of colonial sovereignty, demonstrating a much more enduring connection with the "territory" than the dominant national (temporal) imaginary and revealing the contingency of current (spatial) boundaries and the coercive force that sustains them. Additionally, the natural–cultural interconnection challenges the anthropocentrism and ethnocentrism that undergird colonial sovereignty (pushing back against the narrative of "colonial civilization" by emphasizing its wasteful and destructive practices). These modes of resistance, however, do not necessarily escape or disavow sovereign power; rather, they strategically employ the tools at their disposal (e.g., ideals of nationalism and, at times, constitutional and legal protections) in pursuit of more radical aims.

18  Dussel is arguing that the reconfiguration of existing social antagonisms— the emergence of a "social bloc of the oppressed"—would legitimate and constitute a qualitatively different form of authority backed by coercive force. Although liberatory visions of a "people's sovereignty" ought to be approached cautiously and critically (see, e.g., Foucault's famous debate with the Maoist revolutionary), I would argue that this alternative sovereignty (driven by an ethos of socioecological justice) is backed by modes of power or knowledge, social norms, and political subjects that are currently excluded from the state of exception driven by an ethos of militarized neoliberalism. As revolutionary movements of the twentieth century have shown, supposedly revolutionary politics come with great risks. But continuing along our current trajectory poses a far greater risk. A state of rebellion appears to provide a promising direction beyond sovereign power as we now know it.

19  Patricia Hynes, for instance, suggests that the populationist equation IPAT (Environmental Impact = Population × Affluence × Technology) could be reformulated as I = C − PAT (Environmental Impact = Conservation − Patriarchy × Affluence × Technology). Her discussion of this alternative equation is too nuanced to do justice to here, but it presents a persuasive case for an alternative vision of respect for environmental limits situated in a critique of structural injustice (Hynes 1999, 62–64). Taking a slightly different tack, Skyler Simmons (2012)—writing on Earth First!'s website—makes an impassioned argument that the current human population is unsustainable but suggests a five-point approach to ameliorating this problem: drastically reduce consumption; smash

patriarchy; separate overpopulation from immigration; class war; and end policies that encourage population growth in countries with low birthrates. Though the environmentalism of migration that I call for would contain room for debate over how socioecological justice relates to population, it seems increasingly clear that any type of population policy needs to focus on empowering (rather than controlling) women.

20 Navajo efforts to "protect the confluence" refer to the place where the Colorado and Little Colorado Rivers meet. It is a sacred place to the Diné (the place where life began) but is threatened by the proposed "Grand Canyon Escalade" development.

21 For example, such an approach would begin by noting that Native Americans were fixed in place by a colonial sovereign. Patterns of nomadic movement and systems of communal property—around which indigenous conceptions of place were often oriented—were deemed threats to private property and the westward march of the American state (see, e.g., Cronon 1983, 62–67).

22 The best example of this is in upper-middle-class and wealthy American cities surrounding wilderness areas. As environmental journalist Jenny Price (2006) puts it, "how much easier is it to keep your air clean when the factories that manufacture your SUVs and Gore-Tex jackets lie in other, distant towns? And you can minimize racial and class confrontations when your own population is white and affluent, while the poor and nonwhite labor force that sustains your city's material life resides safely far away. . . . Boulder couldn't be the town Boulder adores without LA."

## CONCLUSION

1 For example, in Jonathan Franzen's novel *Freedom,* one of the main characters, Walter, is an environmental restrictionist. Walter is genuine in his commitment to nature, does not appear to be racist, and is too likable to be a social nativist or econativist. Walter is, in many ways, the model of the ecocommunitarians that I've talked to and studied; saving nature comes to be seen as an end that is both detached from political economic processes and overrides every alternative ethical commitment.

2 The ecocommunitarian restrictionist discourse is very apparent on the websites of these organizations. See http://www.populationmatters .org/2012/population-matters-news/immigration-economic-fix-sideef fects/ and http://www.populationparty.org.au/.

# BIBLIOGRAPHY

Abbey, Edward. 1988. "Immigration and Liberal Taboos." In *One Life at a Time, Please,* 41–44. New York: Henry Holt.

Abernethy, Virginia. 2006. "Immigration Reduction Offers Chance for Softer Landing." *Ecological Economics* 59, no. 2: 226–30.

Adler, Ben. 2004. "Sierra Club Votes for Its Future." *The Nation,* April 26.

Agamben, Giorgio. 1995. "We Refugees." *Symposium: A Quarterly Journal in Modern Literatures* 49, no. 2: 114–19.

———. 1998. *Homo Sacer: Sovereign Power and Bare Life.* Trans. Daniel Heller-Roazen. Stanford, Calif.: Stanford University Press.

———. 2005. *State of Exception.* Trans. Kevin Attell. Chicago: University of Chicago Press.

Agnew, John. 2009. *Globalization and Sovereignty.* Lanham, Md.: Rowman and Littlefield.

Albo, Gregory. 2007. "The Limits of Eco-Localism: Scale, Strategy, Socialism." In *Socialist Register,* edited by L. Panitch and C. Leys, 337–63. New York: Monthly Review Press.

Alexander, Robin. 2011. "Letter to the C of CC." http://cofcc.org/2011/07/letter-to-the-cofcc/.

Alkon, Alison, and Julian Agyeman. 2011. *Cultivating Food Justice: Race, Class, and Sustainability.* Cambridge, Mass.: MIT Press.

Allen, Garland. 2013. "'Culling the Herd': Eugenics and the Conservation Movement in the United States, 1900–1940." *Journal of the History of Biology* 46: 31–72.

American Rivers. 2008. "America's Most Endangered Rivers." http://www.americanrivers.org/wp-content/uploads/2013/10/mer_2008.pdf.

America's Leadership Team for Long Range Population-Immigration-Resource Planning. 2009. "Americans May Eventually Find a Way to Live without Oil. Water Is Another Story." http://web.archive.org/web/20101225083555/http://www.capsweb.org/content_elements/recent_advertising/Water_Print.pdf.

Anderson, Sarah. 2011. "Complex Constituencies: Intense Environmentalists and Representation." *Environmental Politics* 20, no. 4: 547–65.

Anderson, Stuart. 2013. *How Many More Deaths? The Moral Case for a Temporary Worker Program.* NFAP Policy Brief. Arlington, Va.: National Foundation for American Policy Reform.

Andreas, Peter. 1996. "US–Mexico: Open Markets, Closed Border." *Foreign Policy* 103: 51–69.

———. 1998–99. "The Escalation of US Immigration Control in the Post-NAFTA Era." *Political Science Quarterly* 113, no. 4: 591–615.

Angus, Ian, and Simon Butler. 2011. *Too Many People? Population, Immigration, and the Environmental Crisis.* Chicago, Ill.: Haymarket Books.

Anzaldúa, Gloria. 1999. *Borderlands/La Frontera: The New Mestiza.* San Francisco: Aunt Lute Books.

Apostolidis, Paul. 2010. *Breaks in the Chain: What Immigrant Workers Can Teach America about Democracy.* Minneapolis: University of Minnesota Press.

Bacon, David. 2012. "Migration: A Product of Free-Market Reforms." America's Program. http://www.cipamericas.org/archives/6038.

Balibar, Etienne. (1991) 2005. "Racism and Nationalism." In *Nations and Nationalism: A Reader,* edited by Philip Spencer and Howard Wollman, 163–72. New Brunswick, N.J.: Rutgers University Press.

Bandarage, Asoka. 1999. "Population and Environment: Toward a Social Justice Agenda." In *Dangerous Intersections: Feminist Perspectives on Population, Environment, and Development,* edited by Jael Silliman and Ynestra King, 24–38. Cambridge, Mass.: South End Press.

Barbier, Edward. 2010. *A Global Green New Deal: Rethinking the Economic Recovery.* New York: Cambridge University Press.

Barker, Joanne, ed. 2005. *Sovereignty Matters: Locations of Contestation and Possibility in Indigenous Struggles for Self-Determination.* Lincoln: University of Nebraska Press.

Barker, Michael. 2011. "William Vogt and Malthusian Conservationism." *Swans Commentary,* October 24. http://www.swans.com/library/art17/barker91.html.

Barria, Carlos. 2013. "A Mongolian Neo-Nazi Environmentalist Walks into a Lingerie Store in Ulan Bator." *The Atlantic.* http://www.theatlantic.com/infocus/2013/07/a-mongolian-neo-nazi-environmentalist-walks-in-to-a-lingerie-store-in-ulan-bator/100547/.

Barringer, Felicity. 2004. "Bitter Division for Sierra Club on Immigration." *New York Times,* March 16.

Barry, John, and Robyn Eckersley, eds. 2005. Introduction to *The State and the Global Ecological Crisis,* ix–xxv. Cambridge, Mass.: MIT Press.

Bartlett, Albert. 2005. "Reflections on Sustainability, Population Growth, and the Environment—Revisited." *The Social Contract* 16, no. 1: 35–54.

Beck, Roy. 1996. "'No' to Immigrant Bashing." NumbersUSA. http://www .numbersusa.com/content/learn/about-us/no-immigrant-bashing/no-immigrant-bashing.html.

———. 2008. "Obama Plan Would Save/Create 2.5 Million Jobs—Much Cheaper Immigration Moratorium Would Save 2.5 Million Jobs." *NumbersUSA,* December 5. https://www.numbersusa.com/content/nusablog/ beckr/november-25-2008/obama-plan-would-savecreate-25-million-jobs-much-cheaper-immigration.

———. 2009. "Testimony to the Senate Judiciary Committee on S. 424, 6/3/2009." http://www.youtube.com/watch?v=_pfZVjD4P3A.

Beck, Roy, and Leon Kolankiewicz. 2000. "The Environmental Movement's Retreat from Advocating U.S. Population Stabilization (1970–1998)." *Journal of Policy History* 12, no. 1: 123–56.

Beck, Roy, Leon Kolankiewicz, and Steve Camarota. 2003. *Outsmarting Smart Growth: Population Growth, Immigration, and the Problem of Sprawl.* Report for the Center for Immigration Studies. http://www .numbersusa.com/content/files/pdf/SprawlPaper.pdf.

Beilenson, Anthony. 1996. "Immigration versus Our Grandchildren." *Las Vegas Sun,* May 30. http://www.lasvegassun.com/news/1996/may/30/ beilensonimmigration-versus-our-grandchildren/.

Beirich, Heidi. 2007. "Federation for American Immigration Reform's Hate Filled Track Record." *Intelligence Report* 128. http://www.splcenter .org/get-informed/intelligence-report/browse-all-issues/2007/winter/ the-teflon-nativists.

———. 2010. "The Hypocrisy of Hate: Nativists and Environmentalism." In *Greenwash: Nativists, Environmentalism, and the Hypocrisy of Hate,* 6–10. Montgomery, Ala.: Southern Poverty Law Center.

Belcher, Oliver, Lauren Martin, Anna Secor, Stephanie Simon, and Tommy Wilson. 2008. "Everywhere and Nowhere: The Exception and the Topological Challenge to Geography." *Antipode* 40, no. 4: 499–503.

Bender, Susan Elizabeth. 2003. "Immigration and the Environment: The Story of a Sierra Club Policy Initiative." PhD diss., University of Nevada, Reno.

Bennett, Jane, and William Chaloupka, eds. 1993. *In the Nature of Things: Language, Politics, and the Environment.* Minneapolis: University of Minnesota Press.

Berg, Bruce. 2007. *Qualitative Research Methods for the Social Sciences.* Boston: Pearson Education.

Bernstein, Oliver. 2006. "What Mexican Activists Can Teach the U.S. about Poverty and the Planet." Grist.org, March 7. http://grist.org/article/bernstein1/.

Berry, Wendell. 1985. "A Few Words in Favor of Edward Abbey." In *Whole Earth Review*, 38–44. http://home2.btconnect.com/tipiglen/abbey.html.

Bettini, G. 2013. "Climate Barbarians at the Gate? A Critique of Apocalyptic Narratives on 'Climate Refugees.'" *Geoforum* 45: 63–72.

Bhatia, Rajani. 2004. "Green or Brown? White Nativist Environmental Movements." In *Home-Grown Hate: Gender and Organized Racism*, edited by Abby Ferber, 194–214. New York: Routledge.

Biehl, Janet. 1994. "'Ecology' and the Modernization of Fascism in the German Ultra-right." *Society and Nature* 2, no. 2: 130–70.

Bier, David. 2013. "New Study Links Anti-Immigration Groups to Pro-Population Control Environmentalists." Competitive Enterprise Institution, January 29. https://cei.org/blog/new-study-links-anti-immigration-groups-pro%E2%80%93population-control-environmentalists.

Biermann, F., and I. Boas. 2010. "Preparing for a Warmer World: Towards a Global Governance System to Protect Climate Refugees." *Global Environmental Politics* 10, no. 1: 60–88.

Biswas, Shampa, and Sheila Nair, eds. 2010. *International Relations and States of Exception: Margins, Peripheries, and Excluded Bodies*. New York: Routledge.

Blue Green Alliance. 2012. "About Us." http://www.bluegreenalliance.org/about.

Boggs, William Robertson. 1993. "The Rise of Islam in America." *American Renaissance* 4, no. 11. http://www.amren.com/ar/1993/11/index.html.

Bonilla-Silva, Eduardo. 2001. *White Supremacy and Racism in the Post–Civil Rights Era*. Boulder, Colo.: Lynne Rienner.

———. 2006. *Racism without Racists: Color-Blind Racism and the Persistence of Racial Inequality in the United States*. 2nd ed. Oxford: Rowman and Littlefield.

Bookchin, Murray. 1980. *Toward an Ecological Society*. Montreal: Black Rose Books.

———. 1991. *Defending the Earth: A Debate between Murray Bookchin and Dave Foreman*. Montreal, Quebec: Black Rose Books.

Bramwell, Anna. 1989. *Ecology in the Twentieth Century: A History*. New Haven, Conn.: Yale University Press.

Braun, Bruce. 2000. "Producing Vertical Territory: Geology and Governmentality in Late Victorian Canada." *Ecumene* 7, no. 1: 7–46.

———. 2002. *The Intemperate Rainforest: Nature, Culture, and Power on Canada's West Coast.* Minneapolis: University of Minnesota Press.

Brechin, Gray. 1996. "Conserving the Race: Natural Aristocracies, Eugenics, and the US Conservation Movement." *Antipode* 28, no. 3: 229–45.

Brimelow, Peter. 1995. *Alien Nation: Common Sense about America's Immigration Disaster.* New York: Random House.

———. 2000. "Eclipsed Environmentalists, by Meredith Burke." *VDARE,* September 20. http://www.vdare.com/articles/vdare-eclipsed-environmentalists-by-meredith-burke.

Brown, Chris. 2010. "The Dream Act: Just Another Amnesty Bill." June 29. http://www.progressivesforimmigrationreform.org/?s=The+Dream+Act+and+Chris+Brown.

Brown, Oli. 2008. *Migration and Climate Change.* IOM Migration Research Series 31. Geneva: International Organization for Migration.

Brown, Wendy. 2010. *Walled States, Waning Sovereignty.* New York: Zone Books.

Brune, Michael, and Allison Chin. 2013. "A Path to the Future." Sierra Club. http://sierraclub.typepad.com/michaelbrune/2013/04/immigration.html.

Bruyneel, Kevin. 2007. *The Third Space of Sovereignty: The Postcolonial Politics of US–Indigenous Relations.* Minneapolis: University of Minnesota Press.

Bryner, Gary. 2008. "Failure and Opportunity: Environmental Groups in US Climate Change Policy." *Environmental Politics* 17, no. 2: 319–36.

Buchanan, Pat. 2006. *State of Emergency: The Third World Invasion and Conquest of America.* New York: St. Martin's Press.

Bullard, Robert. 1994. "Environmental Justice for All." In *Unequal Protection: Environmental Justice and Communities of Color,* edited by Robert Bullard, 9–10. San Francisco: Sierra Club Books.

———. 2000. *Dumping in Dixie: Race, Class, and Environmental Quality.* Boulder, Colo.: Westview Press.

Burke, B. M. 2000. "Immigrations Dire Effect on the Environment." *Seattle Times,* June 15. http://www.commondreams.org/views/061500-104.htm.

Butler, Judith. 2004. *Precarious Life: The Powers of Mourning and Violence.* New York: Verso.

Cafaro, Philip. 2010a. "Why I Am an Environmentalist—for Immigration Reduction." NumbersUSA. April 22. https://www.numbersusa.com/content/nusablog/cafarop/april-21-2010/why-i-am-environmentalist-immigration-reduction.html.

———. 2010b. "Patriotism as an Environmental Virtue." *Journal of Agricultural and Environmental Ethics* 23: 185–206.

———. 2010c. "Hypocrisy and Responsibility." *Progressives for Immigration Reform Blog.* September 28. http://www.progressivesforimmigrationreform.org/2010/09/28/hypocrisy-and-responsibility/.

———. 2011. Personal interview. February 8.

Cafaro, Philip, and Winthrop Staples III. 2009. "The Environmental Argument for Reducing Immigration into the United States." *Environmental Ethics* 31: 5–30.

Cairns, John, Jr. 2003. "Sovereignty, Individuality, and Sustainability." *Ethics in Science and Environmental Politics* 3: 71–77.

———. 2004. "Sustainability Ethics: Zero Net Immigration." *The Social Contract,* Fall, 58–71.

Californians for Population Stabilization. 2008a. "Ecological Footprint." http://www.youtube.com/watch?v=eDFFbiIbm2c&feature=player_embedded.

———. 2008b. "Mass Immigration and Global Warming: Gives the Term Melting Pot a Whole New Meaning." http://www.capsweb.org/about/our-tv-ads/mass-immigration-and-global-warming-gives-term-melting-pot-whole-new-meaning.

———. 2008c. "One of America's Best Selling Vehicles." http://www.capsweb.org/about/our-tv-ads/bulldozer-one-americas-best-selling-vehicles.

Camarota, Steven, Philip Cafaro, Don Weeden, and Andrew Light. 2009. "Immigration, Population, and the Environment: Experts to Debate Impacts of Current Policies." Panel organized by the Center for Immigration Studies. http://cis.org/Transcript/EnvironmentalPanel.

Carrillo-Guerrero, Yamilett, Karl Flessa, Osvel Hinojosa-Huerta, and Laura Lopez-Hoffman. 2013. "From Accident to Management: The Cienega de Santa Clara Ecosystem." *Ecological Engineering* 59: 84–92.

Carrying Capacity Network. 2010a. "Homepage." http://www.carryingcapacity.org/.

———. 2010b. "Cultural Marxism: A Threat to the USA?" July Action Alert. http://www.carryingcapacity.org/alerts/alert07110.html.

Carter, Eric, Bianca Silva, and Graciela Guzman. 2013. "Migration, Acculturation, and Environmental Values: The Case of Mexican Immigrants in Central Iowa." *Annals of the Association of American Geographers* 103, no. 1: 129–47.

Castree, Noel. 2008. "Neoliberalising Nature: The Logics of Deregulation and Reregulation." *Environment and Planning A* 40, no. 1: 131–52.

Castree, Noel, and Bruce Braun, eds. 2001. *Social Nature: Theory, Practice, and Politics.* Malden, Mass.: Blackwell.

Center for Immigration Studies. 2011. "Who We Are." http://www.cis.org/About.

Center for New Community. 2009. "The John Tanton Network." http://www.newcomm.org/pdf/CNC-Tanton_Network_2009.pdf.

———. 2010. *The Green War on Immigrants.* Chicago: Do Tell Productions.

Chaloupka, W. 2003. "The Irrepressible Lightness and Joy of Being Green: Empire and Environmentalism." *Strategies* 16, no. 2: 147–61.

———. 2008. "The Environmentalist 'What Is to Be Done.'" *Environmental Politics* 17, no. 2: 237–53.

Chandler DeYoung, Marilyn. 2011. Personal interview. May 23.

Chapman, Robert. 2006. "Confessions of a Malthusian Restrictionist." *Ecological Economics* 59, no. 2: 214–19.

Chavez, Leo. 2008. *The Latino Threat: Constructing Immigrants, Citizens, and the Nation.* Stanford, Calif.: Stanford University Press.

Chavkin, Sasha. 2009. "Cash for Thunder: Bolivia Demands Climate Reparations." *Mother Jones.* November/December. http://www.motherjones.com/environment/2009/11/bolivia-paying-rain.

Chernillo, Daniel. 2006. "Social Theory's Methodological Nationalism: Myth and Reality." *European Journal of Social Theory* 9, no. 1: 5–22.

Christian Aid. 2007. "Human Tide: The Real Migration Crisis." http://www.christianaid.org.uk/images/human-tide.pdf.

*Colbert Report.* 2012. "United We Can't Stand Them." April 25. http://thecolbertreport.cc.com/videos/6xkuod/the-word---united-we-can-t-stand-them.

Coleman, Mathew. 2005. "US Statecraft and the Mexico–US Border as Security/Economy Nexus." *Political Geography* 24: 184–209.

———. 2007. "Immigration Geopolitics beyond the Mexico–US Border." *Antipode* 39, no. 1: 54–76.

Collins, Donald. 2011. "Immigrant Assimilation or Blind Growth Mania." *VDARE,* September 15. http://www.vdare.com/articles/immigrant-assimilation-or-blind-growth-mania.

Comaroff, Jean, and John Comaroff. 2001. "Naturing the Nation: Aliens, Apocalypse, and the Post-colonial State." *Journal of Southern African Studies* 27, no. 3: 627–51.

Commission on Population Growth and the American Future [Rockefeller Commission]. 1969. "Population and the American Future." http://www.population-security.org/rockefeller/001_population_growth_and_the_american_future.htm.

Committee on Women, Population, and Environment. 2006. "Political Ecology Group's Immigration and Environment Campaign Position Statement." http://cwpe.org/node/148.

Conca, Ken. 1994. "Rethinking the Ecology–Sovereignty Debate." *Millennium: Journal of International Studies* 23, no. 3: 701–11.

Connolly, William. 2004. "The Complexity of Sovereignty." In *Sovereign Lives: Power in Global Politics,* edited by Jenny Edkins, Veronique Pin-Fat, and Michael Shapiro, 23–40. New York: Routledge.

Coolidge, Calvin. 1921. "Whose Country Is This?" *Good Housekeeping* 72, no. 2: 13–14. http://hearth.library.cornell.edu/h/hearth/browse/articles/arts-cookesontv.html.

Cooper, Chloe. 2010. "Indigenous Peoples Take a Stand against SB1070." *Imagine 2050,* June 15. http://imagine2050.newcomm.org/2010/06/15/indigenous_communities_take_stand_against_nativism/.

Council of Conservative Citizens. 2010a. "Congress Shocker: Democrats Buck Obama, Introduce Bill to Repeal NAFTA." March 8. http://cofcc.org/2010/03/congress-shocker-democrat-blue-dogs-buck-obama-introduce-bill-to-repeal-nafta/.

———. 2010b. "Another Animal Preserve Wiped Out in Africa." September 28. http://cofcc.org/2010/09/another-animal-preserve-wiped-out-in-africa/.

———. 2010c. "European Soil." *Citizens Informer,* April–June 2010, 10. http://cofcc.org/newspaper/june10ci.pdf.

———. 2011. "J-Street: American Jews Will Stand by Obama." August 19. http://cofcc.org/2011/08/j-street-american-jews-will-stand-by-obama/.

Council on Hemispheric Affairs. 2012. "The Failures of NAFTA." http://www.coha.org/the-failures-of-nafta/.

Cronon, William. 1983. *Changes in the Land: Indians, Colonists, and the Ecology of New England.* New York: Hill and Wang.

———. 1996. "The Trouble with Wilderness: Or, Getting Back to the Wrong Nature." *Environmental History* 1, no. 1: 7–28.

Dalby, Simon. 2002. *Environmental Security.* Minneapolis: University of Minneapolis Press.

———. 2004. "Ecological Politics, Violence, and the Theme of Empire." *Global Environmental Politics* 4, no. 2: 1–11.

Daly, Herman. 1974. "The Economics of the Steady State." *The American Economic Review* 64, no. 2: 15–21.

———. 2006. "Population, Migration, and Globalization." *Ecological Economics* 59, no. 2: 187–90.

Darwin, Charles. (1876) 2005. *The Autobiography of Charles Darwin.* New York: Barnes and Noble.

De Genova, N. 2005. *Working the Boundaries: Race, Space, and "Illegality" in Mexican Chicago.* Durham, N.C.: Duke University Press.

Deloria, Vine, Jr., and Clifford Lytle. 1984. *The Nations Within: The Past and Future of American Indian Sovereignty.* Austin: University of Texas Press.

Demeritt, David. 2001. "Being Constructive about Nature." In *Social Nature: Theory, Practice, and Politics,* edited by Noel Castree and Bruce Braun, 22–40. Malden, Mass.: Blackwell.

Deparle, Jason. 2011. "Immigration Opponent Withdraws from Group." *New York Times,* April 29, A12.

Department of Defense. 2010. "Quadrennial Defense Report." http://www.defense.gov/qdr/QDR%20as%20of%2026JAN10%200700.pdf.

Desrochers, Pierre, and Christine Hoffbauer. 2009. "The Post-war Intellectual Roots of the Population Bomb: Fairfield Osborn's 'Our Plundered Planet' and William Vogt's 'Road to Survival' in Retrospect." *The Electronic Journal of Sustainable Development* 1, no. 3: 37–61.

Deudney, Daniel. 1998. "Global Village Sovereignty: Intergenerational Sovereign Publics, Federal-Republican Earth Constitutions, and Planetary Identities." In *The Greening of Sovereignty in World Politics,* edited by Karen Litfin, 299–325. Cambridge, Mass.: MIT Press.

Devall, Bill, and George Sessions. 1985. *Deep Ecology: Living as If Nature Mattered.* Salt Lake City, Utah: Peregrine Smith Books.

DeYoung, Marilyn Chandler. 2011a. "Open Letter to the Funders of the Center for New Community." August 22. http://www.caps-blog.org/articles/2011/08/22/letter-to-the-funders-of-the-center-for-new-community/.

———. 2011b. Personal interview. May 23.

Di Chiro, Giovanna. 2008. "Living Environmentalisms: Coalition Politics, Social Reproduction, and Environmental Justice." *Environmental Politics* 17, no. 2: 276–98.

Dinalt, Jason. 1997. "The Environmental Impact of Immigration into the United States." *Focus* 4, no. 2. http://www.carryingcapacity.org/DinAlt.htm.

Distaso, Cheryl. 2011. Personal interview. February 22.

Donato, Ruben. 2003. "Sugar Beets, Segregation, and Schools: Mexican Americans in a Northern Colorado Community, 1920–1960." *Journal of Latinos and Education* 2, no. 2: 69–88.

Dorsey, Michael. 2011. Personal interview. October 5.

Doty, Roxanne. 1996. "The Double-Writing of Statecraft: Exploring State Responses to Illegal Immigration." *Alternatives* 21, no. 2: 171–89.

———. 1999. "Racism, Desire, and the Politics of Immigration." *Millennium: Journal of International Studies* 28: 585–606.

———. 2001. "Desert Tracts: Statecraft in Remote Places." *Alternatives* 26: 523–43.

———. 2007. "States of Exception on the Mexico–US Border: Security, 'Decisions,' and Civilian Border Patrols." *International Political Sociology* 1: 113–37.

———. 2009. *The Law into Their Own Hands: Immigration and the Politics of Exceptionalism.* Tucson: University of Arizona Press.

Draper, William. 1966. "Parks?—Or More People?" *National Parks Magazine* 40: 10–13.

Dunaway, Brian. 2001. "A Reader Comments on Environmentalism vs. Conservation." *VDARE*, April 28. http://www.vdare.com/node/18443.

Duncan, Richard. 2007. "America: A Frog in the Kettle Slowly Coming to a Boil." *The Social Contract* 18, no. 1.

Dunlap, Riley, Chenyang Xiao, and Aaron McCright. 2001. "Politics and Environment in America: Partisan and Ideological Cleavages in Public Support for Environmentalism." *Environmental Politics* 10, no. 4: 23–48.

Dunn, T. J. 1996. *The Militarization of the US–Mexico Border, 1978–1992: Low Intensity Conflict Doctrine Comes Home.* Austin, Tex.: CMAS Books.

Durant, Leah. 2010. "Bolton's Ruling a Major Miscarriage of Justice." Progressives for Immigration Reform. July 28. http://www.progressivesforimmigrationreform.org/boltons-ruling-a-major-miscarriage-of-justice/.

Dussel, Enrique. 2008. *Twenty Theses on Politics.* Durham, N.C.: Duke University Press.

Earth First! 2011. "Earth First! Means a World without Borders." http://earthfirstjournal.org/newswire/2011/04/29/earth-first-means-a-world-without-borders/.

Eberhard, M. J. W. 1975. "The Evolution of Social Behavior by Kin Selection." *The Quarterly Review of Biology* 50, no. 1: 1–33.

Eckersley, Robyn. 2004. *The Green State: Rethinking Democracy and Sovereignty.* Cambridge: Massachusetts Institute of Technology.

———. 2006. "The State as Gatekeeper: A Reply." *Politics and Ethics Review* 2, no. 2: 127–38.

———. 2007a. "From Cosmopolitan Nationalism to Cosmopolitan Democracy." *Review of International Studies* 33: 675–92.

———. 2007b. "Environmentalism and Patriotism: An Unholy Alliance?" In *Patriotism: Philosophical and Political Perspectives,* edited by Igor Primoratz and Aleksandar Pavkovic, 183–200. Burlington, Vt.: Ashgate.

Edkins, Jenny, and Veronique Pin-Fat. 2004. "Introduction: Life, Power, Resistance." In *Sovereign Lives: Power in Global Politics,* edited by Jenny Edkins, Veronique Pin-Fat, and Michael Shapiro, 1–22. New York: Routledge.

Ehrlich, Paul. 1968. *The Population Bomb.* Cutchogue, N.Y.: Buccaneer Books.

Ehrlich, Paul, and Anne Ehrlich. 2004. *One with Ninevah: Politics, Consumption, and the Human Future*. Washington, D.C.: Island Press.

Ehrlich, Paul, Loy Bilderback, and Anne Erhlich. 1979. *The Golden Door: International Migration, Mexico, and the United States*. New York: Ballantine Books.

Ehrlich, Paul, Anne Ehrlich, and John Holdren. 1977. *Ecoscience: Population, Resources, Environment*. San Francisco: Freeman.

Elbel, Fred. 2007. "Consequences of Misinterpreting the 14th Amendment to the United States Constitution." http://www.14thamendment.us/birthright_citizenship/consequences.html.

Elder, Bill. 2001. "Testimony to United States Congress." House Judiciary Committee's Subcommittee on Immigration and Claims. *U.S. Population and Immigration*. 107th Cong., 1st sess.

Environmental Health Coalition. 2012. "Border Environmental Justice Campaign." http://www.environmentalhealth.org/BorderEHC/index.html.

Fahrenthold, David. 2012. "Self-Deportation Proponents Kris Kobach, Michael Hethmon Facing Time of Trial." *Washington Post,* April 24. http://www.washingtonpost.com/politics/2012/04/24/gIQAe6lheT_story.html.

Federation for American Immigration Reform. 2008. "Immigration and Population Growth." http://www.fairus.org/site/News2?page=NewsArticle&id=16919&security=1601&news_iv_ctrl=1009.

———. 2010. "Birthright Citizenship." http://www.fairus.org/issue/birthright-citizenship.

Ferber, Abbey. 1998. *White Man Falling: Race, Gender, and White Supremacy*. Lanham, Md.: Rowman and Littlefield.

———. 2004. *Home Grown Hate: Gender and Organized Racism*. New York: Routledge.

Fernandez, Luis, and Joel Olson. 2011. "To Live, Love, and Work Anywhere You Please." *Contemporary Political Theory* 10: 412–19.

Fischer, Irving. 1909. *Report on National Vitality, Its Wastes and Conservation*. Bulletin 30 of the Committee of One Hundred on National Health. Washington, D.C.: Government Printing Office.

Foreman, Dave. 1983. "Reducing Population." *Earth First!* 3, no. 6: 3.

———. 1987. "Is Sanctuary the Answer?" *Earth First!* 8, no. 1: 21–22.

Fort Collins History Connection. n.d. "Sugar Beets, Streetcar Suburbs, and the City Beautiful, 1900–1919." http://history.fcgov.com/archive/contexts/sugar.php.

Foucault, Michel. 1980. *Power/Knowledge: Selected Interviews and Other Writings, 1972–77*. Edited by Colin Gordon. New York: Pantheon Books.

———. (1978) 1990. *The History of Sexuality, Volume 1.* Translated by Robert Hurley. New York: Vintage Books.

———. (1977) 1995. *Discipline and Punish: The Birth of the Prison.* Translated by Alan Sheridan. New York: Vintage Books.

———. (1979) 2008. *The Birth of Biopolitics: Lectures at the College de France, 1978–79.* Translated by Graham Burchell. New York: Palgrave Macmillan.

Francis, Sam. 2004. "When the State Is the Enemy of the Nation." *VDARE,* July 19. http://www.vdare.com/articles/when-the-state-is-the-enemy-of-the-nation.

———. 2005. "Statement of Principles." Council of Conservative Citizens. http://cofcc.org/introduction/statement-of-principles/.

Frank, Brian. 2010. "Downstream: Death of the Mighty Colorado." http://www.brianfrankphoto.com/index.php.

Franklin, Benjamin. 1751. "Observations Concerning the Increase of Mankind, Peopling of Countries, etc." http://www.indiana.edu/~kdhist/H105-documents-web/week06/Franklin1751.html.

Gardner, Dave. 2011. "Comments on 'Network Takes Aim at Growthbusters, Allows Anti-contraception Advocate to Mislead.'" September 11. http://www.growthbusters.org/2011/11/network_takes_aim_at_growthbusters/.

Garling, Spiro. 1998. "Immigration Policy and the Environment: The Washington DC Metropolitan Area." *Population and Environment* 20, no. 1: 23–54.

Garvey, Jill. 2010. "The Green War on Immigrants." *Imagine2050,* August 25. http://imagine2050.newcomm.org/2010/08/25/the-green-war-on-immigrants/.

Gelobter, Michel. 2005. "The Soul of Environmentalism: Rediscovering Transformational Politics in the 21st Century." https://www.energyactioncoalition.org/sites/wearepowershift.org/files/Soul_of_Environmentalism.pdf.

Gibson-Wood, Hilary, and Sarah Wakefield. 2013. "'Participation,' White Privilege, and Environmental Justice: Understanding Environmentalism among Hispanics in Toronto." *Antipode* 45, no. 3: 641–62.

Gill, Stephen. 1995. "Globalization, Market Civilization, and Disciplinary Neoliberalism." *Millennium: Journal of International Studies* 24, no. 3: 399–423.

Giroux, Henri. 2006. "Reading Hurricane Katrina: Race, Class, and the Biopolitics of Disposability." *College Literature* 33, no. 3: 171–96.

Glissant, Édouard. (1990) 1997. *Poetics of Relation.* Translated by Betsy Wing. Ann Arbor: University of Michigan Press.

Goldman, Michael. 2006. *Imperial Nature: The World Bank and Struggles for Social Justice in the Age of Globalization*. New Haven, Conn.: Yale University Press.

Gordon, Linda. 1976. *Woman's Body, Woman's Right: A Social History of Birth Control in America*. New York: Grossman.

Gottlieb, Robert. 1993. *Forcing the Spring: The Transformation of the American Environmental Movement*. Washington, D.C.: Island Press.

———. 2001. *Environmentalism Unbound: Exploring New Pathways for Change*. Cambridge, Mass.: MIT Press.

Gould, Carol. 2006. "Ecological Democracy: Statist or Transnational?" *Politics and Ethics Review* 2, no. 2: 119–26.

Grant, Madison. 1921. *The Passing of the Great Race*. New York: Charles Scribner's Sons.

Gregory, Dick. 1971. "My Answer to Genocide." *Ebony*, October, 66–72.

Gregson, Nicky, and Gillian Rose. 2000. "Taking Butler Elsewhere: Performativity, Spatialities, Subjectivities." *Environment and Planning D: Society and Space* 18, no. 4: 433–52.

Grove, Richard. 1996. *Green Imperialism: Colonial Expansion, Tropical Island Edens, and the Origins of Western Environmentalism, 1600–1860*. New York: Cambridge University Press.

Hajer, Maarten. 1995. *The Politics of Environmental Discourse: Ecological Modernization and the Policy Process*. Oxford: Oxford University Press.

Hall, Stuart. 1985. "Signification, Representation, Ideology: Althusser and the Post-Structuralist Debates." *Critical Studies in Mass Communication* 2, no. 2: 91–114.

Hamilton, Paul. 2002. "The Greening of Nationalism: Nationalizing Nature in Europe." *Environmental Politics* 11, no. 2: 27–48.

Handy, Ryan. 2014. "Plan for Massive New Reservoir Delayed Again." *Fort Collins Coloradoan*, November 9.

Hannigan, John. 2011. "Implacable Foes or Strange Bedfellows? The Promise and Pitfalls of Eco-Nationalism in a Globalized World." In *Against Orthodoxy: Studies in Nationalism*, edited by Trevor Harrison and Slobodan Drakulic, 314–32. Vancouver: UBC Press.

Hardin, Garrett. 1968. "The Tragedy of the Commons." http://www.garretthardinsociety.org/articles/art_tragedy_of_the_commons.html.

———. 1974. "Lifeboat Ethics: The Case against Helping the Poor." *Psychology Today*. http://www.garretthardinsociety.org/articles/art_lifeboat_ethics_case_against_helping_poor.html.

———. 1986. "Cultural Carrying Capacity." http://www.garretthardinsociety.org/articles/art_cultural_carrying_capacity.html.

————. 1989. "There Is No Global Population Problem." http://www.gar retthardinsociety.org/articles/art_no_global_pop_problem.html.

————. (1989) 2001. "There Is No Colored Population Problem." *The Social Contract* 12, no. 1: 19–22.

Hardt, Michael, and Antonio Negri. 2000. *Empire.* Cambridge, Mass.: Harvard University Press.

————. 2004. *Multitude.* New York: Penguin Press.

Hartmann, Betsy. 1995. *Reproductive Rights and Wrongs: The Global Politics of Population Control.* Boston, Mass.: South End Press.

————. 2004. "Conserving Racism: The Greening of Hate at Home and Abroad." *Different Takes* 27: 1–4.

————. 2010. "The Greening of Hate: An Environmentalist's Essay." Southern Poverty Law Center. http://www.splcenter.org/greenwash-nativists-environmentalism-and-the-hypocrisy-of-hate/the-greening-of-hate-an-essay.

Harvey, David. 1974. "Population, Resources, and the Ideology of Science." *Economic Geography* 50, no. 3: 256–77.

Hayes, Chris. 2006. "Keeping America Empty: How One Small-Town Conservationist Launched Today's Anti-immigration Movement." *In These Times,* April 26. http://www.inthesetimes.com/article/2608/.

————. 2014. "The New Abolitionism." *The Nation,* May 12. http://www .thenation.com/article/179461/new-abolitionism?page=full.

Hernandez, Kelly. 2010. *Migra! A History of the U.S. Border Patrol.* Berkeley: University of California Press.

Higham, John. 1983. *Strangers in the Land: Patterns of American Nativism, 1860–1925.* New Brunswick, N.J.: Rutgers University Press.

Hing, Bill Ong. 2010. *Ethical Borders: NAFTA, Globalization, and Mexican Migration.* Philadelphia: Temple University Press.

Hornborg, Alf. 1998. "Towards an Ecological Theory of Unequal Exchange: Articulating World Systems Theory and Ecological Economics." *Ecological Economics* 25: 127–36.

Horowitz, Carl. 2005. "La Reconquista: Amnesty's Elephant in the Living Room." *The Social Contract* 15, no. 3: 198–206.

Hugo, Graeme. 1996. "Environmental Concerns and International Migration." *International Migration Review* 30, no. 1: 105–31.

Hull, Diana. 2008. "Anchor Babies, Birthright Citizenship, and the 14th Amendment." http://www.14thamendment.us/info/videos.html.

Hunold, Christian, and John Dryzek. 2005. "Green Political Strategy and the State: Combining Political Theory and Comparative History." In *The State and the Global Ecological Crisis,* edited by John

Barry and Robyn Eckersley, 75–96. Cambridge, Mass.: MIT Press.

Hunter, Lori. 2005. "Migration and Environmental Hazards." *Population and Environment* 26, no. 4: 273–302.

Hurlbert, Stewart. 2006. "Immigration, Population, and the Environment: Homage to Louise Monroe Wood." http://www.capsweb.org/content .php?id=56&menu_id=7&menu_item_id=60.

Huslin, Anita. 2006. "On Immigration, a Theorist Who's No Fence-Sitter." *Washington Post*, September 26.

Hynes, H. Patricia. 1999. "Taking Population Out of the Equation: Reformulating I=PAT." In *Dangerous Intersections: Feminist Perspectives on Population, Environment, and Development*, edited by Jael Silliman and Ynestra King, 39–73. Cambridge, Mass.: South End Press.

*Imagine2050*. 2012. "Who We Are." http://imagine2050.newcomm.org/ about/.

Intergovernmental Panel on Climate Change. 2014. "Summary for Policymakers." In Climate Change 2014: Impacts, Adaptation, and Vulnerability, Part A: Global and Sectoral Aspects. Contribution of Working Group II to the Fifth Assessment Report of the Intergovernmental Panel on Climate Change 20. Cambridge: Cambridge University Press.

International Labor Organization. 2014. "Labor Migration." http://www .ilo.org/global/topics/labour-migration/lang—en/index.htm.

Jacobson, Robin. 2008. *The New Nativism: Proposition 187 and the Debate over Immigration*. Minneapolis: University of Minnesota Press.

Jacoby, Karl. 2001. *Crimes against Nature: Squatters, Poachers, Thieves, and the Hidden History of American Conservation*. Berkeley: University of California Press.

Jakopovich, Dan. 2009. "Uniting to Win: Labor–Environmental Alliances." *Capitalism, Nature, Socialism* 20, no. 2: 74–96.

Jazeel, Tariq. 2011. "Spatializing Difference beyond Cosmopolitanism: Rethinking Planetary Futures." *Theory, Culture, and Society* 28, no. 5: 75–97.

Jobling, Ian. 2004. "Conference Draws a Record Turnout." *American Renaissance* 15, no. 4: 1–4.

Johnson, Fawn. 2013. "Why GOP Sees a Conspiracy as Environmental Groups Join Fight Against Immigration." *National Journal*, February 13. http://www.nationaljournal.com/daily/why-gop-sees-a-conspiracy-as-environmental-groups-join-fight-against-immigration-20130213.

Johnson, Kevin. 1997. "The New Nativism: Something Old, Something New, Something Borrowed, Something Blue." In *Immigrants Out! The New Nativism and the Anti-immigrant Impulse in the United States*, edited by Juan Perea, 165–89. New York: New York University Press.

Jones, Van. 2008. *The Green Collar Economy: How One Solution Can Fix Our Two Biggest Problems*. New York: HarperCollins.

Jowit, Juliette. 2011. "Paul Ehrlich: A Prophet of Global Population Doom Who Is Gloomier Than Ever." *The Guardian,* October 23. http://www.guardian.co.uk/environment/2011/oct/23/paul-ehrlich-global-collapse-warning?newsfeed=true.

Kaplan, Robert. 1994. "The Coming Anarchy." *The Atlantic Magazine,* February.

King, Leslie. 2007. "Charting a Discursive Field: Environmentalists for US Population Stabilization." *Sociological Inquiry* 27, no. 3: 301–25.

———. 2008. "Ideology, Strategy, and Conflict in a Social Movement Organization: The Sierra Club Immigration Wars." *Mobilization* 13, no. 1: 45–61.

Klein, Naomi. 2014. "The Change Within: The Obstacles We Face Are Not Just External." *The Nation,* May 12. http://www.thenation.com/article/179460/change-within-obstacles-we-face-are-not-just-external#.

Koerner, Lisbet. 1999. *Linnaeus: Nature and Nation*. Cambridge, Mass.: Harvard University Press.

Kohoutek, Bethany. 2004. "Border Wars Go Green." *Rocky Mountain Bullhorn,* December 16.

Kolankiewicz, Leon, and Steven Camarota. 2008. "Immigration to the United States and World-Wide Greenhouse Gas Emissions." Center for Immigration Studies Backgrounder. http://www.cis.org/sites/cis.org/files/articles/2008/back1008.pdf.

Kosek, Jake. 2006. *Understories: The Political Life of Forests in Northern New Mexico*. Durham, N.C.: Duke University Press.

Kraly, Ellen P. 1995. *US Immigration and the Environment: Scientific Research and Analytic Issues*. Washington, D.C.: US Commission on Immigration Reform.

———. 1998. "Immigration and Environment: A Framework for Establishing a *Possible* Relationship." *Population Research and Policy Review* 17, no. 5: 421–37.

Kuehls, Thom. 1996. *Beyond Sovereign Territory: The Space of Ecopolitics*. Minneapolis: University of Minnesota Press.

Lal, Prerna. 2009. "Passing the Dream Act, It's a No-Brainer." *Imagine2050,* August 14. http://imagine2050.newcomm.org/2009/08/14/passing-the-dream-act-its-a-no-brainer/.

Latour, Bruno. 1993. *We Have Never Been Modern*. Translated by Catherine Porter. Cambridge, Mass.: Harvard University Press.

———. 2004. *The Politics of Nature: How to Bring the Sciences into Democracy.* Cambridge, Mass.: Harvard University Press.

Lazzarato, Maurizio. 2006. "From Biopower to Biopolitics." *Tailoring Biotechnologies* 2, no. 2: 11–20.

Lee, Martha. 1995. *Earth First! Environmental Apocalypse.* Syracuse, N.Y.: Syracuse University Press.

Leopold, Aldo. (1949) 1970. *A Sand County Almanac: With Essays on Conservation from Round River.* New York: Ballantine Books.

Levison, Jenny, Stephen Piggott, Rebecca Poswolsky, and Eric Ward. 2010. *Apply the Brakes: Anti-immigrant Co-optation of the Environmental Movement.* Chicago: Center for New Community.

Levy, Marc. 1995. "Is the Environment a National Security Issue?" *International Security* 20, no. 2: 35–62.

Lindner, Keith. 2012. "Returning the Commons: Resource Access and Environmental Governance in San Luis, Colorado." PhD diss., Syracuse University.

Lindsley, Syd. 2001a. "The Greening of Hate Continues." *Political Environments* 8: 15–20.

———. 2001b. "Mainstream Environmental Organizations Sign on to Anti-immigrant Alliance." *Political Environments* 8: 19.

Lipschutz, Ronnie. 1998. "The Nature of Sovereignty and the Sovereignty of Nature." In *The Greening of Sovereignty in World Politics,* edited by Karen Litfin, 109–39. Cambridge, Mass.: MIT Press.

Litfin, Karen, ed. 1998. *The Greening of Sovereignty in World Politics.* Cambridge: Massachusetts Institute of Technology.

Lombardo, Paul. 2003. "Taking Eugenics Seriously: Three Generations of ??? Are Enough?" *Florida State University Law Review* 30: 191–218.

Ludden, Jennifer. 2008. "Ads Warn That All Immigration Must Be Reduced." National Public Radio. September 12. http://www.npr.org/templates/story/story.php?storyId=94545604.

Lutton, Wayne. 1996. "Anchor Babies." *The Social Contract* 6, no. 4. http://www.thesocialcontract.com/artman2/publish/tsc0604/article_582.shtml.

MacDonald, Kevin. 2004. "Can the Jewish Model Help the West Survive?" http://www.kevinmacdonald.net/WestSurvive.htm.

———. 2010. "Recent Jewish and Muslim Pro-immigration Activism." *Occidental Observer,* September 30. http://www.theoccidentalobserver.net/2010/11/recent-jewish-and-muslim-pro-immigration-activism/.

———. 2011. "Phillip Weiss on the Disintegration of WASP Society."

*Occidental Observer,* August 19. http://www.theoccidentalobserver
.net/2011/08/philip-weiss-on-the-disintegration-of-wasp-society/.

Majority Rights. 2008. "Nationalism and the Environment." http://ma
jorityrights.com/weblog/comments/nationalism_and_the_environment/.

Malthus, Thomas. 1826. *Essay on the Principle of Population.* Edinburgh:
Ballantyne Press.

Mamdani, Mahmood. 1972. *The Myth of Population Control: Family,
Caste, and Class in an Indian Village.* New York: Monthly Review Press.

Massey, Douglass, Jorge Durand, and Nolan Malone. 2003. *Beyond Smoke
and Mirrors: Mexican Migration in an Era of Economic Integration.*
New York: Russell Sage Foundation.

McAfee, Kathleen. 2003. "Neoliberalism on the Molecular Scale: Economic
and Genetic Reductionism in Biotechnology Battles." *Geoforum* 34:
203–19.

McCarthy, James. 2004. "Privatizing Conditions of Production: Trade
Agreements as Neoliberal Economic Governance." *Geoforum* 35: 327–
41.

———. 2005. "Scale, Sovereignty, and Strategy in Environmental Governance." *Antipode* 37, no. 4: 731–53.

McCarthy, James, and Scott Prudham. 2004. "Neoliberal Nature and the
Nature of Neoliberalism." *Geoforum* 35: 275–83.

McClintock, Anne. 1995. *Imperial Leather: Race, Gender, and Sexuality
in the Colonial Contest.* New York: Routledge.

McGinnis, John. 1997. "The Origin of Conservatism." *National Review*
49, no. 24: 31.

McKibben, Bill. 2013. "Immigration Reform—For the Climate." *Los Angeles Times,* March 14. http://articles.latimes.com/2013/mar/14/opinion/
la-oe-mckibben-immigration-environment-20130314.

McMahon, Minnie, and Jesse Sanes. 2011. *Race, Migration, and the Environment.* Chicago: Center for New Community. http://www.newcomm
.org/images/stories/ATB/rme_paper_final.pdf.

Meadowcroft, James. 2005. "From Welfare State to Ecostate." In *The State
and the Global Ecological Crisis,* edited by John Barry and Robyn
Eckersley, 3–24. Cambridge, Mass.: MIT Press.

Medina, Kim Baker. 2012. Personal interview. January 7.

Miele, Frank. 1995. "Darwin's Dangerous Disciple: An Interview with
Richard Dawkins." *Skeptic* 3, no. 4: 80–85. http://www.scepsis.ru/eng/
articles/id_3.php.

Mignolo, Walter. 2000. "The Many Faces of Cosmo-Polis: Border Thinking and Critical Cosmopolitanism." *Public Culture* 12, no. 3: 721–48.

Miller, Adam. 1994–95. "The Pioneer Fund: Bankrolling the Professors of Hate." *Journal of Blacks in Higher Education* 6: 58–61.

Milliken, Jennifer. 2001. "Discourse Study: Bringing Rigor to Critical Theory." In *Constructing International Relations: The Next Generation*, edited by Karin Fierke and Knud Erik Jorgensen, 136–59. Armonk, N.Y.: M. E. Sharpe.

Millis, Dan. 2011. Personal interview. January 12.

Minkoff-Zern, Laura. 2012. "Knowing 'Good Food': Immigrant Knowledge and the Racial Politics of Farmworker Food Insecurity." *Antipode* 46, no. 5: 1190–204.

Mische, Patricia. 1989. "Ecological Security and the Need to Reconceptualize Sovereignty." *Alternatives* 14: 389–427.

Miss Ann Thropy. 1987. "Population and AIDS." *Earth First!* 7, no. 5: 32.

Mitchell, Timothy. 1991. "The Limits of the State: Beyond Statist Approaches and Their Critics." *The American Political Science Review* 85, no. 1: 77–96.

Mongia, Rhadika. 1999. "Race, Nationality, Mobility: A History of the Passport." *Public Culture* 11, no. 3: 527–56.

———. 2007. "Historicizing State Sovereignty: Inequality and the Form of Equivalence." *Comparative Studies in Society and History* 49, no. 2: 384–411.

Moore, D., J. Kosek, and A. Pandian. 2003. "Introduction: The Cultural Politics of Race and Nature: Terrains of Power and Practice." In *Race, Nature, and the Politics of Difference*, edited by D. Moore, J. Kosek, and A. Pandian, 1–70. Durham, N.C.: Duke University Press.

Muehlman, Shaylih. 2013. *Where the River Ends: Contested Indigeneity in the Mexican Colorado Delta*. Durham, N.C.: Duke University Press.

Muradian, Roldan. 2006. "Immigration and the Environment: Underlying Values and Scope of Analysis." *Ecological Economics* 59, no. 2: 208–13.

Myers, Norman. 1993. "Environmental Refugees in a Globally Warmed World." *Bioscience* 43, no. 11: 752–61.

Naess, Arne. 1973. "The Shallow and Deep Long-Range Ecology Movement." *Inquiry: An Interdisciplinary Journal of Philosophy* 16: 95–100.

Nelson, Diane. 1999. *A Finger in the Wound: Body Politics in Quincentennial Guatemala*. Berkeley: University of California Press.

Neumann, Roderick. 1998. *Imposing Wilderness: Struggles over Livelihood and Nature Preservation in Africa*. Berkeley: University of California Press.

Neumayer, Eric. 2006. "An Empirical Test of a Neo-Malthusian Theory of Fertility Change." *Population and Environment* 27, no. 4: 327–36.

Nevins, Joseph. (2002) 2010. *Operation Gatekeeper and Beyond: The War on "Illegals" and the Remaking of the US–Mexico Boundary.* New York: Routledge.

*New York Times.* 2008. "America's Leadership Team for Long-Range Population-Immigration-Resource Planning." September 23, A21.

Ngai, Mae. 1999. "The Architecture of Race in American Immigration Law: A Re-examination of the Immigration Act of 1924." *Journal of American History* 86, no. 1: 67–92.

———. 2004. *Impossible Subjects: Illegal Aliens and the Making of Modern America.* Princeton, N.J.: Princeton University Press.

*Occidental Observer.* 2010. "Mission Statement." http://www.theoccidentalobserver.net/archives/MissionStatement.html.

O'Connor, Lydia. 2014. "Blame Immigrants for California's Environmental Woes, Says Bizarre Earth Day Ad." *Huffington Post,* April 18.

Oelschlaeger, Max. 1991. *The Idea of Wilderness: The Prehistory to the Age of Ecology.* New Haven, Conn.: Yale University Press.

Olsen, Jonathan. 1999. *Nature and Nationalism: Right Wing Ecology and the Politics of Identity in Contemporary Germany.* New York: St. Martin's Press.

Olson, Joel. 2004. *The Abolition of White Democracy.* Minneapolis: University of Minnesota Press.

Ong, Aihwa. 2006. *Neoliberalism as Exception: Mutations in Citizenship and Sovereignty.* Durham, N.C.: Duke University Press.

Osborne, Fairfield. 1948. *Our Plundered Planet.* New York: Little, Brown.

Pachirat, Timothy. 2011. *Every Twelve Seconds: Industrialized Slaughter and the Politics of Sight.* New Haven, Conn.: Yale University Press.

Parenti, Christian. 2011. *Tropic of Chaos: Climate Change and the New Geography of Violence.* New York: Nation Books.

Park, Brian. 2007. "Friends in Low Places." *The Rocky Mountain Chronicle,* September 7. http://www.rmchronicle.com/index.php?id=1359&option=com_content&task=view.

Park, Lisa Sun-Hee, and David Pellow. 2004. "Racial Formation, Environmental Racism, and the Emergence of Silicon Valley." *Ethnicities* 4, no. 3: 403–24.

———. 2011. *The Slums of Aspen: Immigrants vs. the Environment in America's Eden.* New York: New York University Press.

Passel, Jeffrey. 2006. "The Size and Characteristics of the Unauthorized Migrant Population in the U.S. Pew Hispanic Research Center." http://www.pewhispanic.org/2006/03/07/size-and-characteristics-of-the-unauthorized-migrant-population-in-the-us/.

Pasternak, Kenneth. 2011. "A Response to the Center for New Community's Immigration Tabloid 'The Borderline.'" Californians for Population Stabilization. August 22. http://www.caps-blog.org/articles/2011/08/22/letter-to-the-funders-of-the-center-for-new-community/.

Paterson, Matthew. 1999. "Interpreting Trends in Global Environmental Governance." *International Affairs* 75, no. 4: 793–802.

————. 2006. "Theoretical Perspectives on International Environmental Politics." In *Palgrave Advances in International Environmental Politics*, edited by M. Betsill, K. Hochstetler, and D. Stevis, 54–81. New York: Palgrave Macmillan.

Pearce, Fred. 2010. *The Coming Population Crash and Our Planet's Surprising Future.* Boston: Beacon Press.

Pellow, David. 2002. *Garbage Wars: The Struggle for Environmental Justice in Chicago.* Cambridge, Mass.: MIT Press.

Peluso, Nancy, and Michael Watts. 2001. *Violent Environments.* Ithaca, N.Y.: Cornell University Press.

Perea, Juan. 1997. *Immigrants Out! The New Nativism and the Anti-immigrant Impulse in the United States.* New York: New York University Press.

Pevnick, R. 2008. "An Exchange: The Morality of Immigration." *Ethics and International Affairs* 22, no. 3: 241–59.

Piggott, Stephen. 2011. "White Nationalist John Tanton Join's FAIR's National Board of Advisors." *Imagine2050*, July 7. http://imagine2050.newcomm.org/2011/07/11/white-nationalist-john-tanton-joins-fair%E2%80%99s-national-board-of-advisors/.

Platt, Tony. 2005. "Engaging the Past: Charles M. Goethe, American Eugenics, and Sacramento State University." *Social Justice* 32, no. 2: 17–33.

Polanyi, Karl. 1957. "The Economy as Instituted Process." In *Trade and Market in the Early Empires: Economies in History and Theory,* edited by Karl Polanyi, Conrad Arensberg, and Harry Pearson, 243–70. Glencoe, Ill.: The Free Press.

————. (1944) 2001. *The Great Transformation: The Political and Economic Origins of Our Time.* Boston: Beacon Press.

Political Ecology Group. 1999. "Immigration and Environment Campaign." In *Dangerous Intersections: Feminist Perspectives on Population, Environment, and Development,* edited by Jael Silliman and Ynestra King, xxii–xxiii. Cambridge, Mass.: South End Press.

————. 2006. "Political Ecology Group's Immigration and Environment Campaign Position Statement." http://www.cwpe.org/resources/environment/politicaleco.

Pope, Carl. 2010. "Water Is Not Waste." September 10. http://sierraclub
.typepad.com/carlpope/2010/09/water-is-not-waste.html.

Population and Consumption Task Force. 1996. "Executive Summary."
http://clinton2.nara.gov/PCSD/Publications/TF_Reports/pop-exec.html.

Population–Environment Balance Inc. 1992. "Why Excess Immigration
Damages the Environment." *Population and Environment* 13, no. 4:
303–12.

Postel, Sandra. 2013. "The Accidental Wetland in the Colorado Delta."
*National Geographic,* April 2. http://voices.nationalgeographic.com/
2013/04/02/the-accidental-wetland-in-the-colorado-delta/.

Poswolsky, Rebecca. 2011. "Social Justice Movements Standing Strong
against Anti-immigrant Inroads." *Different Takes* 68 (Spring): 1–4.

Potok, Mark. 2003. "Letter from Mark Potok, Editor of SLPC *Intelligence
Report* to Sierra Club President Larry Fahn." Southern Poverty Law
Center. October 21.

———. 2010. "Executive Summary." In *Greenwash: Nativists, Environmentalism, and the Hypocrisy of Hate,* 4–5. Montgomery, Ala.: Southern
Poverty Law Center.

Pratt, Geraldine. 2005. "Abandoned Women and Spaces of Exception."
*Antipode* 37, no. 5: 1052–78.

Price, Carmel, and Ben Feldmeyer. 2012. "The Environmental Impact of
Immigration: An Analysis of the Effects of Immigrant Concentration
on Air Pollution Levels." *Population Research and Policy Review* 31,
no. 1: 119–40.

Price, Jennifer. 2006. "Thirteen Ways of Seeing Nature in L.A." *The Believer,*
April/May. http://www.believermag.com/issues/200604/?read=article_
price.

Prudham, Scott. 2004. "Poisoning the Well: Neoliberalism and the Con-
tamination of Municipal Water in Walkerton, Ontario." *Geoforum* 35,
no. 3: 343–59.

Pskowski, Martha. 2010. "Got Water? Immigrants Blamed for Water Shortages in the Southwest." *Imagine2050,* December 3. http://imagine2050
.newcomm.org/2010/12/03/got-water-immigrants-blamed-for-water-
shortages-in-the-southwest/.

———. 2011. "Youth Environmentalists Connecting the Dots: This Is a
Movement for Everyone." *Imagine2050,* April 22. http://imagine2050
.newcomm.org/2011/04/22/youth-environmentalists-connecting-the-
dots-this-is-a-movement-for-everyone/.

Pulido, Laura. 1996. *Environmentalism and Economic Justice: Two Chi-
cano Struggles in the Southwest.* Tucson: University of Arizona Press.

———. 2000. "Rethinking Environmental Racism: White Privilege and Urban Development in Southern California." *Annals of the Association of American Geographers* 90, no. 1: 12–40.

Radford, Philip. 2013. "The Environmental Case for a Path to Citizenship." *Huffington Post.* http://www.huffingtonpost.com/philip-radford/the-environmental-case-fo_b_2876324.html.

Randall, Steven. 2011. "Geert Wilders's Message to Americans." *American Renaissance,* May 20. http://www.amren.com/commentary/2011/05/geert_wilderss/.

Raspail, Jean. (1975) 1994. *The Camp of the Saints.* Petoskey, Mich.: The Social Contract Press.

———. 2004. "La Patrie Trahie par la République." *Le Figaro,* June 17.

Rees, William. 2006. "Globalization, Trade and Migration: Undermining Sustainability." *Ecological Economics* 59: 220–25.

———.2011. Personal interview. October 11.

Reimers, David. 1998. *Unwelcome Strangers: American Identity and the Turn against Immigration.* New York: Columbia University Press.

Rich, Carlos. 2011a. "Fear and Loathing on the Killing Room Floor." *Imagine 2050,* June 15. http://imagine2050.newcomm.org/2011/06/15/fear-and-loathing-on-the-killing-room-floor/.

———. 2011b. "Meatpacking Workers Ready for Struggle in 2011." *Imagine2050,* January 5. http://imagine2050.newcomm.org/2011/01/05/meatpacking-workers-ready-for-struggle-in-2011/.

Risse, Mathias. 2008. "On the Morality of Immigration." *Ethics and International Affairs* 22, no. 1: 25–33.

Robertson, Thomas. 2012. *The Malthusian Moment: Global Population Growth and the Birth of American Environmentalism.* Piscataway, N.J.: Rutgers University Press.

Rome, Adam. 2008. "Nature Wars, Culture Wars: Immigration and Environmental Reform in the Progressive Era." *Environmental History* 13: 432–53.

Roosevelt, Theodore, and Ernest Hamlin Abbott. 1910. *The New Nationalism.* New York: The Outlook Company.

Rose, Nikolas. 1996. "Governing Advanced Liberal Democracies." In *Foucault and Political Reason: Liberalism, Neoliberalism, and Rationalities of Government,* edited by Andrew Barry, Thomas Osborne, and Nikolas Rose, 37–64. Chicago: University of Chicago Press.

Ross, Andrew. 2010. "Greenwashing Nativism." *The Nation,* August 16.

Ross, Eric. 1998. *The Malthus Factor: Poverty, Politics, and Population in Capitalist Development.* New York: St. Martin's Press.

Rowe, John. 2002. *Mary Lou and John Tanton: A Journey into American Conservation.* Washington, D.C.: FAIR Horizon Press.

Ruggie, John Gerard. 1982. "International Regimes, Transactions, and Change: Embedded Liberalism in the Postwar Economic Order." *International Organization* 36, no. 2: 379–415.

———. 1993. "Territoriality and Beyond: Problematizing Modernity in International Relations." *International Organization* 47, no. 1: 139–74.

———. 2003. "Taking Embedded Liberalism Global: The Corporate Connection." In T*aming Globalization: Frontiers of Governance,* edited by David Held and Mathias Koenig-Archibugi, 93–129. Malden, Mass.: Polity Press.

Rushdie, Salman. 2002. *Step across this Line.* The Tanner Lectures on Human Values. New Haven, Conn.: Yale University Press. http://www.tannerlectures.utah.edu/lectures/documents/volume24/rushdie_2002.pdf.

Rutherford, Stephanie. 2005. "Constructing Global and National Nature Population: Immigration and the Green-Washing of Racism and Misogyny." *Women and Environments,* Fall/Winter, 20–21.

Ryerson, William. 2011. Personal interview. October 17.

Sailer, Steve. 2001. "Conservatives versus Conservation: How the GOP Drives Off White Voters." *VDARE,* April 16. http://www.vdare.com/articles/conservatives-vs-conservation-how-the-gop-drives-off-white-voters.

———. 2004. "Where Dawkins Fears to Tread: Ethnic Nepotism and the Reality of Race." *VDARE,* October 3. http://www.vdare.com/articles/where-dawkins-fears-to-tread-ethnic-nepotism-and-the-reality-of-race.

Salazar, Debra, and John Hewitt. 2001. "Think Globally, Secure the Borders: The Oregon Environmental Movement and the Population/Immigration Debate." *Organization and Environment* 14, no. 3: 290–310.

Sandilands, Catriona. 1999. *The Good Natured Feminist: Ecofeminism and the Quest for Democracy.* Minneapolis: University of Minnesota Press.

Sasser, Jade. 2014. "From Darkness into Light: Race, Population, and Environmental Advocacy." *Antipode* 46, no. 5: 1240–57.

Sawyer, Suzana. 2004. *Crude Chronicles: Indigenous Politics, Multinational Oil, and Neoliberalism in Ecuador.* Durham, N.C.: Duke University Press.

Sayre, Nathan. 2008. "The Genesis, History, and Limits of Carrying Capacity." *Annals of the Association of American Geographers* 98, no. 1: 120–34.

Scherr, Sonia. 2008. "Anti-immigrant Hate Groups Place Ads in the New York Times." *Southern Poverty Law Center Hatewatch,* June 27. http://www

.splcenter.org/blog/2008/06/27/anti-immigration-hate-groups-place-ads-in-the-new-york-times/.

Schlosser, Eric. 2001. "The Chain Never Stops." *Mother Jones,* July/August, 38–47, 86–87.

Schneider, Francois, Giorgos Kallis, and Joan Martinez-Alier. 2010. "Crisis or Opportunity? Economic Degrowth for Social Equity and Ecological Sustainability." *Journal of Cleaner Production* 18: 511–18.

Schoen, Johanna. 2001. "Between Choice and Coercion: Women and the Politics of Sterilization in North Carolina, 1929–1975." *Journal of Women's History* 13, no. 1: 132–56.

Selle, Caroline. 2013. "Why Bill McKibben Is Wrong about Immigration." http://www.wearepowershift.org/blogs/why-bill-mckibben-wrong-about-immigration.

Shapiro, David. 2011. "Banking on Bondage: Private Prisons and Mass Incarceration." American Civil Liberties Union National Prison Project and Center for Justice. http://www.aclu.org/prisoners-rights/banking-bondage-private-prisons-and-mass-incarceration.

Shapiro, Michael. 2004. *Methods and Nations: Cultural Governance and the Indigenous Subject.* New York: Routledge.

Shaw, Karena. 2004. "The Global/Local Politics of the Great Bear Rainforest." *Environmental Politics* 13, no. 2: 373–92.

———. 2008. *Indigeneity and Political Theory: Sovereignty and the Limits of the Political.* New York: Routledge.

Sierra Club. 2008. "Population FAQ." http://www.sierraclub.org/population/faq/.

———. 2011. "Immigration Policy." http://www.sierraclub.org/policy/conservation/immigration.pdf.

Sierra Club Borderlands Campaign. 2009. "Wild versus Wall." http://www.sierraclub.org/borderlands/film.aspx.

———. 2012a. "Faces of the Borderlands." http://www.sierraclub.org/borderlands/faces/default.aspx.

———. 2012b. "Real ID Act." http://www.sierraclub.org/borderlands/realID.aspx.

Sierra Club Population Committee. 1989. "US Population Growth and Immigration." http://www.susps.org/history/popreport1989.html.

Sierrans for U.S. Population Stabilization. 2011. "Official Sierra Club Population Policy." http://www.susps.org/history/scpolicy.html.

Silliman, Jael, and Ynestra King. 1999. *Dangerous Intersections: Feminist Perspectives on Population, Environment, and Development.* Cambridge, Mass.: South End Press.

Simmons, Skyler. 2012. "Does Earth First! Carry the Capacity for a Justice-Based Approach to Overpopulation?" *Earth First!* http://earthfirstjour nal.org/newswire/articles/we-are-the-00018-percent-does-earth-first-carry-the-capacity-for-a-justice-based-approach-to-overpopulation/.

Smith, Mick. 2008. "Suspended Animation: Radical Ecology, Sovereign Powers, and Saving the (Natural) World." *Journal for the Study of Radicalism* 2, no. 1: 1–25.

———. 2009. "Against Ecological Sovereignty: Agamben, Politics, and Globalisation." *Environmental Politics* 18, no. 1: 99–116.

———. 2011. *Against Ecological Sovereignty: Ethics, Biopolitics, and Saving the Natural World.* Minneapolis: University of Minnesota Press.

Southern Poverty Law Center. 2001. "Anti-immigration Groups." Intelligence Report 101. http://www.splcenter.org/get-informed/intelligence-report/browse-all-issues/2001/spring/blood-on-the-border/anti-immi gration-.

———. 2002a. "Witan Memo 3." Intelligence Report 106. http://www .splcenter.org/get-informed/intelligence-report/browse-all-issues/2002/summer/the-puppeteer/witan-memo-iii.

———. 2002b. "John Tanton's Network." Intelligence Report 106. http:// www.splcenter.org/get-informed/intelligence-report/browse-all-issues /2002/summer/the-puppeteer/john-tantons-network.

———. 2008. "The Tanton Files." Intelligence Report 132. http://www .splcenter.org/get-informed/intelligence-\report/browse-all-issues/2008/winter/the-tanton-files.

Soguk, Nevzat, and Geoffrey Whitehall. 1999. "Wandering Grounds: Transversality, Identity, Territoriality, and Movement." *Millennium: Journal of International Studies* 28, no. 3: 678–98.

Southern Poverty Law Center. 2010. "Nativists and Environmentalists: A Timeline." http://www.splcenter.org/greenwash-nativists-environmen talism-and-the-hypocrisy-of-hate/greenwashing-a-timeline.

Sparke, Matthew. 2006. "A Neoliberal Nexus: Economy, Security, and the Biopolitics of Citizenship on the Border." *Political Geography* 25, no. 3: 151–80.

Spence, Mark. 1999. *Dispossessing the Wilderness: Indian Removal and the Making of the National Parks.* Oxford: Oxford University Press.

Spencer, C. 1992. "Interview with Garrett Hardin." *Omni* 14, no. 9: 55–63.

Spiro, Jonathan. 2009. *Defending the Master Race: Conservation, Eugenics, and the Legacy of Madison Grant.* Lebanon, N.H.: University Press of New England.

Sqaulli, Jay. 2009. "Immigration and Environmental Emissions: A U.S. County-Level Analysis." *Population and Environment* 30: 247–60.

———. 2010. "An Empirical Analysis of U.S. State-Level Immigration and Environmental Emissions." *Ecological Economics* 69: 1170–75.

Steele, D. F. 2008. "Globalization and Cooperative Activity between National Labor Unions and National Environmental Organizations in the United States." *International Journal of Social Inquiry* 1, no. 2: 179–200.

Stein, Jill. 2012. "A Green New Deal for America." http://www.gp.org/GreenNewDeal/.

Stern, Alexandra Minna. 2005. *Eugenic Nation: Faults and Frontiers of Better Breeding in Modern America*. Berkeley: University of California Press.

Sullivan, Eileen. 2007. "Chertoff: Illegals 'Degrade' Environment." *USA Today*, October 1. http://usatoday30.usatoday.com/news/washington/2007-10-01-1156407265_x.htm.

Sunic, Tomislav. 2010. "Cultural or Political Hegemony: The USA and Europe." *Citizens Informer*, April–June, 6. http://cofcc.org/newspaper/june10ci.pdf.

Swanson, Evadene. 1975. *Fort Collins Yesterdays*. Privately published.

Tacoli, Cecelia. 2009. "Crisis or Adaptation? Migration and Climate Change in a Context of High Mobility." *Environment and Urbanization* 21, no. 2: 513–25.

Taylor, Dorceta. 2002. *Race, Class, Gender, and American Environmentalism*. U.S. Department of Agriculture Forest Service, Pacific Northwest Research Station.

Taylor, Jared. 2006. "Jews and American Renaissance." *American Renaissance* 17, no. 5. http://amren.com/oldnews/archives/2006/04/jews_and_americ.php.

Taylor, Lauren. 2014. "Don't Let Population Control Alarmists Derail Earth Day." *Imagine2050*, April 17. http://imagine2050.newcomm.org/2014/04/17/dont-let-population-control-alarmists-derail-earth-day/.

Thomas, Adam. 2003. *Hang Your Wagon to a Star: Hispanics in Fort Collins, 1900–2000*. State Historical Fund Project 01-02-065. Westminster, Colo.: SWCA Environmental Consultants.

Tomorrow's America. 2010. "Discussion Series, Episode 2: How Much Growth Is Too Much?" http://www.tomorrowsamerica.com/discussion/episode-2/.

Trask, H. A. Scott. 2001. "The Christian Doctrine of Nations: Biblical Law Respects Boundaries of Race and Nation." *American Renaissance* 12, no. 7. http://www.amren.com/ar/2001/07/index.html.

Troost, Cornelius. 2009. "Hijacking Darwin." *VDARE*, October 7. http://www.vdare.com/articles/hijacking-darwin.

Tsing, Anna. 2005. *Friction: An Ethnography of Global Connection.* Princeton, N.J.: Princeton University Press.

Tully, James. 1995. *Strange Multiplicity: Constitutionalism in an Age of Diversity.* Cambridge: Cambridge University Press.

Turk, Ana. 2009. "Migrant Workers: The Last, Best Hope for the Labor Movement." *Imagine2050,* February 15. http://imagine2050.newcomm.org/2009/02/15/migrant-workers-the-last-best-hope-for-labor-movement/.

Tweit, Susan. 2009. "Water across the Divide." *High Country News,* October 14. https://www.hcn.org/issues/41.17/water-across-the-divide.

Twitty, Eric. 2003. *Silver Wedge: The Sugar Beet Industry in Fort Collins.* State Historical Fund Project 01-02-065. Westminster, Colo.: SWCA Consultants.

United Nations Economic and Social Affairs. 2013. *International Migration Report 2013.* https://www.un.org/en/development/desa/population/publications/migration/migration-report-2013.shtml.

Urban, Jessica Leann. 2007. "Interrogating Privilege: Challenging the 'Greening of Hate.'" *International Feminist Journal of Politics* 9, no. 2: 251–64.

———. 2008. *Nation, Immigration, and Environmental Security.* New York: Palgrave Macmillan.

*USA Today.* 2005. "Rival Factions Compete to Control Powerful Sierra Club." February 18. http://www.usatoday.com/news/washington/2004-02-18-sierra-club_x.htm.

U.S. Department of Homeland Security. 2011. *Yearbook of Immigration Statistics: 2010.* Washington, D.C.: U.S. DHS Office of Immigration Statistics.

U.S. Congress. 1995. *Congressional Record,* Extensions of Remarks. 104th Cong., 1st sess. July 18. http://www.gpo.gov/fdsys/pkg/CREC-1995-07-18/pdf/CREC-1995-07-18-pt1-PgE1456-3.pdf.

U.S. Congress. House. 2001. "U.S. Population and Environment Hearing." Subcommittee on Immigration and Claims of the Committee on the Judiciary. August 2. http://commdocs.house.gov/committees/judiciary/hju74238.000/hju74238_0f.htm.

U.S. Trade Representative. 2008. "NAFTA: Myth versus Fact." http://www.ustr.gov/sites/default/files/NAFTA-Myth-versus-Fact.pdf.

Vaughan-Williams, Nick. 2009. "The Generalized Bio-political Border: Reconceptualizing the Limits of Sovereign Power." *Review of International Studies* 35, no. 4: 729–49.

Villarreal, M. Angeles, and Ian Fergusson. 2014. "NAFTA at Twenty:

Overview and Trade Effects." *Congressional Research Service* R42965. http://fas.org/sgp/crs/row/R42965.pdf.

Vinson, John. 1998. "Europhobia: The Racism of Anti-racists." *The Social Contract* 8, no. 4. http://www.thesocialcontract.com/artman2/publish/tsc0804/article_765.shtml.

Vogt, William. 1948. *Road to Survival.* New York: William Sloan Associates.

Wainwright, Joel, and Geoff Mann. 2013. "Climate Leviathan." *Antipode* 45, no. 1: 1–22.

Walia, Harsha. 2013. *Undoing Border Imperialism.* Oakland, Calif.: AK Press and the Institute for Anarchist Studies.

Walker, Brenda. 2004. "Save the Sierra Club from the Treason Lobby—Act Now!" *VDARE,* January 8. http://www.vdare.com/articles/save-the-sierra-club-from-the-treason-lobby-act-now.

———. 2005. "Why Multiculturalism Is a Fraud and a Disaster for Women's Rights." http://www.limitstogrowth.org/WEB-text/multiculturalism-fraud.html.

———. 2007. "An Environmentalist Talks to School Kids about the Need for Patriotic Immigration Reform." *VDARE,* August 6. http://www.vdare.com/walker/070806_reform.htm.

Walker, R. B. J. 1992. *Inside/Outside: International Relations as Political Theory.* Cambridge: Cambridge University Press.

Ward, Eric. 2009. "On Earth Day, Environmentalists Must Not Link Arms with Anti-immigrant Forces." *The Progressive,* April 21. http://www.progressive.org/mpward042109.html.

Warner, K. 2010. "Global Environmental Change and Migration: Governance Challenges." *Global Environmental Change* 20: 402–13.

Waterman, Jonathan. 2010. *Running Dry: A Journal from Source to Sea Down the Colorado River.* Washington, D.C.: National Geographic Society.

Weber, Cynthia. 1995. *Simulating Sovereignty: Intervention, the State, and Symbolic Exchange.* Cambridge: Cambridge University Press.

Weissberg, Robert. 2011. "Why Biology Is the Friend of Liberty—and the Enemy of 'Totalitarian Creep.'" *VDARE,* January 27. http://www.vdare.com/articles/why-biology-is-the-friend-of-liberty-and-the-enemy-of-totalitarian-creep.

White, Richard. 1995. "Are You an Environmentalist or Do You Work for a Living?" In *Uncommon Ground,* edited by William Cronon, 172–85. New York: W. W. Norton.

Wilken-Robertson, Michael. 2004. *The US–Mexican Border Environment: Tribal Environmental Issues of the Border Region.* Southwest Center for Environmental Research and Policy Monograph Series 9. San Diego, Calif.: San Diego State University Press.

Williams, Raymond. (1972) 2005. "Ideas of Nature." In *Nature: Thinking the Natural,* edited by David Inglis, John Bone, and Rhoda Wilkie, 47–62. New York: Routledge.

Williamson, Chilton. 2001. "When Will They Ever Learn?" *VDARE,* March 28. http://www.vdare.com/articles/when-will-they-ever-learn.

Wohlforth, Charles. 2010. "Conservation and Eugenics: The Environmental Movement's Dirty Secret." *Orion Magazine,* July/August.

Wooldridge, Frosty. 2004. *Immigration's Unarmed Invasion: Deadly Consequences.* Bloomington, Ind.: AuthorHouse.

———. 2006. "21st Century Paul Revere Ride." http://www.youtube.com/watch?v=djau_pI1bZA.

———. 2009. *America on the Brink: The Next Added 100 Million Americans.* Bloomington, Ind.: AuthorHouse.

———. 2011. Personal interview. May 19.

Worster, Donald. 1994. *Nature's Economy: A History of Ecological Ideas.* 2nd ed. Cambridge: Cambridge University Press.

Yang, JoShing. 2008. "Illegal Mexican Immigrants or Water Refugees?" *Truthout.* http://truth-out.org/archive/component/k2/item/81071:illegal -mexican-immigrants-or-water-refugees.

Yeh, Ling Ling. 2011. Personal interview. May 19.

Young, Iris Marion. 2006. "Responsibility and Global Justice: A Social Connection Model." *Social Philosophy and Policy* 23, no. 1: 102–30.

Zacarias, Andrew. 2014. "El Mercado de Sueños: A Small Glimpse into Flagstaff's Flourishing Rhizome." MA thesis, Northern Arizona University.

Ziarek, Ewa. 2008. "Bare Life on Strike: Notes on the Biopolitics of Race and Gender." *South Atlantic Quarterly* 107, no. 1: 89–105.

Zimmerman, Michael. 1994. *Contesting Earth's Futures: Radical Ecology and Postmodernity.* Berkeley: University of California Press.

# INDEX

**John Hultgren** is a lecturer in the Department of Politics and International Affairs at Northern Arizona University.